About Island Press

Island Press is the only nonprofit organization in the United States whose principal purpose is the publication of books on environmental issues and natural resource management. We provide solutions-oriented information to professionals, public officials, business and community leaders, and concerned citizens who are shaping responses to environmental problems.

In 2001, Island Press celebrates its seventeenth anniversary as the leading provider of timely and practical books that take a multidisciplinary approach to critical environmental concerns. Our growing list of titles reflects our commitment to bringing the best of an expanding body of literature to the environmental community throughout North America and the world.

Support for Island Press is provided by The Bullitt Foundation, The Mary Flagler Cary Charitable Trust, The Nathan Cummings Foundation, Geraldine R. Dodge Foundation, Doris Duke Charitable Foundation, The Charles Engelhard Foundation, The Ford Foundation, The George Gund Foundation, The Vira I. Heinz Endowment, The William and Flora Hewlett Foundation, W. Alton Jones Foundation, The John D. and Catherine T. MacArthur Foundation, The Andrew W. Mellon Foundation, The Charles Stewart Mott Foundation, The Curtis and Edith Munson Foundation, National Fish and Wildlife Foundation, The New-Land Foundation, Oak Foundation, The Overbrook Foundation, The David and Lucile Packard Foundation, The Pew Charitable Trusts, Rockefeller Brothers Fund, The Winslow Foundation, and other generous donors.

About the Rails-to-Trails Conservancy

The mission of the Rails-to-Trails Conservancy (RTC) is to enhance America's communities and countrysides by converting thousands of miles of abandoned rail corridors, and the connecting open space, into a nationwide network of public trails.

Established in 1985, the Rails-to-Trails Conservancy is a national nonprofit organization with more than 80,000 members. In addition to a staff of thirty based in Washington, D.C., the Rails-to-Trails Conservancy has five field offices in California, Florida, Michigan, Ohio, and Pennsylvania as well as a field representative in the New England region.

The Rails-to-Trails Conservancy notifies trail advocates and local governments of upcoming railroad abandonments; assists public and private agencies in the legalities of trail corridor acquisition; provides technical assistance to private citizens as well as trail planners, designers, and managers on trail design, development, and protection; and publicizes rails-to-trails issues throughout the country.

For additional information, contact the Rails-to-Trails Conservancy at 1100 17th Street, N.W., 10th Floor, Washington, DC 20036, call (202) 331-9696, or view the Web site at www.railtrails.org.

FHWA Disclaimer

Trails for the Twenty-First Century

Trails for the Twenty-First Century

SECOND EDITION

Planning, Design, and Management Manual for Multi-Use Trails

CHARLES A. FLINK

KRISTINE OLKA

ROBERT M. SEARNS

RAILS-TO-TRAILS CONSERVANCY

ISLAND PRESS

Washington • Covelo • London

ISLAND PRESS is a trademark of The Center for Resource Economics.

Library of Congress Cataloging-in-Publication Data
Trails for the twenty-first century / Charles A. Flink, II,
Robert M. Searns, Kristine Olka ; Rails-to-Trails Conservancy.—2nd ed.
p.   cm.
ISBN 1–55963–818–4 — ISBN 1–55963–819–2 (pbk.)
1. Trails—United States—Planning. 2. Trails—United
States—Design.   I. Title: Trails for the 21st century.
II. Flink, Charles A.   III. Searns, Robert M.   IV. Olka, Kristine V.
Rails-to-Trails Conservancy.
GV191.4 .T73   2001
796.5'0973—dc21
00-012958
CIP

British Cataloguing-in-Publication Data available.
Printed on recycled, acid-free paper ♲

Manufactured in the United States of America
10 9 8 7 6 5 4 3 2

Contents

Chapter 2: Planning and Public Involvement   30

Chapter 3: Designing Your Trail   51

Acknowledgments

We offer special recognition to Hugh Morris, Betsy Goodrich, Kate Bickert, Karen Stewart, Barbara Richey, Jeff Ciabotti, and Nancy Krupiarz for their contributions to the manuscript on behalf of Rails-to-Trails Conservancy. Thanks to those dedicated individuals whose expertise provided insight into the design and management of trails: Ursula Lemanski, Chris Abbett, and Bryan Bowden, RTCA; Bill O'Neill, East Coast Greenways; Jennifer Barefoot, Rails-to-Trails of Central Pennsylvania; Michael Kelley, International Mountain Biking Association; Ed McBrayer, PATH Foundation; John Dugger, Coalition for the Capital Crescent Trail; Renee Graham, Columbia Missouri Convention and Visitors Bureau; and Jim Schmid, South Carolina Department of Parks, Recreation and Tourism. A special recognition goes to Balmori Associates, Inc., whose artwork and graphics grace the pages of this publication.

Sponsors

National Park Service Rivers, Trails, and Conservation Assistance (RTCA) Rivers & Trails is a national network of conservation- and recreation-planning professionals who assist interested communities with nature-based recreation development and environmental, historic, and cultural conservation projects. Rivers & Trails does not direct or fund projects, but when a community has decided to conserve close-to-home landscapes, the program can help get it started. The Rivers & Trails Program implements the National Park Service's mission in communities across America. Its vision is a network of protected rivers, trails, and greenways that promotes quality of life and links Americans to their natural and cultural heritage.

The Federal Highway Administration (FHWA) coordinates highway transportation programs in cooperation with states and other partners to enhance the country's safety, economic vitality, quality of life, and the environment. The Federal-Aid Highway Program provides federal financial assistance to the states to construct and improve the National Highway System, other major roads, bridges, bicycle and pedestrian facilities, and trails. The Federal Lands Highway Program provides access to and within national forests, national parks, Indian reservations, and other public lands. The FHWA also manages a comprehensive transportation research, development, and technology program. Web site: www.fhwa.dot.gov

Foreword

In the spring of 1999 Island Press informed us that the first edition of *Trails for the Twenty-First Century* was sold out and asked if we wished to provide an update. We were pleased that Rails-to-Trails, the National Center for Recreation and Conservation Division of the National Park Service, and our partner authors had succeeded in producing a useful book of continuing, significant public interest.

The twenty-first century is now a reality—and so is the vision of an emerging national system of interconnected trails and greenways. Demand for trails—and trail systems—is exploding as communities across the country seek opportunities to improve the livability, utility, and beauty of their hometowns. The creation of multi-use trails allows walkers, runners, skaters, cyclists, people with disabilities, equestrians, and skiers—everybody—to access and enjoy their local landscapes.

The expansion of trail development activity to include trail networks, or green infrastructure, presents significant new design challenges. These networks offer connections to a variety of community features such as schools, libraries, and parks, as well as link residential neighborhoods with commercial centers. This adds purposeful transportation as a new design criterion, requiring integration of on-road and off-road pathways, coordination with bicycle facility guidelines, and methods for planning trail systems across political jurisdictions. Add to this a variety of new purposes for trails and greenways—habitat preservation, ecosystem restoration, and buffer zones to protect rivers and streams from highway and farm runoff—and you have some tough design issues.

For these reasons, we are very pleased to have the Federal Highway Administration join the Rails-to-Trails Conservancy and the National Park Service as a sponsor of this new edition of *Trails for the Twenty-First Century.* These three organizations share a common devotion to helping communities meet new public demand for open space, improved quality of life, economic development, and smarter growth, as well as transportation choices that support these objectives. We know that trails advance these goals, but we also understand that the trail-building process can be daunting and complex. We continue to seek ways to streamline this process. In the meantime, this new book will help you get your trail, or your trail and greenway system, under way now.

Trails for the Twenty-First Century was written to help those who are planning, designing, building, and managing multi-use trails. It provides a guide through the process of creating a trail from start to finish and managing the trail for the future. This edition includes new regulations and guidelines for designing well-built trails for users of all types, and people of all abilities, in a manner that also heals the landscape and restores ecological integrity.

We salute the authors of this book, Chuck Flink and Kristine Olka of Greenways, Inc., and Bob Searns of Urban Edges, Inc., for their valuable contributions and knowledge of multi-use trail development and management. We commend the people across our country who are taking advantage of these unique opportunities to change the face of their communities. We look forward to a new century of trail building, and trail partnering, with them.

DAVID G. BURWELL
President, Rails-to-Trails Conservancy

D. THOMAS ROSS
Assistant Director for Recreation and Conservation, National Park Service

CYNTHIA J. BURBANK
Program Manager, Planning and Environment, Federal Highway Administration

Introduction

Trails for the Twenty-First Century was first published in 1991. With the new millennium, trail advocates, planners, and managers thought it was time to reflect on what the trails movement has accomplished, to take stock of new tools and planning and design techniques, and to embrace future challenges and opportunities. This book was written primarily for developing rail-trails, but it applies to all multi-use trails. Rail-trails are built within railroad rights-of-way to accommodate a variety of trail users. Many of the trails take the place of abandoned railroad lines, while others parallel active rail lines.

The trails movement has accomplished much in the last nine years. Since this book announced the appearance of "a new kind of public space" across this country's landscape, the Rails-to-Trails Conservancy estimates that 10,000 miles of trails have been developed within railroad corridors. Doubtless, hundreds more miles of trails have been developed as well within other corridors, such as along rivers, canals, and streams. The *Rails-to-Trails Conservancy, American Trails,* and other national, state, and local organizations advocating for the creation of multi-use trails have experienced growth, expanding into new geographic areas and gaining more grassroots support. The combined efforts of trail advocates helped ensure the passage of TEA21, the next-generation federal surface transportation legislation. This program has been the largest source of funding ever approved for trails and other nonhighway transportation routes.

Cities and towns across the country have worked hard to improve their quality of life through developing trail systems—connecting individual trail segments to form larger recreation and transportation networks. While the benefits of any trail cannot be discounted, creating linkages among trails multiplies their effect.

These trails and trails networks have been providing opportunities for more people to walk to the store, bike to work, get some exercise, learn about their community, observe local wildlife, and experience the outdoors with their families. For example, the KATY Trail that now crosses almost the entire state of Missouri has literally transformed the regions through which it passes, improving the economies of the local towns and providing a wonderful recreational attraction for millions of visitors from the local areas and nationwide. Similarly, major rail-trail corridors are improving the quality of life in Washington State, California, Florida, and Iowa. Greenways and greenway networks, many of which include rail-trails, have left lasting legacies in both major and smaller metropolitan areas, and the movement continues. Towns such as Springfield, Missouri, are building trail networks, and Raleigh, North Carolina, has allocated funding for the "missing pieces" in its existing 30-mile system of trails. Denver now boasts a 200-mile network—one of the finest systems in the nation.

The trail and greenway movement has also evolved. While initially the focus was on trails

Margarite Hoefler

Katy Trail State Park, Missouri

and trail recreation, a new multi-objective movement has emerged. Trail advocates now work in partnership with transportation engineers, drainage and flood control officials, ecologists, and open space advocates. We now think in terms of trail and greenway corridors that provide wildlife habitat and movement corridors, open space vistas, places for rivers and streams to meander in more natural landscapes, places to preserve and interpret history and culture, and many other benefits.

Indeed, trails and their associated greenway corridors are increasingly viewed as vital infrastructure, taking their place along with roads, parks, utilities, and storm drainage improvements as important and essential public assets and resources. The trails movement has spawned a much larger range of benefits that will transform and enhance the urban landscapes of the new century.

Many of us look with enthusiasm on the tremendous opportunities ahead. With trail-type activities including walking, running, and bicycling (the most popular forms of outdoor recreation), trail advocates, planners, builders, and managers have a vital role to play. They will address many important issues, opportunities, and challenges as cities and suburbs continue to grow and new technologies continue to emerge:

- *Promoting a systems approach to trail development.* With the ever-increasing popularity of trails, we should strive to create interconnected trail systems linking the places where people work, live, and play.

- *Using trail and greenway to shape the urban fabric.* The rapid growth of America's urban areas, especially the suburbs, has increased the importance of promoting remedies for sprawl. Trails, as alternative transportation pathways, offer ways to link us to resources close to home and work. As linear parks, these corri-

Colorado's 8-mile Salida Trail system is used daily by hundreds of residents seeking safe recreation and transportation. When the trail system is complete, it will connect the town of Salida, its golf course, lakes, and countryside, with the Arkansas River and other area rail-trails.

dors protect natural resources and can help make our cities more livable. The decline of our inner cities and the effects of past environmental degradation have resulted in the abandonment of disturbed and contaminated landscapes, sometimes described as "brownfields." As communities wrestle with the issues of cleanup and restoration, trails and greenways should be promoted as a way of revitalizing these areas, helping to return their social, economic, and environmental vibrance.

- *Finding ways to empower, enable, and encourage communities to build trails and greenways.* Creating inspiring trail plans, negotiating rights-of-way, and finding money to build trails

remain challenges, especially for smaller communities that may feel they do not have the means or wherewithal to build and maintain trails. We need more success stories and more models in many different kinds of communities. We need to get the word out and expand the availability of local know-how and technical skills.

- *Using technology to better visualize and promote trails.* Ten years ago, many people had never heard of the Internet, computer-based mapping, or readily available satellite imagery. Now, we regularly use the World Wide Web to communicate, work, shop, and find information. New technologies are emerging daily. Trail supporters, planners, and managers should take full advantage of the Internet to promote existing trails and advocate for the development of new ones. We should also capture the possibilities of Geographic Information Systems (GIS) software, 3-D imaging programs, and other technological tools to better analyze, plan, design, and visually communicate our ideas of what trails could be and how they could function.

- *Inspiring the next generation to become involved in trails.* Trails and trail recreation emerged with the baby-boomer generation. We need trail opportunities and positive trail experiences—not only recreating on them but also building them and enhancing them for the next generation, one raised on virtual (computer) experiences and programmed sports.

They and their children need those close-to-home outdoor experiences that can only be found in "wild" places where a kid can still ride a bike, catch a salamander, or create his or her own adventure.

If the last nine years serves as a measurement of success, the trails movement will continue to share experiences, expand support for multi-use trails, and achieve great accomplishments in the twenty-first century.

This book will help people meet the coming challenges and take advantage of future opportunities. Perhaps you have already identified a potential multi-use trail corridor or you are envisioning a trail and greenway network for your community. If so, this book will help guide you toward your goal. It has been developed to guide you through a step-by-step process to plan, design, build, and manage your trail, and to maximize its potential. The information provided here has been culled from the experiences of scores of trail managers and trail enthusiasts across the nation. In addition to the body of knowledge provided here, this book contains a comprehensive list of resources for trail advocates and professionals.

While the guidelines presented in this book should be extremely useful, they also have limitations. You cannot set parameters for your trail without taking into account your corridor's individual setting. This book strives to offer a range of possibilities and acceptable alternatives wherever possible. As you plan, design, and manage your multi-use trail, consider all the possibilities and work with local residents and trail neighbors to determine what will ultimately work best in your community.

Finally, this introduction would not be complete without acknowledging our predecessors who helped make this book possible: David Burwell for his visionary leadership in launching this project; Karen Lee Ryan for the herculean task of managing and editing the first edition of *Trails for the Twenty-First Century;* and Peter Lagerway and Diana Belmori, who contributed heavily to the first edition.

CHAPTER

1

Getting Started

SOURCES OF INFORMATION

1. User Groups
2. Community Organizations
3. Utility Agencies
4. Railroad Company
5. Local Government
   - Planning Department
   - Zoning Department
   - Transportation Department
   - Parks/Recreation Department
6. State Government
   - Department of Natural Resources
   - Historic Preservation Office
   - Bicycle/Pedestrian Coordinator (usually within the State Department of Transportation)
   - State Trail Planner (usually within the State Resource Agency)
7. Federal Government
   - Army Corps of Engineers
   - Environmental Protection Agency
   - U.S. Department of Agriculture
   - U.S. Forest Service
   - Natural Resources Conservation District
   - Surface Transportation Board
   - Federal Highway Administration
   - U.S. Coast Guard
   - U.S. Geological Survey
   - U.S. Fish and Wildlife Service
   - National Park Service/Bureau of Land Management

So you want to build a trail. Congratulations! You join thousands of other advocates, elected officials, and professionals who want to improve their communities by developing trails as new recreation and off-road transportation facilities, outdoor public health facilities, and public resources.

At the beginning of any trail project, keep in mind that you are undertaking a significant community enhancement project that will be enjoyed for generations to come. For this reason, trail development can have all of the physical, social, political, and financial challenges of building a major highway: rights-of-way negotiations, grading, underpasses, overpasses, surfacing, and landscaping issues.

The trail may be built quickly, but more likely the effort will take years of persistent hard work that will be well worthwhile in the end. You will have created not merely a pathway but an experience—a place of enjoyment, a place of solace, a place of discovery to be enjoyed by thousands for generations to come. A well-designed trail can be a work of art, a legacy.

The genesis of a trail project may occur in a number of different ways. The route may be identified in a statewide, regional, or local master plan. It may be a specific corridor identified by a community group, or it could be the result of a serendipitous opportunity created by rail abandonment. This book focuses on developing trails within human-built corridors, including former rail beds, canals, and roads.

In any case, the first step in building a trail is determining the route. Once you have identified the route, give it a name—an inspiring name—even if it is only temporary, so that you and others can speak in terms of a specific trail corridor instead of a nondescript area. Also identify the context into which the route fits, considering the larger plan of a community system of trails, as well as nearby resources that may be connected by the trail (see Case Study 1). You should also start to think about the vision of the trail and how to involve the larger community in creating this vision (see "Community Involvement" in Chapter 2).

Your next step is to gather as much information as you can about the corridor, the people who will use the corridor, and the surrounding community. This can be accomplished through conducting research on the people and conditions in the area, and by completing an inventory of the corridor and surrounding environments.

Your Trail and the Community

Background research of the community goes hand in hand with a field inventory of your future trail corridor. You can find this information by contacting user groups, nonprofit organizations (environmental, education, health, community development), local planning, zoning, transportation, public health, education, and parks departments, or state environmental, transportation, or parks agencies. You should also obtain copies of any recent planning efforts conducted for the area, including land-use plans, park plans, or transportation plans, that may contain useful information about future site conditions. For example, a transportation plan may reveal a proposal for a new roadway that will cross the trail corridor. A parks plan may provide information about recreational needs in the community. Obtain any existing trail master plans. Is your trail part of a proposed system? Who is identified to build and maintain trails in the community?

It is important to examine the local community because the trail corridor will not function in a vacuum—a variety of individuals, businesses, and government agencies will have an interest in what happens along the way. When planning your trail, be sure you know who is likely to be affected by it and who has an interest in it. This knowledge will help you plan effectively and avoid possible setbacks by exposing potential conflicts or opposition early in the process. You may also find opportunities for joint ventures and other mutual benefits with those holding a stake in the corridor.

You will be talking with a variety of people as you carry out your community assessment. Try to develop good relationships with all those who hold a stake in the trail corridor. As you talk with them, try to be sensitive to the corridor's history, its politics, its community character, and the sentiment of adjacent landowners.

Identifying Stakeholders

Stakeholders are individuals, groups, or agencies that will be impacted by, benefit from, or otherwise be interested in your trail corridor. Building rapport with stakeholders will be vital to your project's success. Identifying these individuals and groups, and later contacting them, can help to avoid unpleasant surprises and build the all-important alliances you will need during the implementation phase.

Building your list of stakeholders can be accomplished in several ways. Talking with key public agencies such as the planning department or city engineer will help. Checking the names of landowners at the tax assessor's office will also provide vital information. Some information can be gleaned during site visits along the trail and through informal talks with local residents and business people. Your presentations at community forums and workshops will also elicit local support and concerns. Bear in mind that you will be gathering information throughout the assessment and public participation process, so be prepared for new names, faces, ideas, and concerns all through the planning phase and even after the trail is built. (See "Public Involvement" in Chapter 2.) Here is a list of some of the typical stakeholders with whom you will likely be working.

COMMUNITY ORGANIZATIONS. Identify and list all community organizations with a potential interest in the project. Include recreation clubs (e.g., bicycling, hiking, equestrian, skiing, and

POTENTIAL STAKEHOLDERS

1. Community Groups
   - Recreational Clubs (bicycling, equestrian)
   - Environmental Organizations
   - Groups for the Elderly
   - Garden Clubs
   - Persons with Disabilities
   - Historical Societies
   - Homeowners Associations
   - Chambers of Commerce
   - Farming Organizations
   - Local PTAs, YMCAs
2. Political Jurisdictions/Agencies
   - City or Town
   - County
   - State
   - Federal
3. Utility Companies
4. Nearby Residents
5. Local Businesses

snowmobiling clubs), environmental organizations, groups for the elderly and disabled, historical societies, homeowners' associations, business associations, civic clubs, chambers of commerce, farmers and farm organizations, educational groups, trade associations, schools, public health groups, community development organizations, art and cultural commissions—anyone who may have a stake in what you are planning. Involve at least one person from each group in your trail development process. Do not try to avoid or exclude anyone, even those opposed to the trail. You need the comments, ideas, and support of a myriad of groups for your trail to succeed.

POLITICAL JURISDICTIONS. Identify and document all political jurisdictions along the corridor, preferably mapping their boundaries in relation to the trail corridor. An up-to-date gas-station-style local road map can be a good place to start identifying jurisdictions. Include special districts (such as schools, water, and sewer districts) as well as cities, towns, counties, states, and federal congressional districts and agencies. Also, try to gather information on the community's politics and history regarding trails. Has a trail ever been proposed/developed in the community and what was the reaction? Discussions with parks, planning, and public works staff can be very helpful as well as a check of newspaper articles, local Web sites, and talking with local residents and business owners.

LOCAL, STATE, FEDERAL, AND UTILITY AGENCIES. List (and contact) all governmental agencies with a potential interest in your project—they may be required to review your trail project for compliance with legislation and regulations. They also may be planning projects such as roads or sewers that will have an impact on your corridor, or they may be a source of potential funding. Your local regional planning agency or council of governments may be able to help with this. Begin thinking about areas of mutual interest and partnership opportunities with these agencies. If applicable, include the U.S. Army Corps of Engineers (if a wetland or waterway is involved), Environmental Protection Agency, Surface Transportation Board (if a rail-trail is involved), federal and state wildlife agencies, state and local parks and planning departments, state and local drainage and flood-control agencies, as well as state and local transportation and highway agencies.

Also list any public or private utility companies that may have an affected interest, including electric companies, irrigation ditch companies, water and sewer utilities, fiber-optic companies, telephone companies, railroads, and gas pipeline companies. Many areas have utility identification companies that may be able to help you in identifying utility corridors. You might also want to check with your state public utilities commission. Many trails have been successfully developed within utility rights-of-way.

RESIDENTS AND BUSINESSES ALONG THE CORRIDOR. What kinds of communities do you find along the corridor? Is the area rural, suburban, urban, or a combination of these? Are the people high-income, lower-income, professional, or blue-collar? Are they highly mobile, or have they lived there for generations? Are the residents elderly, middle-aged, or young families in starter homes? For demographic information, consult local planning agencies. Also consider reading recent U.S. Census reports and visiting areas to get a feel for the people and the neighborhoods. Studies have shown that the majority of trail users are nearby residents, so gathering information about them will be useful in understanding their needs and concerns, and in choosing appropriate uses for the trail.

Try to get a sense of how the people along the corridor view their neighborhood or community and how they see the trail fitting into their long-range objectives. How will the trail benefit them? Do they want access? If so, where? Be sure you are aware of and understand any community fears and concerns about the trail. Anticipate possible resistance, especially from nearby residents or businesses along the corridor. Nothing can hold up a project faster than opposition by adjacent landowners. Get to know them, and find out what they really want and what they care about. (See "Meeting the Needs of Adjacent Landowners" in Chapter 2.)

Ownership and Land Use

It is critical that you gather information about the ownership of the corridor, as well as adjacent lands. Ownership of the corridor may be difficult to define, especially if the corridor is a former rail bed, since deed information may be very old and properties may have changed hands many times. In some cases, the land is owned by a single landowner; however, most corridors are owned by numerous individuals, and ownership may constitute an easement instead of a deed. You may need to enlist the services of a real estate attorney or title company to complete this task. Refer to *Secrets of Successful Rail-Trails* and *Acquiring Rail Corridors* by the Rails-to-Trails Conservancy, Washington, D.C., for more information on investigating the ownership of human-made corridors.

Compile an orderly list of key owners of adjacent lands, including information on their interests, concerns, and how to contact them. Tax assessor maps at city hall or the county courthouse will be helpful. While these maps are not always reliable, and should not be considered precise legal descriptions of property lines, they are usually sufficient for identifying most of the property owners. Also, be sure to keep in mind renters of land and buildings, even though you may not be able to identify all of them.

To make sure that your trail becomes part of a viable alternative transportation system, consider existing and proposed land uses (see Figure 1.1). Pay special attention to properties directly

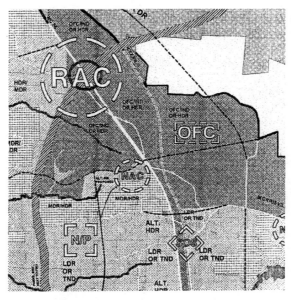

Figure 1.1. Example of a land-use map. Legends: RAC—Regional Activity Center; OFC—Office; HDR—High-Density Residential; MDR—Medium-Density Residential; LDR—Low-Density Residential; TND—Traditional Neighborhood Development; NAC—Neighborhood Activity Center; SOS—Special Opportunity Site; N/P—Neighborhood Park.

LAND USES

- Residential (neighborhoods, homes)
- Commercial (shopping, offices)
- Parks and Recreational (ball fields, preserves)
- Agricultural (farmland)
- Institutional (schools, colleges)
- Industrial (factory, rail yard)
- Open Space/Vacant Properties

abutting the corridor. As you inventory land use, consider the trail's role in linking residential neighborhoods to other community resources, such as shopping centers, parks, schools, transit stops, and offices. Also assess whether these areas present opportunities for or constraints on trail development. Identify and map planned public and private projects that may affect the corridor. These may include the following:

Greenways Inc.

Figure 1.2. Trails can connect to parks and other recreation resources.

RESIDENTIAL. If possible, identify the type and density of housing near the corridor: single-family, townhouse, low-rise, high-rise, senior housing. Acknowledge any potential privacy or security concerns arising from the trail corridor's use.

COMMERCIAL. Include offices, theaters, restaurants, and stores, noting likely destination points, such as a shopping mall. Linkages to commercial areas can boost economic activity.

RECREATIONAL. Include important recreational destinations such as parks, ball fields, forest preserves, museums, and recreation centers (Figure 1.2). Note the facilities present, including rest rooms, water fountains, and parking. Certain recreation areas, such as golf courses, can present a potential hazard to trail users. You do not want trail users to be struck by an errant golf shot.

AGRICULTURAL. The size and kind of agricultural activity are important. Consider potential conflicts arising from users trespassing on private farms, the use of toxic or noxious chemicals, and livestock wandering onto the trail.

INSTITUTIONAL. Note schools by type—elementary, middle, high school, and college. Schools can be important destination points, and trail links to schools may go a long way toward helping you sell your project as safe off-road transportation. Other institutional resources include libraries, cultural centers, civic buildings, and public health facilities.

INDUSTRIAL. Identify heavy, medium, and light industrial uses of adjacent land, and note any possible conflicts, including any safety hazards, targets for vandalism, noise pollution, and so on. A trail next to a railroad switching yard, for example, could create a potentially hazardous situation if children using the trail were attracted into the rail yard. Identify any abandoned industrial areas that might be environmentally contaminated (see "Environmental Contamination Issues" in this chapter).

VACANT PROPERTIES AND OPEN SPACE. Take special note of vacant properties adjoining the trail corridor. Are any in public ownership, and do they have the potential to be developed as trailside parks or future trailheads? Is any future development planned on large vacant tracts? Do opportunities exist for future trail-related development? Can proposed developments be linked to the trail? Are there efforts to preserve natural areas along the way?

Historic and Cultural Considerations

Trail builders and historians make great partners. More often than not, trail corridors follow routes steeped in history. River valleys, canals, and, later, rail lines were the routes of settlement, the first passages for travel and commerce by indigenous people and early settlers (Figure 1.3). They are often rich in artifacts and lore, and they offer unique paths to the past if their histories are preserved and interpreted. Think about opportunities to provide interpretive waysides, displays of artifacts, or other ways to tell stories of the past (see "Understanding the History of Your Trail" in Chapter 3). Consider contacting local arts organizations or museums to explore possibilities for incorporating into your trail project public art that highlights its history and culture. Here are some key historic and cultural considerations and information sources.

LOCAL HISTORY OF THE CORRIDOR. Most communities have local history books. You can probably ascertain what is available by visiting your local library or historical society. Try to

Figure 1.3. Originally built in 1883 for the Minneapolis Union Railway Company, the Stone Arch Bridge is now a majestic bicycle and pedestrian thoroughfare linking the University of Minnesota with downtown Minneapolis.

find local rail or canal enthusiasts, and talk with teachers. You might convince a high school class or college student to research the corridor's history as a school project. Meet with adjacent property owners who may have interesting records or anecdotal material.

STATE AND NATIONAL RESOURCES. Contact your state's historic preservation office, which is likely to have statewide historic surveys and knowledgeable contacts throughout your state. Federal programs such as the National Register of Historic Places maintain listings of sites, structures, and objects significant in American history. Consider also the Historic American Engineering Record/Historic American Buildings Survey (HAER/HABS) collection at the

Library of Congress, which includes numerous drawings, photographs, and histories. All of this information is available to the public.

IMPORTANT STRUCTURES AND PLACES. Inventory the artifacts, structures, and places of aesthetic and cultural interest along the corridor. Does a retaining wall have especially attractive stonework? Are there old railroad artifacts? Who owns these resources? Can they be safely restored, repainted, or otherwise preserved as a permanent part of the trail experience?

Trails can provide a wonderful way to connect people to one another and the cultural institutions that make up our communities. Take note of any museums, special neighborhood gathering places, or multicultural neighborhoods along the way. Often these neighbors and community institutions have something to contribute to the trail, such as ethnic festivals or a local artist specializing in mural painting that could be integrated into trail use.

ARCHAEOLOGICAL ELEMENTS. Check with local historians and your state archaeologist to determine whether any places of archaeological significance exist along the corridor. Consider how to protect, interpret, and integrate archaeological elements into your trail.

Transportation System

Many trails serve a transportation purpose by providing alternative routes among the places

where people live, work, learn, visit, shop, and play. The majority of trails in this country are funded through federal programs that encourage the development of off-road transportation facilities (see "Funding Sources for Trail Development" in Chapter 4). To promote your trail, you will need to understand how it fits into the larger transportation system (see "Comprehensive Trail Planning" in Chapter 2).

Contact city or county planning departments or state departments of transportation for information. Your local Metropolitan Planning Organization (MPO) and state Department of Transportation (DOT) will have information on existing and proposed transportation facilities, including those slated for development in the Transportation Improvements Program (TIP) listing. Federal transportation legislation requires each state to employ a bicycle and pedestrian coordinator, who can offer expertise and useful information. Some larger metropolitan areas also employ a bicycle and pedestrian transportation planner. Consider the following elements of the transportation system.

EXISTING SYSTEMS. Begin your analysis by inventorying the existing system of roadways, railroads, trails, sidewalks, bicycle routes, and other transportation facilities. How does the current transportation system work? Where are the important "trip generators"—schools, places of employment, and large residential enclaves? Can you identify heavily traveled corridors, such as those between a large bedroom community and a downtown area? How might your trail fit into these corridors?

MOTORIZED COUNTS VS. NONMOTORIZED COUNTS. Is there any data in your community comparing motorized travel with nonmotorized travel in general and within certain corridors? Nationwide, bicycle trips account for about 1 percent of all trips, and walking trips account for about 5 percent of all trips, according to the U.S. Department of Transportation. Is the percentage higher in your community? Could it be higher, reducing fuel consumption and pollution, if a trail system were put in place?

FUTURE PLANS AND INTERMODAL OPPORTUNITIES. What are future plans for the transportation system? And how can your trail be part of this system? Consider mass transit as well as auto travel (Figure 1.4). Can your trail act as a feeder into a major mass-transit station, serving as a component in a "bike and ride" system in which users ride their bicycles from home to the transit station and store them in bicycle lockers? Will it tie into a countywide or statewide trail system or transportation network?

Economic Development Factors

The popularity of multi-use trails has steadily increased, and many trails attract tens of thou-

Figure 1.4. A trail in Research Triangle Park, North Carolina, encourages the use of alternative transportation by connecting to a transit stop.

sands of users. This growth has enriched adjoining neighborhoods beyond the obvious recreation and transportation benefits that these corridors provide. A recent study of the Little Miami Scenic Trail in Warren County, Ohio, revealed that trail users spend an average of $13.54 per person per visit on trip-related expenditures—food, lodging, retail items, auto expenses—generating more than $2 million per year for local communities. In addition, these 150,000 to 175,000 trail users also spend an average of $277 each per year on durable goods directly related to the existence of the trail, including clothing, equipment, and accessories.[1] (See the Annotated Resource Directory at the

end of this book for more information on this, and other, publications.)

Another study, on the Montour Trail in Allegheny County, Pennsylvania, focused on the impact of the trail on local businesses. Total spending by trail users was estimated at approximately $10 million in 1998, with revenue expected to increase by $1–2 million when the trail is expanded. Local businesses reported direct economic benefits from trail-related activity—resulting in an estimated $7.9 million in receipts and $1 million in wages. The study also revealed that several companies had been attracted to the region because of the existence of the trail, including "The Waterfront," a $300 million commercial and residential development project along the Montour Trail.[2]

Homebuilders and realtors often market trails as amenities because they increase the value of adjacent properties and attract businesses to a community (Figure 1.5). Talk with business people and community residents to get a sense of how a trail might benefit the area economically, through increased tourism, property values, and business attraction.

Trails also benefit the economy through helping to reduce the costs of health care. The U.S. Centers for Disease Control and the surgeon general recommend regular, moderate-intensity exercise as an effective way of reducing the risk of developing cancer, diabetes, and heart disease. Trails offer

[1] Ohio-Kentucky-Indiana Regional Council of Governments, *Little Miami Scenic Trail Users Study* (Cincinnati, OH: Ohio-Kentucky-Indiana Regional Council of Governments, 1999).
[2] Pennsylvania Economy League and University of Pittsburgh, "An Economic Impact Study for the Allegheny Trail Alliance" (U.S. Department of Transportation, 1999).

Figure 1.5. Trails and greenways can improve the value of nearby properties.

opportunities to improve physical health, which in turn reduces health care costs. People who exercise regularly have fewer claims against their medical insurance and spend less time in the hospital than those who do not exercise.

Assessing Trail Demand

"If you build it, they will come!" Or will they? Like any major capital undertaking, building a trail requires some thought about how to market the trail. Marketing is about increasing the demand for a product by making the public aware of it and promoting its positive attributes. In the case of trails, parks, and other public amenities where tax dollars are involved, marketing takes on an additional dimension—the political dimension. Many taxpayers may never use the trail but must sanction the project or, at least, not put roadblocks in its way. Here are some key marketing considerations:

MARKET DEMAND INVESTIGATION. There are several ways to assess the demand for your trail:

- Contact your state's department of natural resources (or equivalent agency), which is required to complete a State Comprehensive Outdoor Recreation Plan (SCORP) approximately every five years. This publication often will document trail user demand.

- Determine the ratio of existing trail miles to the user population in the communities along the corridor. Compare this to the National Recreation and Park Association's "Open Space Standards," which suggest a ratio of 1 trail mile per 2,000 people for bicycling/jogging trails. (This number is intended only as a rough guideline and does not necessarily reflect local demographics, changing trends, uniqueness of the trail corridor, or myriad other factors. Such data may, however, help you make your case before community decision makers.)

- Contact the Rails-to-Trails Conservancy, American Hiking Society, National Park Service, American Trails, American Recreation Coalition, United Ski Industries Association, and other groups that may have literature about user trends related to trails.

- Obtain user information from another trail in your community, or a similar trail in your region or state. The Rails-to-Trails Conservancy maintains a national database of rail-trail managers.

- Check data from national opinion polls, which periodically survey participation in trail-related activities. In 1994, a Gallup poll survey estimated that 131 million Americans, almost half of the population, regularly walk, run, or bicycle for fitness, recreation, and commuting.

- To generate a rough estimate of potential users, calculate the number of people living within 2 miles of the trail. In many cases, the majority of trail users are nearby residents. Combine this information with any existing public opinion surveys to calculate an approximate number of local users, then add in an estimate of out-of-town users based on current tourism data. To generate precise data, refer to the *Guidebook on Methods to Estimate Non-Motorized Travel* recently published by the Federal Highway Administration[3] (see Case

---

[3] W. L. Schwartz et al., *Guidebook on Methods to Estimate Non-Motorized Travel* (U.S. Department of Transportation, 1999).

SITE ASSESSMENT CHECKLIST:

- Green Infrastructure
  - ☐ Vegetation
  - ☐ Soils
  - ☐ Topography
  - ☐ Waterways
  - ☐ Significant Natural Features
- Built Features
  - ☐ Bridges
  - ☐ Tunnels
  - ☐ Canals
  - ☐ Buildings
  - ☐ Other Structures
- Potentially Contaminated Sites
- Above- and Belowground Utilities
- Intersections
  - ☐ Roadways
  - ☐ Rail Lines or Canals
  - ☐ Driveways
  - ☐ Other Trails
- Access Points
  - ☐ Automobile
  - ☐ Bicycle
  - ☐ Pedestrian
  - ☐ Transit
- Animal Life
- Corridor Composition
- Spatial Values

Study 2), or consider enlisting the services of economic forecasting professionals.

- Most important, determine community interest by talking with any local potential user groups. Bicycling, walking, running, equestrian, and other groups are a good start.

DETERMINING USER GROUPS. Demand for your trail will depend on how you present it. Consider the full range of potential user groups—bicyclists, hikers, runners, nature enthusiasts, equestrians, in-line skaters, people in wheelchairs, parents with strollers, cross-country skiers, anglers, snowmobilers, students, conservationists, and elderly people—and their needs. Throughout the planning process, think about how you can make the trail and its associated benefits appeal to users, supporters, and opponents (see "Promoting and Marketing Your Trail" in Chapter 6).

Site Considerations: Inventory and Assessment

Now that you've completed researching the community, you are ready to conduct a physical assessment of the natural resources and built features within the corridor (see "Site Assessment Checklist"). This includes an accurate description and documentation of the landscape's native elements, the built features of the corridor, the corridor's location in relation to other major natural or developed facilities, and the route or layout of the corridor as it traverses your community, region, or state.

To conduct an assessment, you need to get out and walk or bicycle your trail corridor and inventory what you observe as you move along it. Use all your senses and record how the corridor looks, sounds, and feels. Try to imagine the perspective of a child, an elderly person, or an athlete. Consider the perspective of both genders. A female's perspective of how a trail feels may be quite different than a male's.

Begin by obtaining large, accurate maps. Mapping can be obtained from a number of sources, including local planning agencies, the U.S. Geological Survey, or even maps purchased at a local bookstore. There are also a number of excellent computer mapping products available (see "Mapping Resources on the World Wide Web"). While you will need more sophisticated mapping when you move into the design phase, elementary mapping is fine at the initial visioning and inventory level. Select maps that illustrate the known features within and surrounding the corridor (Figure 1.6), and plan to record your findings. Written descriptions, tape-recorded comments, photographs, and video are excellent ways to document your findings.

Make sure you obtain permission from landowners if you are traveling on private property. Be tactful when approaching adjacent landowners with the trail concept. They can become the most enthusiastic advocates or the most formidable opponents to your trail (see "Meeting the Needs of Adjacent Landowners" in Chapter 2). If you are

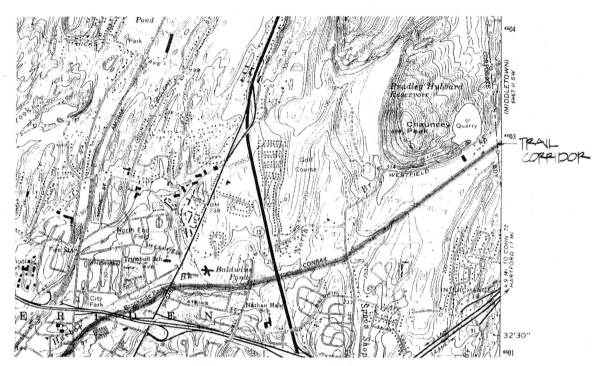

Figure 1.6. United States Geological Survey map.

MAPPING RESOURCES ON THE WORLD WIDE WEB

Obtaining information about your trail corridor has gotten a bit easier and more efficient with the emergence of the World Wide Web. From the comfort of your home or office, you can download information to a personal computer that can help you better determine the existing conditions, opportunities, and constraints associated with your trail project. Many cities, counties, regions, states, and federal government agencies are making a tremendous amount of information available to the public through their Web sites.

Web sites, such as the U.S. Geological Survey (www.usgs.org), can provide detailed maps, known as 7.5-minute-series quadrangle maps, of your community. These maps show topographic lines, vegetation, lakes, rivers and streams, roadways, buildings, utility transmission lines, and other important data. Maps are available in different software file types. You should check to see if the software that you have is compatible with the file type available on the Web.

Because the World Wide Web is a dynamic, ever-changing source of information, it is impossible to list all of the sites that could be applicable to your project. The best way to find these sites on the Internet is to use your Web browser to search for them on any common search engine, such as www.yahoo.com. Just type in a few key words describing what you are looking for, and a list of Web sites will then be provided that meet your criteria.

not ready to approach landowners, or if your corridor is especially long, you can examine the corridor from roadway intersections, bridges, adjacent parks, and other areas of public access. Many corridors, especially those in urban areas, will contain enough of these access points to allow you to conduct an accurate inventory and assessment. Also consider obtaining aerial photographs from a local planning department to assist in your on-site investigations.

As you examine the natural and built elements of the corridor, you will notice areas where trail development is compatible or in conflict with existing resources, or the physical "opportunities" and "constraints" within the corridor. Assess the following elements in terms of what opportunities they present or what constraints they pose for development of a multi-use trail.

Green Infrastructure

Begin the actual assessment with an examination of the natural features, or "green infrastructure," within and adjacent to the corridor. How might these natural features affect, or be affected by, the development of your multi-use trail? Consider the following green infrastructure elements:

EXISTING VEGETATION. In evaluating the vegetation, define the various plant species. (Pay particular attention to any endangered or rare species, and to any nonnative invasive species.) Record any significant characteristics. This information will be used later to define landscape modifications and additions that should be made to your completed multi-use trail (see "Landscaping" in Chapter 3). If you cannot identify a particular plant, collect sample leaves, flowers and take them to a botanist or horticulturist for proper assessment.

Investigate whether railroad companies or local transportation agencies sprayed growth retardants or poisons to reduce leaf mass or exterminate naturally occurring vegetation. If so, the vegetation that led to these practices may still be present. The herbicides that were sprayed may present a threat to new trees or shrubs, and possibly to human health as well, so try to obtain information on which chemicals were used and for how long (see "Environmental Contamination Issues" in this chapter).

EXISTING SOILS. The characteristics of underlying soils help determine landscaping, drainage, surfacing, and appropriate types of structures associated with trail development. You can iden-

tify the soils within your trail corridor by obtaining a Soil Survey from the local office of the U.S. Department of Agriculture, Natural Resources Conservation Service (USDA NRCS), usually associated with a local university. This survey will give you information on soil type, depth, groundwater level, drainage, native vegetation, and stability of the soil.

SURROUNDING TOPOGRAPHY. An accurate assessment of surrounding topography should be done to define the type of drainage controls needed to facilitate safe multi-use trail development. The surrounding topography, or slopes, affects the amount of surface water flowing into and through the corridor (as does frequency and intensity of precipitation), so you need to know where off-site water collects and drains through the corridor. If necessary, employ the services of a hydrologist, an engineer, a landscape architect, or a land surveyor to help you properly assess the drainage patterns through the corridor. Controlling surface water is one of the most important aspects of trail design and development.

There may be areas prone to hazard of falling rock. You may need to consult a geotechnical engineer if potential problems are identified, such as steep rocky slopes above the corridor or evidence of fallen rocks on the right-of-way.

ADJACENT OR INTERSECTING STREAMS. Streams and rivers present challenges to proper drainage within the corridor. The first step is to find out

whether the corridor is within a flood-prone area. Where is it parallel to or intersected by watercourses? Are they likely to damage the trail corridor when in flood (look for high water lines or debris in trees)? Answers to these questions help to determine whether you should develop the trail on the existing natural grade or whether you will need to build a bridge, culvert, or boardwalk to cross a flood-prone area. Also investigate whether the area is prone to flash flooding that might pose a hazard to trail users.

Begin by obtaining maps from your local Federal Emergency Management Agency (FEMA) office showing the boundaries of the 100-year floodplain and general locations of wetland areas (Figure 1.7). You may need to consult a hydrological engineer. You should also contact your local division of water quality to obtain information on what permits are

Figure 1.7. This wetland, adjacent to a railroad corridor, offers educational opportunities and scenic benefits.

required for trail or bridge construction. In many states, buffer requirements now in place to protect stream corridors may also affect the design and development of the trail or trail structures that cross or lie adjacent to waterways.

If a corridor has no bridges and crosses a stream, you need to determine the stream's width from top of bank to top of bank. Also, measure the width of the floodplain in the area, the depth of the stream from top of bank to bottom of channel, and locate the stream's origin. If possible, determine the velocity and volume of the stream. This information will be used later when you design the appropriate stream crossing for your trail. Perform a similar analysis for adjacent streams. You may want to employ the services of a hydrological engineer to assist with this analysis, too.

Stream access is another major issue to consider when conducting your assessment. Where are existing access points? Interesting views? Fishing and swimming spots? Canoe or boat launch and recovery? Where can new ones be placed?

You should also take note of the condition of the stream and its banks. Obtain any water quality studies that have been completed. How clean is the water? Is swimming or fishing allowed? Is there evidence of washouts or stream erosion (Figure 1.8)? Are slopes to the waterway steep or gradual? This information will help you determine whether bank stabilization measures will be necessary.

Figure 1.8. Example of degraded, eroded stream banks.

SIGNIFICANT NATURAL FEATURES. Lakes and ponds, rock outcroppings, old-growth forests, wetlands, or other natural features in your region are important attractions. In completing your evaluation, note the size, shape, location, ownership, and other aspects of these features. Some of the features you discover may be on private lands, especially if the right-of-way is narrow. Are they accessible to the public? Will public use result in their deterioration? Often, significant natural features are the highlights of a trail, but they can also be developmental constraints.

CLIMATE. Is the climate in the area extremely hot or cold, or is it mild? How much rain does your area receive? Will the trail be used year-round, or will the weather discourage use during one or more seasons? It may be helpful to check local weather records or weather data sources available on the Internet and build a climate table showing monthly temperature ranges and precipitation.

Built Features within the Corridor

Built features associated with a rail or canal corridor are structures that are usually significant, whether a trestle bridge across a river, a tunnel through a mountain, or a canal lock. Some built structures, such as abandoned railroad depots, whistle posts, and defunct mills, may no longer be used but are objects of cultural and historic interest.

To evaluate the integrity of these structures, employ a qualified structural engineer or architect with historic structure experience. Unless you are professionally qualified, do not evaluate them yourself—the potential legal liability is enormous. To help assess historic significance, seek out a historian through your local office of historic preservation, state historic office, the National Trust for Historic Preservation, or even your local library. You should also contact local historical societies as well as railroad and canal historical societies, which may have special insight into the significance of corridor-related structures.

Consider the following questions for each tunnel, trestle, or building: What is its dominant characteristic? How old is it? Who owns it? Given its current condition, can it safely support future trail use? Is it accessible to people with disabilities? What modifications are needed so that the structure remains an asset for trail use? When you have answered these questions,

Figure 1.9. A bridge along the Allegheny River Trail in Pennsylvania.

you can decide which structures should be incorporated into the trail's development and which should be removed. It is important to remember that structures that have received historic designation may be difficult and expensive to restore and may not be removable. The following kinds of structures are commonly associated with rail and canal corridors.

BRIDGES. Your corridor may have one bridge or several (Figure 1.9), constructed of wood, steel, or concrete. The structural engineer you employ to evaluate each bridge should inspect the footings or piers that support it, the bridge's superstructure, and its approaches. You should obtain a certified report from the engineer describing the bridge's current condition and what is needed to bring the bridge into compliance with local, state, and federal laws. Remind your struc-

tural engineer that the live load for future trail use may be less than what the bridge was built to support. Reducing the live load rating can result in a different evaluation of the bridge's capacity and capability. This information will be important when you actually begin designing your bridges for trail use (see "Bridges and Railings for Multi-Use Trails" in Chapter 3).

TUNNELS. These are complicated and unique structures. Most were originally constructed to meet site-specific requirements. If possible, locate the tunnel's original engineering drawings. These will describe significant structural features of the tunnel that are not readily apparent from visual inspection. Again, as with bridges, obtain a certified report from a structural engineer describing the current condition of the tunnel. This information will help you make sure your tunnel can be safely and successfully adapted for trail design (see "Tunnels" in Chapter 3).

CANALS. A variety of materials have been used to construct locks and canals. A canal's structural integrity is dependent on the material used in construction and on the settling or shifting of the earth that surrounds the structure. Core samples of the soil mass behind these structures are as important as the evaluation of the joints and mass of the walls, channel bottom, and locks (Figure 1.10). Again, obtain a certified report from a qualified structural engineer describing the canal's condition and its working and nonworking components.

Figure 1.10. A preserved canal lock along the Farmington Canal Linear State Park Trail in Connecticut.

BUILDINGS. Buildings that were developed during your corridor's previous uses may be historically significant. A qualified historian or architect best makes such an evaluation. A structural engineer, architect, or local building inspector should also perform a structural evaluation of a building's foundation and other components to determine whether the building can be integrated safely into the completed trail.

In addition to evaluating the integrity of buildings, give some thought to possible trail-related adaptations you can make. For example, what will an industrial building look like as a snack shop, restaurant, or bike shop? Can a building within the corridor be converted into a trail visitor center (Figures 1.11 and 1.12)?

Before

After

Figures 1.11 and 1.12. Before and after views of the restored train depot at Bloomington, Michigan, that serves as the midpoint for the Kal-Haven Trail.

OTHER RELATED STRUCTURES AND FACILITIES. These include mechanical devices associated with the corridor's prior use—millstones from a flour mill, fences built as a boundary, railroad switches, and other facilities adjacent to the corridor. Note the location, size, former purpose, and current status of these structures and facilities, and determine whether they are opportunities for or constraints on your trail design.

Environmental Contamination Issues

Corridors of land once used for industrial purposes may contain areas of environmental contamination, resulting from past use of chemicals, toxic spills, or leakage from storage tanks. It is important that these areas be identified and cleaned up to a level suitable for human contact. An overview of these issues is provided in this chapter; however, a professional should be consulted to ensure that you are adequately addressing all the legal, public health, and environmental ramifications associated with areas that are contaminated. See Case Study 3 for more information about assessing potential environmental contamination issues. The following text offers key steps to take in determining the influence that contaminated sites may have on your trail project.

ASSESSMENT. If you suspect environmental contamination within or adjacent to a trail corridor, enlist the services of an environmental expert to

conduct a Phase I Environmental Site Assessment. This assessment is limited to a visual inspection, examination of relevant public records, and sampling of possible problem areas. If the Phase I study identifies problem areas, a Phase II assessment may be required, including tests to determine contamination levels. An alternative to this second, more expensive study would be to convince the current owner of the property (e.g., the railroad) to retain responsibility for contamination predating the acquisition of the property for a trail, and to clean up the land before ownership is transferred (See Rails-to-Trails Conservancy's *Secrets of Successful Rail Trails*, "Negotiating with a Railroad.")

BROWNFIELD DESIGNATION. *Brownfield* is a term developed by environmental planners, including the U.S. Environmental Protection Agency (EPA), to describe areas of abandoned or underused land that are perceived to be, or are in fact, environmentally contaminated due to past industrial or commercial use. An abandoned warehouse, an old municipal dump, or a defunct mill are all examples of potential brownfield sites (Figures 1.13 and 1.14). Railroad corridors, or sections of corridors, can also be considered brownfields. Redevelopment of these areas can be complicated by the liability and cost associated with environmental cleanup. However, government programs have been established to assist with these issues.

If you suspect your corridor or an adjacent

Figures 1.13 and 1.14. Once home to stockyards, fertilizer plants, and meat packing and rendering facilities, Herrs' Island in Pittsburgh, Pennsylvania, was transformed into an upscale development. The Three Rivers Heritage Trail circles the island and connects it to the city via a renovated railroad bridge.

property to be a brownfield, contact your state natural resources agency and ask them to make a determination. The property may already be identified as a brownfield. If not, the agency will need to conduct a Phase 1, and possibly a Phase 2, environmental assessment. Once a property is designated as a brownfield, it may qualify under federal law for program assistance from the EPA, and may also qualify for any existing state brownfield assistance. Such assistance can include funding for cleanup and site restoration.

The ultimate goal of brownfields assistance programs is the redevelopment of these areas for appropriate industrial or commercial use, although portions of these sites can be converted into residential use, parks, open space, and trails.

Human-Made Infrastructure

Human-made infrastructure includes built elements that provide specific services such as

drainage structures (culverts and pipes); gas, water, and sewer lines; and electrical, telephone, and cable television wires. Document infrastructure elements that are within the corridor, run parallel to it, or cross it (Figure 1.15). Evaluate the potential compatibility or conflict between existing or proposed utilities and your multi-use trail project.

Water, sanitary sewers, and electrical and telephone lines may be useful on your trail. Are these utilities already present within the corridor

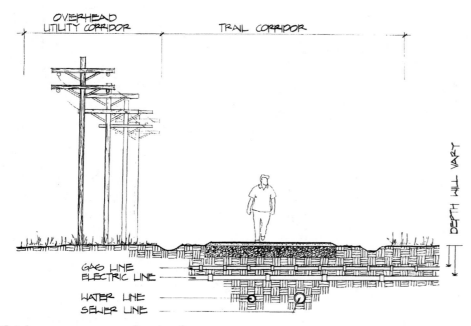

Figure 1.15. Infrastructure surrounding a trail.

or nearby? If so, are they capable of supporting additional use? Who operates the utilities? What is required to provide local connections for trail use?

Certain utility equipment, such as natural gas pipelines and high-voltage electrical lines, can pose a formidable challenge to trail development. A utility-locating service can accurately determine the route and depth of these and other potentially hazardous utilities, so you can appropriately plan, design, and develop your trail around them. Do not underestimate the importance of this step! Such lines cannot be

simply spliced if broken—the consequences can be very serious.

Finally, when considering utilities, note not only the potential conflicts but the potential mutual benefits and economic opportunities of joint corridor use. (See "Joint Ventures within Your Multi-Use Trail Corridor" in Chapter 5.)

Intersections

Intersections can pose challenges during trail design and development, but they can also provide trail access. It is critical that you avoid end-

ing your trail at hazardous intersections or those without safe crossing facilities. There are many types of intersections, and if you evaluate them properly, you can incorporate them successfully into your trail design. Here are some important intersection considerations.

ROADWAYS. Roads are the most hazardous and frequently encountered trail intersection. Consider how the trail will cross the road: at grade, below grade, or overhead. Is the traffic on the roadway too heavy to facilitate a safe at-grade crossing? How many lanes are there? How wide are they? What is the posted speed? Is there a median? Is there enough sight distance so motorists can react to a trail user in the roadway? Is there a signalized intersection nearby, and does it have crosswalks or pedestrian signals? If so, how much time is allowed to cross? Is it adequate for trail users such as children and the elderly? Could someone safely bicycle or walk along the road to get to the trail? Are there sidewalks or bicycle facilities along the road? What is the available clearance of any overpass? Also find out if these roadways are scheduled to be widened or otherwise changed in the near future (you may be able to include trail improvements as part of proposed roadway projects). These answers will enable you to design appropriate and safe road crossings (see "Road Crossings" in Chapter 3).

When evaluating your trail route, also think about avoiding "dumping" trail users into a hazardous situation—for example, having the trail terminate at a very busy road before reaching a desired destination such as a park, school, or other activity center. This may entice users, especially children, into an undesirable situation.

ACTIVE RAIL LINES. Existing railroad routes crossing trails present a unique situation. These rights-of-way often are difficult to cross because their owners fear the liability associated with public access. Some states may refuse a new at-grade crossing because of state policies. Determine the frequency of activity associated with the route, and take note of existing topography, considering the feasibility of going over or under the existing right-of-way (see "Rails-with-Trails" in Chapter 3).

DRIVEWAYS. These may be residential, commercial, or industrial access points to properties adjacent to the trail corridor. Determine the type and frequency of driveways, the type of traffic, the sight distance, and the frequency of use on a daily or monthly basis. Clearly, a driveway cut for a fast-food restaurant or strip mall will have significantly more traffic than a residential driveway. Try to avoid frequent encounters with driveways along your trail.

OTHER TRAIL CORRIDORS. Nearby trails allow you to link trails together. Assess any intersecting trails for compatibility and conflict, based on types of use, surface, level of difficulty, signs, and regulations.

Figure 1.16. Look for worn paths created by bicyclists or pedestrians to indicate potential connections to your trail.

Access Points

It is important to take stock of all access points located within the corridor, including those associated with cars, bicycles, pedestrians, and transit users (Figure 1.16). Determine the impact of these access points on your corridor. Do people currently use the corridor for transportation, and how do they get there? Will it be possible for mass transit riders to access the trail easily? In addition to existing access points, where will new ones need to be located? Assess current and potential access points for the trail.

Animal and Plant Communities within the Corridor

Corridors cut through the habitats of a variety of domesticated and wild animals. They may also

pass through sensitive landscapes such as remnant prairies or communities of rare or threatened plant species. In evaluating the corridor, try to quantify and describe the different types of animal and plant life present. Also take note of all animal crossings and the frequency with which they are used. This information will help you determine your trail's route. For example, if your investigation shows that the nesting area for a wildlife species will be permanently disturbed by nearby trail development, you will want to reroute the trail to avoid this environmentally sensitive area. (See "Wildlife and Multi-Use Trails" in Chapter 3). Keep the following considerations in mind.

DOMESTICATED ANIMALS OR LIVESTOCK. Catalog the domesticated animals and livestock you encounter, and describe their habitat—meadow, cultivated field, natural forest, and so forth. Also make note of any existing livestock crossings and talk with farmers and ranchers about their needs with respect to the corridor and trail development. Does the trail cut across two pastures? Will cattle crossings take place along the corridor? Are appropriate gates in place? How permanent or temporary are these animal populations? Will they pose any danger to future trail users?

WILDLIFE. Numerous species of birds, mammals, reptiles, and insects occupy the vegetated edges and adjacent lands of corridors in rural and urban landscapes. Seek professional assistance to identify wildlife within the corridor. In completing your wildlife evaluation, understand

Figure 1.17. A blue heron nesting area adjacent to the West Bloomfield Trail network in Michigan.

the potential impact of a trail on wildlife nesting, breeding, and migratory habits (Figure 1.17).

Remember to conduct your investigation at different times of the year in order to observe wildlife and other species during different seasons. Note particular wildlife that may be harmful to trail users, and vice versa. Look for ways in which trail development might improve wildlife habitat (see "Wildlife and Multi-Use Trails" in Chapter 3).

ENDANGERED OR RARE SPECIES. Because of the accelerating loss of ecologically sensitive species, it is important for you to use extreme care to identify species threatened by human activity. Check with your state wildlife department and U.S. Fish and Wildlife Service to identify any threatened or endangered animal or plant

species. Be sure to allow time to schedule any required surveys or inventories (some of these can be conducted only at certain times of the year). Many states and counties have conducted natural heritage inventories that may contain known locations of rare and endangered plant and animal species. Note any endangered or rare species that exist in the area, identify potential threats to that species, and investigate trail routing or development options that would eliminate or minimize those threats. Your trail's development may be affected by federal or state legislation regarding rare, threatened, or endangered species (see "Compliance with Legislation and Permitting" in Chapter 4).

Corridor Composition

In many transportation and utility corridors, the corridor's original surface has been altered significantly. The alterations can make it difficult to determine slopes as well as soil composition and texture of the corridor surface. If your corridor has been altered, you should analyze its surface and subsurface materials to determine composition and structural integrity. Here are some important corridor composition considerations.

COMPOSITION. This refers to the materials that were used to form the subsurface and surface of the corridor. The composition of railroad beds, for example, includes ballast stone and, in certain cases, a surface-washed stone. A structural engineer

and a geotechnical testing laboratory can properly identify these materials and their integrity.

CROSS-SECTION SLOPE. This is the slope across the corridor perpendicular to the path of travel. You will most likely encounter four types of cross section as you evaluate your corridor: convex (or raised bed), flat, concave (or carved-out bed), and terraced (along a side slope) (Figures 1.18–1.20). Determine where each type of cross section is located within your corridor. How will this slope affect drainage along the corridor? Will the slopes prevent anyone from using the trail? Cross-section slopes are especially important in accommodating wheelchair users (see "Making Your Trail Accessible" in Chapter 3).

LONGITUDINAL SLOPE. This is the slope that runs along the centerline of the path of travel, often called the profile. For most former transportation corridors, the longitudinal slope is generally flat to gently rolling (3 percent), depending on the type of prior use the corridor served. In evaluating the longitudinal slopes of your corridor, you will encounter three types: uphill slopes,

Figure 1.18. Convex (raised) cross section.

Figure 1.19. Concave (carved-out) cross section.

Figure 1.20. Terraced cross section.

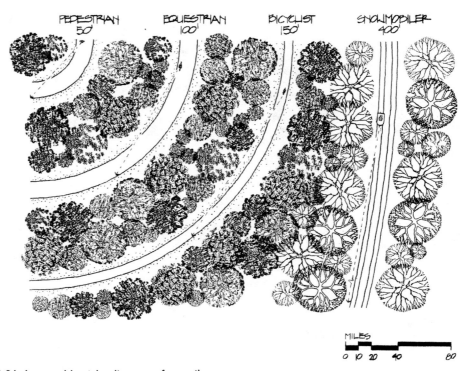

Figure 1.21. Acceptable sight distances for trail users.

Spatial Values of the Trail Corridor Landscape

flat slopes, and downhill slopes. To evaluate these slopes, you must determine the percentage of longitudinal slope (consider enlisting the assistance of a local engineer). In general, an acceptable, accessible longitudinal slope is less than 5 percent, although it may be less for natural surface trails (see "The Trail Surface" in Chapter 3).

Spatial Values of the Trail Corridor Landscape

The sequence of different landscapes that compose a trail corridor makes it an interesting place to walk, bike, and ride. As you evaluate your trail corridor, pay particular attention to the spatial components of its environment.

VIEWSHEDS. Lines of sight within a corridor or out to a landscape or adjacent built feature are called viewsheds. Evaluate not only the view from the proposed trail, but also the view *from* adjacent lands *into* the corridor. Doing this is particularly important when you have a feature that should be highlighted or security concerns, or when an adjacent landowner objects to the view of the trail.

Two viewshed issues are of concern to future trail users. The first is safety: the need for an unobstructed forward and rear view at all times. Here are the minimum acceptable sight distances: pedestrians, 50 linear feet each way; equestrians, 100 linear feet each way; bicyclists, 150 linear feet each way; snowmobilers, 400 linear feet each way (Figure 1.21).

The second important viewshed issue is the

need for trail users to see their surroundings, preferably wide views of the natural and built features of adjacent landscapes. Because viewsheds from the trail affect the quality of users' experience, you may consider creating view opportunities, even constructing an observation tower if your corridor is flat and potentially "boring."

LIGHT AREAS AND DARK AREAS. These are determined by sun exposure, topography, surrounding vegetation, and adjacent structures. Both light and dark areas alter the trail's environment, offering respite or energy for the user. They also affect the soil's moisture content, influence temperature, and vary the visual quality of the trail's features. Ideally, an assessment of both light and dark areas should be made during different seasons and at various times of the day. The ideal from a user's perspective is a mixture of light areas and dark

areas. Note also that shaded areas may result in snow or ice buildup in winter, and this may need to be addressed in trail planning and design.

OPEN OR CLOSED LANDSCAPES. These affect viewsheds and light, provide structure, and heavily influence the spatial sequence of a route's environment. Whether a landscape is open or closed is most often defined by vegetation, although topography and built structures can also be determinants. An example of an open landscape is an agricultural field or naturally occurring meadow. A closed landscape may be a segment of the corridor surrounded by thick, overhanging vegetation, which creates a tunnel effect.

Open or closed landscapes affect the trail user's experience and should be carefully considered when you are designing the trail. An ideal trail has a contrasting sequence of open and

closed landscapes as well as light areas and dark areas. Once you understand the spatial sequence of the trail environment, you can alter it or leave it intact to provide trail users with a satisfying trail experience.

Using Your Assessment

After completing this assessment you should understand the existing constraints and opportunities, compatibilities and conflicts within and surrounding your corridor. The information you have collected, evaluated, and assembled during this analysis will be used throughout the design process, so store it in an easily accessible location. The conclusions of your evaluation will serve as the starting point for designing your multi-use trail.

CASE STUDY 1

Ballenger Creek Trail: Getting Started

Frederick County, Maryland, possesses a rich diversity of historic, cultural, and natural resources. However, due to its location within commuting distance of Washington, D.C., and Baltimore, the county has been experiencing explosive growth that is consuming the landscape and straining local resources. County resi-

dents are beginning to feel more and more pressure to identify potential trail corridors, greenway linkages, and critical open space before it is lost permanently to development.

In spring 1998, the county embarked on a countywide bikeway and trail planning process in a first attempt to identify potential off-road

trails and on-road bikeway opportunities. Early in the planning process, the Ballenger Creek watershed was identified as an area experiencing some of the highest rates of growth and having a good potential for trail development. The Ballenger Creek corridor became a top priority of Frederick County Trails Inc (FCTI), a nonprofit 501(C)3, multi-user trail interest group.

In January 1999, the Maryland Greenways Commission announced a new pilot program to assist local jurisdictions with trail planning, using a portion of the state's Recreational Trail Funds. FCTI proposed to county staff that an application be submitted for Ballenger Creek, specifically, to assist in the development of a greenway and trail master plan for the corridor.

County staff did not feel the timing was right to begin work on a specific corridor, since the overall county plan had not yet been completed and adopted by the county commissioners. Given the rate of development and the fact that the state's assistance program may not be funded in future years, FCTI did not feel it was in the best interest of the county to wait. A second alternative was proposed—FCTI would apply for the grant.

FCTI approached the county commissioners directly, explained the urgency of its request, and was successful in receiving a letter of support to accompany the application. In June, when the winning projects were announced, Ballenger Creek was included on the list. With the help of the Maryland Greenways Commission and the National Park Service Rivers, Trails, and Conservation Assistance Program, a local landscape architect was hired and fieldwork began. During the summer, FCTI discussed the proposal informally with area residents and walked the corridor with the design consultant. A resource assessment of the corridor was conducted and base maps were developed showing existing features.

In December 1999, the county completed and adopted the Frederick County Bikeways and Trails Plan. With preliminary fieldwork already begun, county staff were able to move directly to work on the development of a trail master plan. The county outlined a master planning process and public involvement strategy, and organized a citizens advisory committee of local residents, homeowner association representatives, and trail interest groups to provide direction in development of the plan.

This case study highlights how working in collaboration allows for more effective and efficient delivery of services to local greenway and trail planning efforts. By working cooperatively with the county, FCTI was able to jump-start the planning process, bringing additional funding and resources to the table. The project shows the value of partnering in achieving common goals. It demonstrates how private-public partnerships can take advantage of opportunities that either entity may miss if acting alone.

CASE STUDY 2
Assessing Trail Demand

Part of your job at this point is to develop ways to sell the trail to other folks. You will need to convince local elected officials as well as any potential funders that the trail you are proposing will be used. Most trails, particularly those in urban and suburban areas, tend to have two types of users: people there for recreation, and people making a trip from one location to another. Proving this latter point is particularly important if you are going to apply for Transportation Enhancements funds.

The recently published *Guidebook on Methods to Estimate Non-Motorized Travel: Overview of Methods* provides a good discussion of the various ways to estimate nonmotorized travel. Methods discussed range from simple, back-of-the-envelope techniques to more complex methods that take into account factors such as trip location, mode choice, route choice, trip schedule, trip length, and land use. While the methods discussed here can be used for both bicycling and walking, some distinct differences exist between trips made by bike and those made on foot. For example, pedestrian trips tend to be shorter than bike trips; a large proportion of pedestrian trips are actually trips to access other modes; and the decision to use a bicycle involves more thought, a greater conceptual leap, than does the decision to walk.

There are five types of demand estimation studies:

1. Comparison studies where the proposed facility is compared to existing facilities in areas similar in population density, land use, topography, and climate.

2. Aggregate behavior studies that relate non-motorized travel in an area to its local population, land use, and other factors through regression analysis.

3. Sketch plan methods that calculate potential demand based on rules of thumb about trip lengths, mode shares, and other aspects of travel behavior.

4. Discrete choice models that predict an individual's travel choice based on characteristics of the alternatives available to them. This technique (and number 5) involves the use of specialized travel demand forecasting software.

5. Regional travel models that predict all trips in a region based on trip purpose, mode, location of trip origin and destination, land use, and population, and on characteristics of the transportation network.

The most rigorous forecasting techniques can

Demand Calculation Techniques Summary

Characteristic	Technique				
	1	*2*	*3*	*4*	*5*
Facility vs. regional level	Fac.	Reg.	Fac.	Both	Both
Ease of use	Easy	Mod.	Mod.	Dif.	Dif.
Data requirements	Mod.	Min.	Min.	Hi.	Hi.
Accuracy	Low	Low	Med.	Hi.	Mod.
Sensitivity to design factors	Low	Low	Low	Hi.	Mod.
Widely used	Yes	No	Yes	Mod.	Mod.

estimate not only the number of facility users but also the attendant reductions on automobile emissions and energy consumption and even the time and cost savings to travelers.

For more information:
Guidebook on Methods to Estimate Non-Motorized Travel: Overview of Methods July 1999.
U.S. Dept. of Transportation
Federal Highway Administration
Publication FHWA-RD-98-165
www.fhwa.dot.gov/tfhrc/safety/pubs/vol1/title.htm

CASE STUDY 3

Ten Tips for Addressing Environmental (Potential Contaminant) Issues

1. Anticipate potential environmental contamination especially in urban areas, along existing and former rail lines, and in drainages and locations with existing or historic industrial activity.

2. The primary key to successful trail development in an environmentally impacted area is to prevent people from coming in contact with contaminated media in a manner that might cause negative health effects. Trails can usually be designed to minimize contaminated media contact by trail users.

3. Include an environmental investigation as part of the "due diligence" process before accepting ownership of any parcels of land. If in doubt, a trail easement may be preferable to accepting land in fee ownership.

4. Look for suspicious indicators along the corridor: areas with no vegetation; storage drums; discolored spots; soils, gravel, or other material that do not match the surrounding terrain; unusual odors; slicks on water surfaces; or nearby activities such as an auto storage yard. Do not handle suspicious materials. Consult an expert who understands American Society for Testing Materials (ASTM, www.astm.org) assessment processes.

5. Perform a complete Phase I Environmental Site Assessment consistent with ASTM standards to identify any potential areas of environmental concerns along the proposed trail route. A Phase I assessment looks at existing and historic land uses, records of contamination events or violations in the area, and a site reconnaissance by an ASTM-certified expert.

6. If areas of interest or concern are identified in the Phase I assessment, you may need to perform a Phase II Environmental Site Assessment. This typically involves surface and subsurface sampling in areas where past activities may have resulted in contamination.

7. The results of the Phase II assessment should be used to evaluate potential routes of contaminants exposure and potential health impacts on both construction workers and long-term public use.

8. Avoid spreading contaminants or other adverse environmental impacts on plants, animals, groundwater, and other resources as a result of trail construction and use. Note also the potential impacts of digging, altering drainage patterns, or introducing irrigation to the site.

9. Do not necessarily be deterred by the presence of surface or subsurface contamination. The question is whether the contaminants pose a health risk or unacceptable risk to area resources such as plants and animals as a result of trail construction and use.

10. Always consult an environmental specialist. These experts can be found in the *Yellow Pages* under "*Environmental & Ecological Services,*" through referral by the American Academy of Environmental Engineers, or there may be qualified environmental consultant who works with your local planning or public works department.

Tips provided by David M. Rau, Principal Engineer, Paragon Consulting Group, Inc., Fort Collins, Colorado.

Planning and Public Involvement

Comprehensive Trail Planning

Planning for a trail, or a system of trails, is the first important step in transforming your vision into reality. It is just as important as proper design, and lays the foundation for successful development of your facilities. Planning presents a vision for a trail or trail system and brings a comprehensive, long-range perspective. Planning also offers the opportunity for the community to participate in helping to envision its future. Whether you want to build a quarter-mile jogging path or a 200-mile network of off-road transportation routes, you will need some type of master plan to guide design, development, and management. Developing your plan can be fun and will be easier than you may think. In fact, the site assessment you just completed is one of the first important components.

Planning Process Terminology

To better understand the planning and design process, it is important to learn the terminology. Defined below are the key steps in any planning process—from idea to construction documents. Note that some trail developers combine a few of these steps or skip some steps, depending on the characteristics of an individual project.

TRAIL VISION OR CONCEPT. This is the first step after you form the idea of building a trail or trail system. The concept usually includes a map showing the proposed trail route(s), some basic goals, objectives, and planning guidelines,

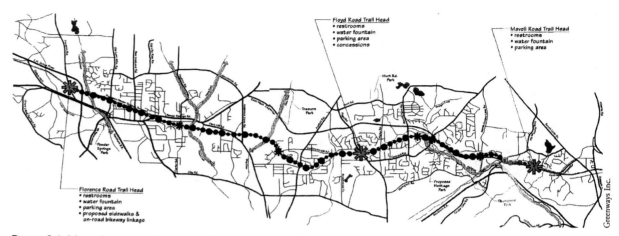

Figure 2.1. Map of proposed trail corridor.

and possibly some typical cross-section sketches and perspectives. Many trail planners employ GIS mapping technology (see Box 2.1). Some trail advocates include this step as part of the master plan. Trail visioning may be a three- to five-day process led by a planning or design professional, or capable volunteers.

THE MASTER PLAN. The master plan is the next level of planning that provides more specific detail to the trail or trail network. It includes a more thorough site analysis that identifies grades, barriers, land ownership, sensitive areas, and other opportunities and constraints. The master plan depicts graphically on a map and in written form where the trail corridors are located, how the trails will be aligned in their corridors, and what amenities will be built (such

as trailheads and other planning details). It usually includes cost estimates, design criteria for key components, and recommendations for project funding, phasing, and management. The master plan should be realistic and address the feasibility of the project. Depending on the size of the project, the master plan may take as long as one year to complete. In general, professionals complete the master plan while working with the community (Figure 2.1).

PRELIMINARY DESIGN. Preliminary design is the first step in "engineering" your trail. Most likely, you will conduct preliminary design only on the trail segments you intend to build in the near future. At the preliminary design stage, you walk the corridor, usually with a professional landscape architect and engineer,

Box 2.1. Using GIS to Map Your Trail Project

Geographic Information Systems (GIS) software is the latest advancement in data collection, analysis, and mapping. GIS combines the ability to produce maps of a given area with databases that contain information about the features shown on the maps. GIS technology is used to collect, store, retrieve, analyze, and display data such as land use, physical infrastructure, utilities, open spaces, and floodplains. Typically, a series of "thematic" maps are produced for the same general area. The maps are stored as individual map "layers" with the same boundaries and scale so that they can be overlaid and displayed simultaneously. These layers may be combined in a variety of ways to produce other maps. The graphics or maps are also linked to a database of computer information that can be displayed on the map.

For example, you could use GIS to display features along your trail corridor such as streams, roads, and buildings. In a separate layer, you could display land use for the same geographic area. In a third layer, you could display parcel ownership boundaries. When overlaid, these three layers (and their associated data) can be queried to show you detailed information, such as the name of the person owning the commercial property with a stream that is adjacent to your trail corridor. The advantage of GIS is that the overlay process is an accurate representation of the data in map form, and the overlay process is conducted digitally on the computer screen.

The most popular GIS software packages are ArcInfo and ArcView, both products of the Environmental Systems Research Institute (ESRI). ArcView permits an intermediate-level computer user, with a minimal amount of training, to display and query a GIS database developed by GIS professionals. ArcInfo permits the trained user to select the map layers to be displayed and query the database tables associated with the map features. The user can also change map colors and symbols, add or modify annotation associated with map features, and make custom layers.

Keep in mind that any GIS map is only as good as the data used to create it. Check the level of precision for base data, as some can be off as much as 100 feet in any direction, depending on how the data was originally collected. Obtain GIS information from local sources, if possible, in order to have the most accurate information available. Start with your city or county planning department. You can also search on the Internet for GIS information.

GIS mapping systems will likely become the standard for digital collection and storage of information about communities in the United States within the next twenty years. You and your organization should become familiar with GIS software and its capabilities, as it will help you to better plan, design, develop, and manage your future trail projects.

to identify specific trail locations, areas where bridges and retaining walls will be needed, ownership of necessary rights-of-way, and other critical details. This stage involves accurate cost estimates, determination of the actual components and materials to be used, and more precise cost estimates. The goal of preliminary design is to know exactly what rights-of-way and permits you will need, and what you can afford to build, given the available resources. The preliminary design stage is a good time to begin rights-of-way negotiations and permit applications because modifications to the plan at this level will be less costly than when construction documents are completed. Products of the preliminary design phase include trail alignment plans, which normally prepare at a scale of 1″ = 200′ or at a larger scale, specific cross sections for components, and a cost estimate spreadsheet. Some field surveying may be required to obtain precise measurements and location.

CONSTRUCTION DRAWINGS AND DOCUMENTS. Sometimes referred to as "bid documents," construction documents are used to guide the contractor during construction. They include all alignments, structures, grading, landscape planting, and amenity details. They also include written design specifications, such as the grade of concrete to be used and the level of soil compaction required.

Note that this chapter addresses the master plan process. Information contained in the preliminary design and construction documents for your trail is discussed in Chapter 3.

Developing a Master Plan

There are two basic types of master plans: those focusing on a system of trails, and those focusing on a specific trail segment or facility. The trail system master plan is usually completed first, followed by more site-specific master plans or preliminary designs for individual trail segments. Although the focus of each type of plan is different, the purpose, process, and components of each are similar.

In general, a communitywide trail plan is the first step toward developing trails. Without the "big picture" guidance that such a plan provides, trail development may result in disjointed or underutilized segments instead of an interconnected, continuous system. Trail systems should be planned as transportation, recreation, and open space networks that traverse a town, city, county, or state. They should connect important origins and destinations such as neighborhoods, schools, parks, natural areas, offices, shopping centers, transit stops, workplaces, museums, libraries, and restaurants. Indeed, the more types of land uses and destinations the trail system connects, the greater the range of trip purposes.

Trail master plans typically identify built corridors, such as rail, highway, and utility rights-of-way, as well as natural corridors, including streams, shorelines, and ridgelines, for trail development. Trails should also link with on-

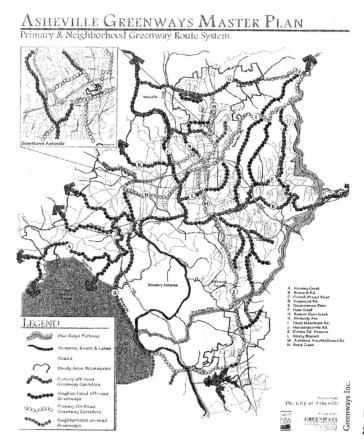

Figure 2.2. Map of community-wide trails and greenways system.

road facilities, such as bike routes, bike lanes, sidewalks, transit stops, park-and-ride facilities, and other modes of travel to create a complete network of off-road transportation facilities.

A comprehensive trail system master plan is typically developed by a public agency, with guidance from citizens. Check with the appropriate entity—usually the planning or parks department—to see if your community has completed such a plan or is in the process of doing so. If there is a plan, see if the trail system or trail corridor you are interested in is mentioned. If not, make a case for your trail and encourage them to include it (Figure 2.2). Note also that trails listed in a system master plan may have been prioritized as to their sequence of development due to monetary or other reasons.

A master plan specific to an individual trail will provide recommendations for the routing, design, development, and management of that facility. If it follows a rail line canal or drainageway, your trail will already have a general route and perhaps a completed site assessment, as described in Chapter 1. Guided by public involvement, a plan will help to conceptually define your route, the location of trail access points, the type of design, appropriate uses, and strategies for implementation. An effective trail master plan will also demonstrate connections among nearby origins and destinations.

The Master Planning Process

To ensure that your final plan provides solid, credible recommendations for developing a trail or trail system that is safe, convenient, well used, supported by local residents, realistic to implement, and customized to meet the needs of the community, you will need to follow a logical planning process. Most important, you will need to involve the public throughout the planning process (see "Public Involvement" in this chapter). The final products of any plan typically include a map, illustrating the trail route or trail system, and an accompanying report, including all relevant recommendations. Be prepared for a lengthy process. Master plans can take from six months to one year to complete. Here are the key master planning elements:

SITE ASSESSMENT. The first step to undertake for any master plan is to complete a site assessment, whether the site is an abandoned rail corridor or an entire county. Inventory the natural and built conditions within the site, as described in Chapter 1. When you are ready to involve local residents, begin your public involvement process by conducting your first meetings and workshops to present your findings.

VISION, GOALS, AND OBJECTIVES. A good plan starts with a guiding vision, goals, and objectives. A vision is something the plan aspires to, such as "The trail system will be interconnected and readily accessible to a broad cross section of the community." Goals are a little more specific than the vision, and describe the ultimate outcome, such as "Complete a paved multi-use trail that encourages alternative forms of transportation." There are usually several goals, with objectives developed for each. Objectives describe key milestones in meeting the goals, such as "Provide a connection from the trail to local bus stops."

A good way to develop your guiding vision, goals, and objectives is to begin with a public forum. This will likely be the first public forum in the planning process. At this session, discuss the benefits of the project, using examples where possible. Talk about not only the recreational and transportation benefits, but also how trails can improve education opportunities, health, the local economy, quality of life, and surrounding natural resources. Find out what the community envisions for the trail or trail system. Should it primarily serve an alternative transportation function, or should it be designed as a tourist attraction, or both? Document the results of this workshop and use this input to draft your guiding vision, goals, and objectives.

ROUTING AND DESIGN. Complete your preliminary routing and design based on the site assessment, goals and objectives, targeted user groups, and the principles of trail planning as described earlier. Show on a map where the trail will be located, its amenities, and its connections to local destinations. Present this to the public and stakeholder groups for their input. This is the "meat" of your plan, so intend spending most of your planning effort in developing and refining the route and design. Try to include maps, drawings, or computer-generated "before and after" photographs in your presentations to help residents envision alternatives.

IMPLEMENTATION STRATEGIES. A plan is more likely to go unnoticed without the inclusion of recommendations for getting the trail, or trail system, built. Every plan should include proposed "action steps" to be taken, identifying the agencies or organizations that will take them, and in what order these actions should be taken. Priority projects, or phases of a project, should be identified along with estimated costs for development. Project funding sources and strategies for maintenance and management should also be included in the plan. In the end, your plan will provide not only a vision of trail possibilities but also direction for how to make the vision a reality.

Principles of Trail Planning

When planning for a trail, or system of trails, keep several factors in mind. Think about how the trail will fit into a comprehensive trail or greenway system, and how that system will function within the context of the larger community as both a recreational and a transportation facility. Trails and trail systems should provide linkages to popular destinations, safely accommodate a variety of users, and be sensitive to any negative impacts on the natural environment and wildlife. Trail planners also need to think about how the trail, or trail system, will function in the future as areas are developed or trail popularity increases. For example, is the right-of-way now in hand wide enough to add a parallel jogging tread? Considering all of these factors during the planning process will ensure the existence of high-quality facilities for years to come.

BUILDING MULTI-OBJECTIVE TRAILS. In your planning, keep in mind that the best trails are multi-objective facilities. Although often viewed as mere pathways for recreational use, trails are so much more. They can serve as nonmotorized transportation routes, providing real alternatives and real choices to those who cannot or prefer not to drive, thus improving air quality while reducing the number of cars on the road. Trails can serve as educational facilities, teaching young and old the importance of local historic, cultural, and natural resources. They can provide opportunities for low-cost, close-to-home exercise that has been proven to significantly improve health. Open space buffers along streams associated with trails can provide an alternative use of floodplains, reducing damages associated with floods and improving water quality by providing natural buffers to filter pollutants from stormwater runoff. Keep all of these potential functions in mind as you plan your trail and advocate for its development.

CONTINUITY. A hundred years ago, Frederick Law Olmstead, who shaped many of our nation's great urban park systems, said that "a connected system of parks and pathways is manifestly far more complete and useful than a series of isolated parks." Trails, too, should be continuous and interconnected. While this may seem obvious, trails sometimes end abruptly—especially in urban areas—with no provision for integrating them into a larger trail system or for linking into the street network.

Multi-use trails should link homes, parks, and open space facilities. Trails should also connect neighborhoods to transit stops, schools, libraries, parks, commercial areas, and employment centers. Bicyclists and walkers generally have the same trip origins and destinations as motorists and need to get to and from the same facilities, services, and places of work and recreation. Using trails to connect residents to bus stops and commuter rail systems will increase the use of these alternative transportation facilities by improving access.

Clearly, the relationship between continuity and trail use is direct. Disjointed, short sections of trail will not be as useful as trails interconnected with a larger trail network and multiple destinations. While it is sometimes necessary to build trails in shorter segments or phases, communities should work to complete all future links and segments to ensure overall continuity.

Note that lack of continuity will likely be an issue while your trail or trail system is under development, and development of a trail may take several years. During that time, it is important to be sure that the segments you build connect logical destination points, even if the distances are short.

POTENTIAL USE. Multi-use trails should be located along corridors that assure maximum use by the intended user groups. User groups can include, for example, road and mountain bicyclists, walkers, snowmobilers (if a motorized trail), runners, equestrians, in-line skaters, and cross-country skiers. And there are many types of users within each category. For example, just within the cycling category are racers, commuters, fitness trainers, family recreational bicyclists, and even children riding to school.

During the planning stage, select the types of trail users to be accommodated. This selection will help determine the trail surface, width, trailside amenities, and other design elements. For example, a rural trail that will primarily be used by equestrians will be designed differently from an urban trail used by commuter cyclists. Most trails can accommodate a variety of users through proper design and management (see "Meeting the Needs of Different Users" in Chapter 3).

SAFETY. Safety considerations should be given top priority when planning trail corridors. If possible, do not locate trails in areas where users must cross busy intersections, negotiate steep grades, or come in contact with other barriers or hazard areas. Be sure to investigate any potential areas of environmental contamination, and make sure they are safe for trail use (see "Environmental Contamination Issues" in Chapter 1).

Trail planners should also avoid leading users into dangerous situations. For example, a trail that leads toward an important destination (such as a park or shopping area) and ends at a busy street (or forces users to cross a dangerous barrier, such as a bridge without sidewalks) may create an unnecessary danger to users. Try to anticipate the existence of popular nearby destinations, and be sure that the safe linkages are made before the trail is opened. (See Chapter 4 for additional comments on safety.)

PLANNING WITH WILDLIFE IN MIND. When planning your rail-trail, canal trail, or utility trail, carefully consider the trail's potential impacts on local wildlife. Begin by examining the information collected during your inventory (see "Site Considerations: Inventory and Assessment" in Chapter 1). Use this information to identify areas (or seasons) of concern for threatened, endangered, or sensitive wildlife; landscapes in need of ecological improvement; and appropriate locations for wildlife interpretive displays or observation points.

Examine the proposed locations of trailheads and other gathering places for impacts to wildlife. Try to avoid, minimize, or mitigate negative impacts on the surrounding habitat and wildlife species. Be aware that such impacts may ultimately be difficult to assess, and the impact of both the short-term construction stage as well as the long-term use stage must be considered. While some of the important wildlife assessment tasks may be completed by a person with general planning experience, some tasks will require a seasoned wildlife expert. (See "Wildlife and Multi-Use Trails" in Chapter 3 for more information on trail design for wildlife.)

Depending on how disturbed your trail corridor and adjacent properties are, set wildlife-related goals for the project. If you are dealing with an urban landscape that is heavily disturbed, restoring habitat may be the principal wildlife goal. In more pristine settings, preserving what is already there and minimizing impacts may be the major concerns. Several trails across the country have incorporated the improvement of wildlife areas through restoring habitat, creating wetlands, and planting native plant species for food, cover, and visual screening.[1]

ANTICIPATE FUTURE DEVELOPMENT AND EXPANSION. There is only one constant for trail planners: Things change! Wise trail planning, therefore, always means looking ahead. Planners eager to get a trail built may be reluctant to think about the trail's surroundings a decade or two hence. However, considering future needs and planning for them are important because an informed decision early on will save dollars and aggravation later.

Try to anticipate trail use levels accurately—the number of people who use the trail can expand explosively as word spreads or nearby vacant land is developed (see "Assessing Trail Demand" in Chapter 1). A new trail may fill to capacity within a few years after opening, leaving trail managers at a loss to accommodate the flood of users and to alleviate conflicts among them. A trail is over "capacity" when crowding and user conflicts degrade the intended trail experience for the bulk of the users. Demographic change should also be considered, as one large segment of the population—the baby boomers—moves into retirement age and their use patterns shift.

Other factors change as well, including equipment used on the trail. The mountain bike introduced a whole new set of opportunities and needs. Now there are racing wheelchairs and in-line skaters. Each sport has its own specialized equipment and user needs. Talk with sporting

[1] Colorado State Parks Trails and Wildlife Task Force, *Planning Trails with Wildlife in Mind* (Denver, CO: Colorado State Parks, 1998).

goods and bicycle shop operators, since they may have a sense of future trends. Look to various trail organizations, national manufacturers associations, and magazines for additional insight. If you have reason to believe that use levels may expand significantly, you may want to plan ahead by securing a wider right-of-way and building key infrastructure such as pedestrian bridges or tunnels wider than is currently needed (i.e., 12 feet wide versus 10 feet wide) to accommodate future expansion.

Future residential, commercial, and industrial development along trail corridors will likely impact trails in two ways. First, projects such as new roads, utility crossings, and drainage projects can make trails impassable—at least temporarily. Second, land-use changes along the corridor will alter the experience or feeling of using the trail. State and local comprehensive plans and land-use plans obtained during your site assessment should give you information about projected growth and development. Learn about project funding, phasing, and schedules by talking with planners.

It is also important to have a detour plan and policies in place that are supported by utility and road agencies. Disrupting a trail is not only an inconvenience, but can be a hazard if trail users are forced onto busy streets or encounter other dangers. Although utility construction may disrupt a trail, consider opportunities for joint use and the benefits for trail builders as well as utility companies (see "Joint Ventures within Your Multi-Use Trail Corridor" in Chap-

ter 5). Note where these projects will intersect your trail corridor. Plan now to develop a policy to protect your trail from development pressure and its impacts so that future projects do not disrupt the trail corridor (see "Protect Your Trail in the Face of Change" in Chapter 5).

Prudent trail planning includes looking at existing land-use maps and the comprehensive plans of the communities involved. How is the corridor currently zoned? What new projects are planned? How will these affect the trail project? Work with local planning and zoning departments. Find out who is requesting building permits for large projects. Where are projects likely to be located? Talk to area developers and realtors as well as planning officials. Many city, county, and regional planning agencies maintain mailing lists for notifying interested agencies and groups when a development project is submitted for review. Be sure your organization or agency is on those lists.

Integrating Your Plan into Existing Documents

Trail proponents realize that the success of comprehensive trail master plans depends on their integration into the policy and planning documents used by planners, engineers, and other decision makers. Integrating a comprehensive trail plan into existing policy and planning documents is an effective institutionalization strategy because it generates familiarity, awareness, and legitimacy.

Perhaps most important, it generates funding opportunities. For example, to use "transportation" dollars (one of the most likely funding sources) to build trails requires trails to be included in transportation plans. The same is true for "recreation" and "open space" dollars. Failure to include trails in these various documents will severely limit possible funding sources for these projects.

Comprehensive trail plans should be integrated into transportation, recreation, open space, commercial, and industrial plans and policies. While the specifics of local and regional policy and planning documents will differ for each community, they will generally fall into one or more of the following categories.

TRANSPORTATION POLICIES AND PLANS. Most state and local governments have transportation policies and plans because they are required for funding. In most cases, a department of transportation (DOT) or public works is responsible for developing and implementing its plan; in some cases, a separate planning department develops it.

Each state DOT is required to have a state planning process and a statewide transportation improvement program (STIP). Each metropolitan area (with an urbanized population base of at least 50,000) has a metropolitan planning organization (MPO) that develops a metropolitan transportation plan and transportation improvement program (TIP), which is a listing of all transportation projects for the region in the next few years. All state and metropolitan plans must address development of bicycle and pedestrian facilities.

Transportation plans are perhaps the most important place in which to include multi-use trails projects because more money is available for transportation than for recreation. When including trails in transportation plans, be sure to identify them as "transportation" facilities and not "recreational" facilities, because federal and state funding guidelines usually require that money spent on nonmotorized facilities be spent for "transportation" purposes. That said, a trail must legitimately meet some transportation need in order to be labeled as such. Clearly, a quarter-mile trail that is a loop inside a park would not meet such criteria. (See "Funding Sources for Trail Development" in Chapter 4.)

RECREATION POLICIES AND PLANS. All states have a statewide comprehensive outdoor recreation plan (SCORP) developed by a state resource agency—a policy plan document but usually not a project-specific document. The state is responsible for implementing the recommendations of the SCORP. This is another important planning document in which to incorporate multi-use trail planning recommendations. When you include a trail in a SCORP plan, define the trail as a "linear park" or "greenway" that connects "active," more traditional parks with natural areas used for "passive" recreation.

OPEN SPACE POLICIES AND PLANS. Open space policies and plans are appearing in more communities as people realize the benefits of protecting natural land in developing areas. Multi-use trails should be part of these plans. Along with drainageways, abandoned railroad rights-of-way and utility corridors are often the only remaining significant undeveloped open spaces in urban areas, so it is important to include them in the plans.

Developing a Plan: In-House Staff or Outside Contractor?

As you enter the planning or design phase of a multi-use trail project, you will need to determine whether you have the staff to complete the project in-house, or whether you need to hire a consultant to do the work. Weigh the advantages and disadvantages of each option. For example, in-house staff provide an agency or organization more direct control over the final product and easily incorporate knowledge of existing facilities, plans, and land use, whereas outside contractors can utilize expertise gained from working on similar projects.

Advantages and Disadvantages

Working with a hired consultant may have advantages. If there have been problems in the past or there is a perceived lack of public trust toward your agency, you may want to consider hiring a consultant who will be viewed as a neutral third party. Many consultants are able to meet tight deadlines and move more quickly than an in-house person, especially if the staff member is already stretched across several projects. If you are feeling pressure to move the project forward quickly, a consultant can often provide the relief you need. In addition, if your staff is small or has little experience with multi-use trail projects, a consultant can provide the necessary expertise.

On the other hand, depending on the previous experience and location of the firm, consultants may be viewed as outsiders who do not understand the needs of a community. For example, residents of a small town may be skeptical of an out-of-town or out-of-state consulting firm, particularly if most of the firm's experience has been centered elsewhere. Since public involvement is an important aspect of the design phase, be sure to hire someone who has significant public involvement experience and with whom the public feels comfortable.

The positive aspects of working with an in-house staff person should also be weighed. If you are fortunate enough to have an experienced staff, make use of their skills. Communication is likely to be better with a close-at-hand staff person than a (possibly) distant consultant, and your staff probably knows the community better than an outside contractor would. In addition, the job can probably be done more cheaply in-house than by a consultant.

Some of the disadvantages of working with

your own staff are that other work priorities can take time away from the trail design effort, and your staff may possibly lack necessary expertise. As you would expect, there can be negative aspects to working with a consultant as well, including possible increases in costs as the project progresses and the potential for gaps in communication.

Many consultants are available to work with in-house staff, incorporating a team approach. This allows in-house staff to contribute available time and resources for certain tasks, while taking advantage of consultant expertise.

How to Find a Good Consultant

You can find a competent consultant by prequalifying a list of consultants (annually or biennially) who can bid on projects for your agency. You can send out a request for qualifications, pare down the list of applicants based on previous experience, and evaluate these prospective consultants based on their ability to meet the needs of your project.

If you have not gone through a prequalification process, and decide to employ the services of a consultant for a complex job, you should issue a "request for proposals" (RFP), which allows a number of consultants to bid on your project by outlining their plan and its associated costs.

From the best proposals submitted, you should interview the two or three finalists. Get acquainted while learning about their relevant experience and assessing their ability to do the job. You should examine the consultant's attitude, understanding of the project, and ability to communicate during the interview. A good consultant will use this time to ask questions and become more familiar with the project.

The decision to use one consultant over another should be based on the quality of the interview and proposal, as well as on recommendations from previous clients. It is extremely important to solicit this information, just as you would if you were hiring a new employee. List questions to ask the previous clients about quality of design, commitment of staff people, timely product delivery, creativity, and enthusiasm. The cost of the contract also will play a role in your decision, but remember that the lowest price is not always the best buy. In fact, some consultants put in a low bid to win contracts, but then add additional expenses as a project progresses.

It is wise to document the factors that entered into the decision to hire so that if it is contested in court, a jury can see the logic of your choice. In hiring any consultant, avoid personal favoritism.

Once you hire a consultant, you will need to ensure that project deadlines are met. One option is to provide incentive payment for submitting portions of the project early. On the other hand, you can stipulate penalties for each day the consultant is late.

University Assistance

If you do not have the money to hire a professional consultant and your staff has little expertise, look into the possibility of a landscape architecture or civil engineering department at a local college or university taking on your multiuse trail design as a class project. This can be a win-win situation for everyone involved. Your agency and the community can benefit because they get design assistance for minimal cost; students get real-world, hands-on experience; the professor has a ready-made project for the semester, and the university is recognized for its expertise.

When considering this option, however, you should realize that your request for a design plan might not result in a completed plan. The professor controls the process, and his or her first priority is providing a valuable learning experience for the students. A project must fit within the academic time frame and meet course objectives. Therefore, your request for assistance should be made well in advance, and with an acceptance of possible constraints. Such a design plan may remain conceptual with construction drawings carried out by others (see Case Study 5).

A university may require a memorandum of agreement that covers costs involved with the project, such as travel expenses related to site visits as well as photography, printing, and administrative expenses. Many universities with planning and design programs offer assistance to communities. Investigate what resources are available in your region.

Public Involvement

Public involvement is the key to any successful trail planning effort. If you institute and carry out a comprehensive public involvement campaign, you will create a plan that meets the needs of the local community while generating trust and support between your agency or organization and the public.

Meeting the Needs of Adjacent Landowners

Remember to involve adjacent landowners first, before going public with your project. You will likely get opposition early on if landowners first learn about the proposed trail from the press. It is critical to communicate with adjacent landowners from the outset and respect their opinions. Their proximity to the corridor often fosters anxiety about the trail's effect on their quality of life. Resistance from even a few opponents can result in both bureaucratic inactivity and financial difficulties. You must provide them with opportunities to express themselves, because only by listening to their fears and concerns can you begin developing solutions and moving toward a successful trail project. Some of the more common concerns of landowners are listed below.

CRIME, PROPERTY VALUES, AND LIABILITY. The overriding concerns most often voiced by potential trail neighbors are fears of increased crime, decreased property values, and liability. Many adjacent owners, particularly those abutting the corridor, may view the trail as a new public thoroughfare that provides quick access to their property by "undesirable" outsiders. Many of these concerns stem from a fear of the unknown and disappear once the trail is open. Be sensitive to landowners' concerns, yet also inform them of the benefits realized by residents near other trails (Figure 2.3). Often, residents who are ambivalent about the trail project become opponents when they hear the concerns of others. Consider inviting a police officer to attend meetings to address the crime issue. Continuing

Greenways Inc.

Figure 2.3. The popular Minuteman Trail passes through the busy suburbs of Boston, Massachusetts, providing recreation and transportation options to hundreds of people.

USEFUL WEB SITES
- Rails-to-Trails Conservancy: www.railtrails.org
- National Park Service: www.nps.gov
- U.S. Department of Transportation Bicycle and Pedestrian Information Centers: www.walkinginfo.org or www.bicyclinginfo.org
- Trails and Greenways Clearinghouse: www.trailsandgreenways.org
- National Bicycle and Pedestrian Clearinghouse: www.bikefed.org/clear.htm
- Greenways Incorporated: www.greenways.com

with the public involvement strategy discussed in this section should help neutralize many fears at the outset and begin building landowners' commitment to the trail. Several organization and government agencies also provide useful information that will help you make the case for your trail (see "Useful Web Sites" on page 39).

Be prepared to address potential landowner concerns and think through your answers to possible questions. You will find extremely useful information in various studies that highlight the realities of rail-trails and refute claims about their negative impact.

A recent comprehensive study conducted by the Rails-to-Trails Conservancy revealed, through statistics and anecdotal data, that trails are some of the safest places in the country. Of the 372 trail managers responding to the study, only 3 percent reported that major criminal activity (crimes against persons) had occurred on their trail. Only 25 percent reported any type of minor crime, such as graffiti or littering, and these problems were quickly corrected as part of routine trail maintenance.

According to national crime statistics, parks and trails are among the safest places to be—people are two to three times safer on a trail than in a parking lot, on the street, or even inside their own homes. Further, the study reproduced letters from twelve law enforcement agencies that have had positive experiences with the trails in their jurisdictions.[2]

The most comprehensive study to date, *The Impacts of Rail-Trails,* looks at the effects of rail-trails in three diverse areas across the country. Overall, landowners agreed that living next to a rail-trail was better than living next to abandoned tracks. Moreover, the vast majority of landowners use the trails frequently. For example, in the East Bay region near San Francisco, 99 percent of neighbors living along the suburban Lafayette/Moraga Trail use it; in fact, members of their households use it an average of 132 days each year.[3] A study of Seattle's Burke-Gilman Trail shows similar results, with adjacent owners making frequent use of the trail. The study points out that two of the trail's most vocal opponents now believe the trail is the best thing that ever happened to the neighborhood.[4]

The studies also addressed concerns about property values. No negative effect on property values has been found, and in some cases property values have increased. Along the Burke-Gilman, homes directly adjacent to the trail showed no increase or decrease, but those located a block from the trail realized a 6 percent increase in property values according to local real estate agents.[5] In *The Impacts of Rail-Trails,* landowners said they believed the trails either increased or had no effect on property values. Some landowners thought their proximity to trails might make their homes easier to sell. In suburban areas of Chicago, Tampa, Washington, D.C., Seattle, and elsewhere, home-sale advertisements promote the properties' proximity to trails as a selling point.

Liability is another common concern among landowners. They fear that a trail user will wander onto their property, get injured, and then sue the landowner for liability. Fortunately, liability has not been much of a problem on multi-use trails, primarily because a person entering an adjacent landowner's property is considered a trespasser and the landowner owes limited duty of care to a trespasser. Further, recreational use statutes (RUS) are on the books in all fifty states. Under these statutes, no landowner is liable for recreational injuries resulting from mere carelessness if they have provided public access to their land for recreation purposes. To recover damages, an injured person needs to prove "willful and wanton misconduct" on the part of the landowner. Also, the recreational use statute typically will apply if the landowner is charging a fee for access to his or her property.

Admittedly, the RUS does not necessarily prevent landowners from being sued, but it will grant them certain protections. Note that homeowners

[2] Rails-to-Trails Conservancy, *Rail Trails and Safe Communities* (Washington, DC: Rails-to-Trails Conservancy, 1998).

[3] Roger L. Moore et al., *The Impacts of Rail-Trails: A Study of Users and Nearby Property Owners from Three Trails* (Washington, DC: National Park Service, 1992), III:9.

[4] Seattle Engineering Department and Office for Planning, *Evaluation of the Burke-Gilman Trail's Effect on Property Values and Crime* (Seattle: Seattle Engineering Department, May 1987), 3.

[5] Ibid.

insurance is often used to defend against such instances. Obtain a copy of your state's statute and find out to what extent it will afford protection or has been tested in court. Also, inform landowners that trail users wandering onto posted private property are considered trespassers under law. Sharing this information with concerned trailside residents, many of whom are probably unfamiliar with the protection they receive under the statute, will do much to alleviate their concerns about liability. It is strongly advised that you consult an attorney knowledgeable in this area to determine the current status of RUS laws in your state.

OTHER CONCERNS. Additional concerns you will likely encounter are fears of careless maintenance, trespassing, and loss of privacy, all of which require specific management solutions.

Although most trails are more attractive than abandoned, rundown corridors, many adjacent landowners fear that a developed trail will not be well maintained after its opening. Trail neighbors are often concerned about weed control, tree pruning, drainage control, and trash pickup. Develop a regular maintenance schedule as part of your master plan, and share it with future trail neighbors to demonstrate that you are addressing their concerns.

Landowners also fear that trail users will leave the trail via their property in search of phones, bathrooms, and trail exits. You can reduce the potential for these problems by locating public parking lots, emergency telephones, access points, rest rooms, and drinking fountains at

Figure 2.4. Berm and planting screen.

regular intervals along the trail. To allay their fears, assure landowners that you will build proper amenities into the trail design.

If funds do not allow all desired amenities to be included at once, seek input from trail neighbors as to which are most crucial from their perspective. You could plan to install temporary facilities (including portable toilets and drinking fountains) until money permits construction of permanent structures.

The New River Trail State Park in southwestern Virginia produced a development plan outlining facilities to be constructed over twenty years. This plan complements the park's "guidelines for opening," which include required features (such as stop signs before road crossings and informational kiosks at major access points) that had to be in place prior to the trail's opening. Together, these documents allowed the trail to open without all facilities in place while they reassured landowners that desired amenities would be installed over time.

Loss of privacy may be one of the most difficult issues you will face because it is so personal for each landowner. The heart of this issue is making people feel comfortable with their proximity to the trail, which is typically accomplished through some form of screening. Undoubtedly, trailside tenants will have different ideas (although some may have no idea at all) of how to shield their properties from the trail—and from the sight of trail users (Figure 2.4).

In residential areas, landowners often insist that fences be installed (at the agency's expense) to prevent trespassing and to maintain privacy. Keep in mind, however, that there are other less costly and more natural options than fencing, such as trees, shrubs, and other plantings (Figure 2.5), that landowners may accept.

Whatever screening works best in your situation, you need to consider the cost and who will cover it. Is there money in the trail development budget to cover plantings for the adjacent landowners? Will the adjacent landowners be

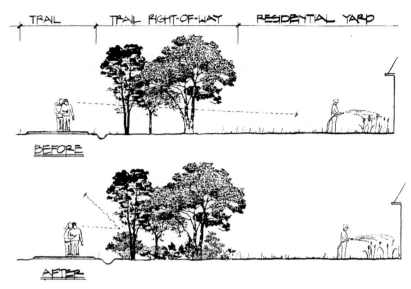

Figure 2.5. Natural screening for trail neighbors.

required to split the cost with you? Who will pay the maintenance costs? No matter how much screening you require, these are critical questions to consider during the planning phase. Typically, fences should be considered as a last resort because of their high cost and aesthetic impact.

The manager of New Jersey's Delaware and Raritan Canal State Park faced a difficult dilemma when adjacent landowners strongly opposed a trail extension. The landowners would agree to it only on the condition that fencing would be installed along the route to keep trespassers off their properties and that breaks would be located in the fence at regular

intervals so the neighbors could access the trail. The manager developed a model solution: The trail would be installed with no fences in place, but at any time landowners could individually request fencing along their properties if they found it necessary. After five years, the trail manager has yet to install a single fence. This example of a change in adjacent landowner attitudes toward a trail once it is developed is not atypical.

If this scenario doesn't satisfy your trail neighbors, urge them to try natural screening on a trial basis. Try an involvement technique to get them on-board: Plan a tree-planting ceremony hosted jointly by the agency and trail neighbors.

Once the trail is open and neighbors' concerns subside, they may be less anxious about fence installation.

In areas where a railroad company constructed or maintained fences (often in livestock grazing areas), you will need to continue the upkeep. But again, talk individually with landowners to ascertain their needs.

After thinking through all of these issues, consider different strategies for working with future trail neighbors. You may want to open lines of communication with adjacent landowners by sending a personalized letter to each one, introducing yourself and the trail concept, and stating that you want to work with him or her in developing the trail. This gets these future trail neighbors involved at the outset, before they can feel shut out of the process.

Strategies for Landowner Involvement

Employ various strategies to gain the support of adjacent landowners and to address any concerns that develop. Individual meetings and trail tours are good ways to involve this critical group of people. In some cases, you may need to move into mitigation and negotiation with certain landowners who are unyielding on a particular issue. In some instances, you may need to consider an alternative routing of the trail.

The best strategy you can undertake is to conduct face-to-face meetings with adjacent landowners. This allows you to make a personal contact with each person and proves that you are making a genuine effort to take his or her feelings into consideration. It also gives the trail a human side—you become the "face of the trail." Also, by isolating possible trail opponents, you may be able to avoid a negative group mentality that can develop at a public meeting when strong negative views or opinions taken out of context are voiced. Another option is to organize a tour of an existing nearby multi-use trail to gain support from adjacent landowners (or to neutralize opponents). Such a visit allows future trail neighbors to experience firsthand an existing facility, and possibly existing trail neighbors, and should allay some of their fears. Speaking directly with other landowners can do more to win people over than any statistics you can offer.

Negotiation and mitigation are other tools that can help you and adjacent landowners develop creative solutions together. Often, a landowner will compromise on an issue in exchange for an amenity connected to the trail. For example, to address fears of increased crime along the route, you might agree to hire a full-time patrol person (to be augmented by volunteer patrols), or you might plant shrubs and trees to shield adjacent properties to relieve privacy concerns.

Listen carefully to the concerns of adjacent landowners and discern in what areas they may be willing to compromise in exchange for some personal benefit. You can develop creative solutions to landowners' problems without hinder-

ing the trail project. In addition to these strategies, include the future trail neighbors in other public involvement efforts (trail advisory committees, community design workshops) to make them part of the entire trail-planning process.

Community Involvement

Most trail projects have numerous stakeholders: trail users, friendly and hostile adjacent landowners, affected agencies, elected officials, and those unaware of the project. Know who the various stakeholders are, whom you need to inform, and from whom you need input (see "Identifying Stakeholders" in Chapter 1). Your goal will be to get all parties involved in the planning and design phase so that all develop a sense of "ownership" and "investment" in the trail. The following suggestions will help you advance your relations with all the various people who have a vested interest in your trail.

First, know more about the corridor than anyone else. This will give you the edge in a public setting: You will be prepared to answer any question that may come up; you (and your agency or organization) will be viewed as credible; and you will be able to defuse potential opposition. Compile a "resource book" for the proposed trail, including information collected during your community and site assessments. What were its previous uses? Did any interesting historic events take place along the route? Are there notable natural features along the route? If a cultural inventory was conducted, much of

this information will already be assembled. Add news clippings and old photos to the book where possible (a three-ring binder works well). Include information about other trails in your region and articles on the national trails movement. Plan to display such a report at public meetings and events to help generate excitement about the project. Include maps of the corridor and photographs to add visual interest.

In addition, develop an introductory manual to sell your project. It should supply interesting background information about the trail. Include maps of the route, highlighting the community resources it links (e.g., schools, libraries, parks, industrial centers). In addition, compile a list of potential user groups and some estimated development and maintenance costs. (A word of caution on cost estimates: Make sure your cost figures are solid before going public with them; your credibility will be undermined if they escalate.) This manual will introduce the trail to new groups. Visual elements, such as slides, are very helpful in a public setting. Also you may consider setting up a Web site, or make use of an existing Web site, so that residents can easily access information and answers to frequently asked questions.

Equipped with knowledge and materials, you are now ready to develop public interest and investment in the trail. Surveys, citizen advisory committees, public meetings, hearings, and meetings with individuals are all good ways to involve the public. A media outreach campaign may also be useful. A successful public involvement program includes an appropriate mix of techniques that maximize inclusion of a large number of people and minimize confrontation.

Before deciding which strategies will work best for you, consider the following questions: What kind of input are you asking the public to provide? What decision-making roles will the public play? And when is public involvement appropriate or most effective?

MEETINGS WITH INDIVIDUALS. To address difficult, emotional issues, one-on-one meetings with individuals can be the most effective technique. Conduct these meetings in a setting that is comfortable and convenient for the individual. Once out of a public setting (where pressure from friends and neighbors can be great), an individual will likely express his or her true feelings about the trail project. Often, people are neutral about a trail, but they are persuaded by others to oppose it. Or those who are truly opposed will not air their actual aversions in an open forum. One-on-one meetings give you and your opposition the opportunity to talk openly and discuss various options. What initially seemed an inflexible position may become quite fluid in this setting. Taking the time to talk with people one-on-one also demonstrates to the community your willingness to listen to different views and to work toward solutions.

CITIZEN ADVISORY COMMITTEES. Citizens advisory committees (CACs) provide an outlet for the views of the many stakeholders to be represented while also developing consensus among groups with differing perspectives. The CAC should serve as a forum for information exchange, citizen advice, and input on the project. Committee members can be selected by an agency or organization and typically have a regularly scheduled meeting time for the duration of the project.

If a CAC does not already exist for this purpose, you should form one at the beginning of your trail project. Select up to fifteen members, representing a variety of stakeholders, including different agencies (parks, planning, law enforcement), community organizations, user groups (hikers, equestrians, snowmobilers, bicyclists), local businesses, and adjacent landowners. The more diverse the group, the better. Political endorsement for the trail project is more likely to be generated when a large cross section of the community is supportive. And, it is possible for this group to evolve into a nonprofit trail development organization following the completion of the planning process (Figure 2.6).

CAC meetings can provide powerful insight to trail design and management. But when planning a meeting, remember that too many meetings, or meetings without a clear purpose, waste time. Don't schedule one unless you know what you want to accomplish. When working with this committee, clearly state each member's role and the decision-making abilities of the group.

PUBLIC WORKSHOPS. The best way to elicit public input and raise public awareness of any trail project is to conduct public workshops. These

Figure 2.6. A citizens advisory committee meeting in progress.

events should be scheduled at different stages of your planning and design process, but should not take place before adjacent landowners have been contacted. If you are creating a communitywide trails master plan, instead of working on a specific corridor, you will not be able to contact potential trail neighbors (because the routes have yet to be identified). Instead, remain conceptual about proposed trail routes and build flexibility and voluntary land acquisition measures into the plan.

Schedule workshops in neighborhood settings—perhaps in a library—rather than at your agency's headquarters. Participants will be more at ease in a familiar setting. Advertise the workshops well in advance. Remember to establish ground rules (e.g., each person must speak in turn, there are no "bad ideas, issues can be listed only once) at the outset of any meeting or public workshop, and be ready to enforce them.

At any type of meeting, plan to use visual aids. This can include maps of the corridor, aerial photographs, and pictures of the corridor or other trails. More and more, people are using 3-D computer modeling or 2-D computer-generated visualizations to illustrate what a trail or trail system will look like when it is fully developed. These tools will help people pinpoint their residences (and community resources) along the route and see how the project fits into the entire community. Consider handing out written response forms with your mailing address on them. Always write down all comments on a large pad. Post comments from previous meetings at subsequent ones.

There are several different types of public workshops that can be held, depending on the purpose and stage in the planning and design process.

- Benefits, Goals, and Objectives Workshop: Describe in detail the various economic, recreational, transportation, health, education, quality of life, and other benefits of trails at this workshop. Then, ask the public to identify goals and objectives related to these benefits for the trail project. You may want to conduct a voting exercise at the end of this workshop to identify the importance that residents assign to each goal or objective. For example, distribute five stickers to each person and have each participant place the stickers next to the five objectives he or she feels are most important. This will give you a better

sense of how the community would like the trail to look and feel.

- Issues Identification Workshop: Similar to a Benefits, Goals, and Objectives Workshop, an Issues Identification Workshop follows the presentation of benefits with the identification of priority concerns about the project. This type of workshop should be used when you anticipate opposition at the beginning of the project. After all issues have been identified and listed on a flip chart, workshop participants vote on which three to five issues are top priority. Allow time for a question-and-answer session with a panel of experts addressing the selected priority issues. Participants should be aware that all the ideas will be considered but that some may not be implemented in the final design.

- Design Workshop: A community design workshop educates the public about the trail while eliciting input on design (see Case Study 6). This workshop can revolve around a large, user-friendly map of the trail corridor (Figure 2.7) and a variety of miniature symbols representing trail-related objects such as signs, rest stops, trailheads, benches, drinking fountains, and trees for landscaping and buffers. With the map spread out on a large table or affixed to a wall, participants are encouraged to place the pieces where they envision them along the trail. This fun technique allows the public substantial input into the trail design and helps them visualize what the trail might look

Figure 2.7. A community design workshop in progress.

like when complete. A design specialist should take notes during the process and incorporate the ideas into the actual design.

- Open House: If your project is controversial or you feel a workshop will not generate enough participants, you may want to bill the gathering as an "open house," with free flow of information for a few hours, rather than a set meeting with a strict agenda. An open house provides more flexibility for people's schedules, as they can come at their convenience during the allotted time period. It also provides a forum for opposing parties to express their concerns in a more personalized setting. More progress will be made by talking with the opposition one-on-one at an open house, than by listening to everyone's concerns at a public workshop setting.

PUBLIC HEARINGS. Many public agencies are mandated by law to incorporate public hearings—usually formal procedures with the air of a legal proceeding—into their planning process. Hearings are one way of developing a permanent, "public" record. If you are required to use public hearings, make your goals very clear. If not, utilize the public workshop forum described above.

Do not expect hearings to be consensus-builders or forums for resolving differences. The hearing format can encourage those testifying to take strong positions from which it may be difficult to back down. Hearings may bring much of the hidden opposition out of the woodwork—be prepared for this. Make sure that trail supporters are aware of any public hearings taking place. If possible, try to schedule public hearings to take place near the end of the public involvement process, making the event more of a formality to show support for the project.

SURVEYS. Although many people do not feel strongly enough about a trail project to attend a hearing or other meeting, they will anonymously express their views in a survey. If you do conduct a survey, make sure your purpose is clear. Do you hope that the results will demonstrate community support for the trail? Show that people prefer the trail to another community improvement? Determine how many peo-

ple will use the trail once it opens? Your purpose will determine the questions to ask. But keep in mind that you may get results you didn't expect.

In northwestern New Jersey, a newspaper conducted a reader's poll to determine whether or not the Paulinskill Valley Trail project was controversial—as had been reported by the local media. The survey results showed the true dimensions of public support: Of those who expressed an opinion, 97 percent (895 area residents) supported the conversion of an abandoned rail line into a trail, compared to 3 percent (27 people) who opposed it.

Keep your questions clear and unambiguous, and avoid asking open-ended questions. Make sure the sample you survey represents the groups you are trying to reach. You will likely get a low response rate—10 to 20 percent is average. Know how you will tabulate, analyze, and utilize every question in your survey.

Accurate survey research requires expertise to ensure a representative sample of a community. And survey research can be costly due to staff time and mailing costs. You may want to obtain assistance from a professional survey researcher or local university. Another option is to conduct a nonscientific survey of individuals "on the street" or workshop participants. The Internet can also be a valuable way to generate pub-

lic feedback—have people e-mail you, or encourage them to use your organization's Web site to "mail in" a standard form to an established database that can be used to tabulate the results.

Mass Media Outreach

The media can help inform the public about your project and generate public input and support. But before reaching out to the media, remember that any newspaper or television coverage can stir up opponents as well as supporters. The media loves controversy, and a reporter is unlikely to take the story without looking at other opinions. As with a survey, be sure that you are communicating a clear message with little danger of being misinterpreted.

Once you feel sure that the time is right for some press coverage, you can use a wide array of techniques to attract the media. Press releases, press conferences, public service announcements (PSAs), newsletters, and public events can all stimulate the attention you are seeking (see "Promoting and Marketing Your Trail" in Chapter 6). Remember to provide contact information, including addresses of any Web sites that provide information about the project.

CASE STUDY 4

Creating a Trail System for Southeast Michigan

Trails developed in isolation provide many benefits to communities. But trail and greenway systems created on a regional scale can transform those isolated trails and greenways into a larger, more dynamic continuous network. This is what the Southeast Michigan Greenways Initiative is all about. This initiative exemplifies the process involved in creating a successful trail and greenway system.

The project was initiated in 1990 by the Rails-to-Trails Conservancy, the National Park Service, the Michigan Department of Natural Resources, and the Michigan Department of Transportation to develop a vision for an interconnected greenway system that connects thousands of miles of trails and acres of open space.

The project included three distinct phases: defining potential greenways and resources, presenting and refining the plan with public participation, and implementing demonstration projects and fund-raising.

Phase one involved two years of public workshops, held in all affected counties of the state, to determine community needs and sentiment about a regional greenway system. Through these workshops, over 2,300 miles of corridor and more than 200,000 acres of open space were identified for their potential inclusion in the greenway system.

The information collected from the workshops was input into a Geographic Information System, which was used to create descriptive tables and preliminary maps showing greenway opportunities. The maps, tables, and a summary of the public input included in draft reports, along with an adopted procedure for evaluating greenway opportunities, were used during phase three of the project.

Phase two, which involved refining the vision, called for establishing the public-private Regional Greenways Advisory Committee, comprised of representatives of key public and private agencies throughout the area. Using the maps and evaluation procedures already developed, the committee drafted the initial Southeast Michigan Greenway network and presented the plan at county meetings where participants reviewed and modified the maps and corridor functions as they saw fit. The updated maps were then circulated to members of the committee and county planning and recreation agencies in the region for review and finalization. Simultaneously, University of Michigan graduate students compared greenway implementation principles used in major metropolitan areas to help frame a plan for the Southeast Michigan system.

During the final phase of the process, the advisory committee nominated two demonstration projects. The Southeast Livingston Greenways includes a looped system of trails and uses greenways to preserve the character of this rapidly developing area. The Southwest Detroit Riverfront Greenway will connect neighborhoods and parks along the river and promote economic revitalization efforts in this area. Steering committees were formed from local agencies to develop the corridor plans to the point of implementation.

Identifying potential funding sources was also a primary objective during this phase of the project. Maps and an overall vision document were also developed to market the greenway plan to potential funders. The Regional Greenways Advisory Committee began to discuss funding mechanisms and operational protocol to implement the system. Funders in the vicinity have new expressed interest in coordinating this project with several other emerging environmental initiatives in the region for a more holistic impact on the ecological health and well-being of the area.

CASE STUDY 5

Building Trails through Creative Partnerships

Cooperating with nontraditional partners is one way to get your trail built and provide valuable training experiences for unlikely parties. Bill O'Neill, trustee of the East Coast Greenway (ECG) and vice chair of the Connecticut Greenways Council, enlisted the help of the Connecticut National Guard and Coast Guard Academy to complete sections of the Charter Oak Greenway, which is the Connecticut portion of the ECG. When completed, the ECG will be a ribbon of connecting greenway corridors extending from Key West, Florida, to Canada, where it will connect with Canada's greenway system.

According to Bill O'Neill, the formula for creating a successful partnership with the military is matching the training needs of these agencies with appropriate elements of the trail project. The Connecticut National Guard was searching for a meaningful project in the community that fulfilled the training requirements for its engineers. Trail construction work offered the perfect solution. With a ten-person crew led by General Dan McGuire (ret.), the guard removed trees, cut brush, improved drainage, and graded the surface along the Charter Oak Greenway. To date, the guard has helped improve 54 miles of trail in Connecticut.

A similar partnership was formed with the Coast Guard Academy for work along the Airline Trail, a section of the Charter Oak Greenway. Bill O'Neill worked with Commander Jonathan Russell to match projects along the trail with the needs of the Coast Guard Academy. Bridge design and construction work needed along the trail turned out to be an ideal project for the final design course for the senior civil engineers at the academy. Two consecutive graduating classes evaluated the existing condition of the bridges, created designs, and estimated the cost and time needed to repair, rehabilitate, or construct all the rail-trail bridges. During the spring semesters of 1999 and 2000, cadets built three bridges, including a 20-foot-long bridge along the Airline Trail. Their work included designing, installing wood girders, and decking the bridge. The Coast Guard Academy and the National Guard continue to work on projects and will help transfer an historic bridge, no longer used for automobile traffic, from the Connecticut roadway system to the trail system.

These two cases exemplify the value of partnerships in building trails and making a difference in communities. The success of the Connecticut case has inspired similar partnerships in Massachusetts and Rhode Island.

CASE STUDY 6

Community Involvement in Liberty Lake, Washington

Getting the people who live and work around a proposed trail project interested and involved is a great way to achieve on-the-ground results. The National Park Service's Rivers, Trails and Conservation Assistance Program (RTCA) routinely incorporates community involvement techniques to help communities all over the country develop trails and protect rivers.

In 1998, the RTCA office in Seattle, Washington, initiated an agreement with the state chapter of the American Society of Landscape Architects (WASLA) to bring pro bono (no cost) expertise to selected RTCA projects in Washington. This landmark agreement is a model in partnering because it serves equally the needs of both parties involved. The RTCA and recipient communities benefit from pro bono expertise provided from landscape architects and allied professionals. The WASLA fulfills its goals for public service and provides community service opportunities for its members without having to organize and manage the projects.

The RTCA staff is skilled in developing community involvement strategies for river and trail projects and recognized that WASLA would be a powerful partner. The RTCA contributes its planning and organizational skills and members of WASLA provide their technical expertise.

Combine that with the knowledge and desires of the residents and you have a powerful planning team.

A highly successful project resulting from this partnership came together in 1999 in the rapidly growing community of Liberty Lake, which is expected to double in population over the next several years to more than 10,000. Community leaders thought it necessary to develop a communitywide trail plan before development pressures overtook such possibilities, and submitted an application for RTCA assistance. The RTCA accepted the application and proposed a design charette, in cooperation with WASLA, as the primary method for conducting the project. A charette is generally an intensive, "illustrated brainstorming session" involving any number of people and lasting from a few hours to a few days.

The trail-planning process started three months prior to the weekend selected for the charette, with a concentrated and focused effort to inform the entire community about the project and secure widespread commitment for the effort. A newsletter and survey mailed to all residents asked about their favorite places and forms of recreation and what path and trail features they desired. Volunteers were recruited to

provide meals, transportation, and overnight lodging and to participate on design teams.

In April, over an intense three-day weekend, twenty-three volunteer landscape architects, engineers, teachers, recreation professionals, and interpreters worked with community members to produce a conceptual trail plan for Liberty Lake. On Friday afternoon, all members of the design team were given an orientation tour of Liberty Lake, followed by an evening meal hosted by the community in a local restaurant. After dinner, a public meeting and "kick-off" was held in which community leaders presented the results of the survey, historical perspective, background on previous local trail efforts, an overview of the charette process, and introductions of all the community and professional volunteers.

On Saturday morning, the volunteers were divided into three teams, each with a range of expertise consisting of WASLA members, other professional experts, and community members. Each of the teams developed a comprehensive trail network scheme, all of which, once complete, were brought back to the group as a whole, discussed, and combined into a composite trail plan for Liberty Lake. The composite plan was divided into three sections, one for each team to develop in more detail. A fourth team was assigned the task of developing ideas for an education and interpretation plan for the entire trail network. Also on Saturday, the community sponsored a bike rodeo outside the building as a method for drawing attention to the charette that was going on inside.

On Sunday afternoon, a second public meeting was held to present the results and close out the event. Each team revealed an array of colorful illustrative plans, detail section drawings, and perspective sketches for their piece of the network. Over a hundred people attended this event, drawn by a bike raffle that was organized specifically to encourage a big crowd at the closing celebration.

The results have been remarkable. Within two months following the design charette, Liberty Lake completed and adopted a trail plan reflecting the community's desired network of pathways and trails. The trail plan has since been adopted by the county into the comprehensive park and transportation plan. In September of the same year, residents of Liberty Lake passed a bond measure establishing a non-motorized transportation district for their community, thereby establishing a source of funding to match and leverage other trail grants and money. One year later, the county engineering department announced plans to construct a pedestrian bridge over a major interstate highway that was identified in the plan. Finally, members of the eastside chapter of WASLA were so thrilled by the success of the Liberty Lake charette that they have embarked on their own to provide similar pro bono technical assistance to communities throughout the northeast region of Washington State.

For more information on the RTCA program, visit www.ncrc.nps.gov/rtca.

3

Designing Your Trail

Once you have completed your site assessment, and you have involved the public in planning for the trail, the next step is to embark upon designing your multi-use trail. At this point, you should decide whether you will do the design work yourself or with your in-house staff or whether you should hire a design consultant (see "How to Find a Good Consultant" in Chapter 2). Either way, the following guidelines can help guide you through the process of designing the trail or working with a design consultant.

Keep in mind that designing a trail can be a lengthy, complicated process that may require numerous iterations before the best design emerges. It is also important to remember that multiple-use trails are public facilities and need to be designed with both the safety of the users and the integrity of the landscape and environment in mind. For this reason, it is important that a design professional review and approve all design work before the trail goes to construction.

In this age of computer technology, consider employing any available digital mapping and imaging tools. Many trail designers are using GIS mapping software (see Box 2.1), Computer-Aided Design (CAD) software, and photographic enhancement applications (Figures 3.1 and 3.2). Newer technologies can even assist in producing virtual "fly-throughs" of a project site, showing viewers a 3-D video of future conditions. These tools allow designers to illustrate and "test" alternatives and the effectiveness of

solutions more efficiently than traditional design techniques.

Meeting the Needs of Different Users

Trails are designed and built for the people who use them. From your planning phase, you should have identified the types of users your trail will serve. As a multi-use facility, your trail is likely to attract a variety of users. They will vary in their needs and expectations, so you should take them into account during the design phase. This is especially important with regard to trail width, surface material, and trail amenities. It is also critical that you develop a design that maximizes safety and comfort for everyone.

This is a good point to refer to the notes you took during your assessment and review the feedback you may have received from local residents. You may want to consider hosting a "community design workshop" during this phase to give the public an opportunity to review preliminary design work (see "Public Involvement" in Chapter 2). A sampling of the trail users you may need to accommodate includes walkers, hikers, runners, road bicyclists, mountain bikers, in-line skaters, equestrians, cross-country skiers, and people in wheelchairs. If you permit motorized uses, you may have ATVs, trail bikes, and snowmobiles. In addition, in accordance with

Before

After

Figures 3.1 and 3.2. Digital imaging software can be used to alter existing photographs to show proposed conditions, like this trail along a roadway.

the Americans with Disabilities Act (ADA), you need to take every reasonable effort to make the trail and associated facilities such as the trailhead, rest rooms, and water fountains accessible to all people, regardless of age or ability.

Pedestrians

Pedestrians include a wide variety of people, such as walkers, hikers, joggers, runners, people pushing baby strollers, and people who want to read interpretive signs or spot birds and other wildlife. These users travel at low speeds (an average of 3 to 7 miles per hour) and tend to have fewer specific design requirements than other users. Many pedestrians prefer a surface that is softer than asphalt or concrete (such as crushed rock or mulch) to prevent knee, shin, and foot strain. Other pedestrians may be attracted to hard surfaces so that they can walk faster (power-walking) or push a stroller more easily.

If you are considering paving as your primary trail surface, provide a 2.5- to 5-foot-wide shoulder on both sides of the trail for pedestrians. This shoulder should be well graded and groomed to avoid bumps, hidden holes, or other obstructions or hazards to safe and comfortable walking or running. If a separate pedestrian-only path is planned, it can consist of graded crushed stone or bare earth. Although it is possible to design a trail as pedestrian-only, unless strictly enforced, bicyclists and other users can be expected. It may be more realistic to design a trail for pedestrians that can, at a minimum, also accommodate mountain bicyclists.

Consider the appropriate trail amenities that accommodate pedestrians, including benches, drinking fountains, rest rooms, shelters, and picnic areas. A high-use pedestrian-only path should have a minimum 6- to 8-foot-wide tread.

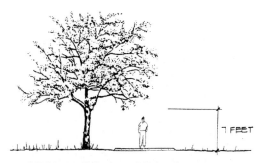

Figure 3.3. Vertical clearance for pedestrians.

Trees, vines, and other vegetation should be trimmed to achieve a 7-foot vertical clearance (Figure 3.3). Ten feet of vertical clearance is needed for equestrians.

Bicyclists

When considering bicyclists' needs, keep in mind the several types of bicyclists: commuting, recreational, and touring, as well as elderly and young cyclists. The different types of bicycles include road or "touring" bikes, all-track bikes, three-wheel and four-wheel bikes, tandem bikes, and mountain bikes. The different types of cyclists and equipment imply somewhat different needs, abilities, and design requirements (Figure 3.4). For example, commuter cyclists usually ride bicycles with narrow, smooth tires that must utilize paved surfaces, whereas all-track cyclists prefer a softer surface. The needs of mountain bikers are addressed on page 55.

The American Association of State Highway

POTENTIAL TRAIL USERS

- Pedestrians
- Bicyclists
- Mountain bikers
- Equestrians
- Cross-country skiers
- Snowmobilers
- In-line skaters (rollerbladers)
- People in wheelchairs

Figure 3.4. A group of bicyclists ride along Kokosing Gap Trail in Ohio.

and Transportation Officials (AASHTO) updated its *Guide for the Development of Bicycle Facilities* in 1999. The AASHTO guidelines are viewed as the national standard for bikeway design, and many of its recommendations have been incorporated into this manual. Many of the AASHTO design guidelines, such as sight distances, trail width, and trail clearances, apply to all bicyclists; however, some aspects (such as

trail surface material) may not apply to mountain bicyclists.

If your trail receives federal or state transportation funding, such as Transportation Enhancement funds (see "Funding Sources for Trail Development" in Chapter 4), your state will most likely require that your trail design follow AASHTO standards. Many transportation agencies will not fund a trail that is not designed to accommodate commuting cyclists, as well as pedestrians and other users. AASHTO's guidelines represent a default national standard for many states, or your state department of transportation may have its own guidelines that are based on AASHTO's recommendations (North Carolina and Oregon have their own bicycle facility standards). If you plan to receive transportation dollars for trail construction, consult your local department of transportation before beginning the design of your trail and obtain a copy of the AASHTO guidelines. You should also consult the AASHTO guidelines as a federal standard for designing any on-road bikeway facilities that may connect to your trail route. In addition, following AASHTO standards can promote safe trail use and reduce your exposure to liability.

AASHTO recommends a minimum 10-foot width for bicycle paths under most conditions, with at least a 2-foot-wide cleared, graded shoulder on either side. Depending on the other anticipated uses on your multi-use trail, a 12- or 14-foot-wide trail with shoulders may be advisable.

An 8-foot-wide path is the absolute minimum for a multi-use trail that accommodates bicyclists, and it should be used only under the following rare conditions: Bicycle traffic will be low even during peak times; the trail will have only occasional pedestrian use; good horizontal and vertical alignments will allow safe and frequent passing; and the path will not be used by heavy maintenance vehicles that may damage the trail edge. If your trail will not meet all of these criteria, develop your trail with a width of at least 10 feet. The vertical clearance for safe bicycle use is at least 8 feet (Figure 3.5), although 10 feet should be the minimum for overpasses and tunnels.

To accommodate the speed of bicyclists, particularly on paved trails, you should develop your trail for a specific design speed, which is the maximum safe speed that a bicyclist can maintain over a specified section of trail. A trail's design speed should be set at a level that is at least as high as the preferred speed of faster cyclists. AASHTO recommends developing

8 FEET

Figure 3.5. Vertical clearance for bicyclists.

shared-use paths for a minimum design speed of 20 miles per hour for level terrain and 30 miles per hour for a downgrade that exceeds 4 percent. On slower, unpaved paths, a 15-mile-per-hour design speed is adequate. High speeds should be strongly discouraged, however, on heavily used urban trails, especially where pedestrians will be present.

Providing adequate stopping sight distance (the distance required to bring a bicycle to a full controlled stop) is critical for bicycle and pedestrian safety. Paved or unpaved multi-use trails should maintain a minimum sight distance of 150 feet for bicyclists. If you are building your trail on a former rail corridor or canal, sight distances may be less of a problem and grades will be minimal. Ideal grades for bicyclists—over long distances—are less than 3 percent (typical for old rail beds and canal routes), although up to 5 percent is acceptable.

Signage along the trail should indicate trail courtesy and *share-the-trail* protocol. For example, bicyclists should yield the right-of-way to pedestrians and equestrians. Signs should also be posted to encourage bicyclists to give a clear warning before passing and to reduce speed or dismount when entering tunnels or culverts. Note that equestrians should receive a voice warning rather than a horn or bell to avoid startling the horse.

Trail support amenities for bicyclists should include bicycle racks and, in some areas, bicycle lockers. Racks should be visible and easy to use, and they should be designed to prevent damage to bicycles (see "Trail Support Facilities" later in this chapter). Lockers, which are particularly helpful near mass transit stations and employment centers, should secure the entire bicycle and protect it from inclement weather. Periodic rest areas, benches, drinking fountains, shelters, and rest rooms are also desirable.

Mountain Bikers

In the early 1980s, the mountain bike took the recreation market by storm, and the sport has continued to grow and diversify. Some mountain bikers enjoy easy trails and some seek out rough, off-road terrain to conquer. Equipment design has evolved to include both simple all-track, or "hybrid" style, bikes that function well on both road and trail, as well as sophisticated machines that include shock-absorbing devices and special tires. Because of the growing popularity and the variety of mountain biking user types, this activity can compromise trail safety, degrade the environment, and increase user conflict, especially on backcountry trails.

Education is the key to solving many potential problems with conflicts between mountain bikers and hikers or equestrians. Fortunately, the International Mountain Bicycling Association is actively working to educate mountain bikers about proper trail use, such as riding only on open trails, yielding the right-of-way to other users, and taking care not to scare animals (see Case Study 7). If mountain bikers will be using your trail, you should develop an educational campaign on proper trail use for all users.

Because mountain bikers often seek a challenging trail experience on steeper grades and softer surfaces than those used by other cyclists, a major complaint is that they tear up certain trail surfaces and cause erosion, particularly after heavy rains or during a thaw (Figure 3.6). However, this is primarily a problem on steeper grades with natural surfaces. The problem can be alleviated through changing the use patterns or locations of trails or reconstructing trails that were not built properly (poor sub-grade and sub-base preparation). If your multi-use trail is on a former railroad, canal, or road, none of these issues should be of great concern. Railroad corridors rarely exceed grades of 4 percent, and railroad engineers improved the sub-grade and sub-base problems when they built the line. (See

Figure 3.6. Mountain bikers enjoy the Midland Trail, Colorado.

"Sub-grade, Sub-base, and Trail Surface" later in this chapter.)

Your facility is more likely to suffer damage from mountain bikers straying off the trail, a situation that can be remedied through education and possibly by trail patrols (see "Trail Management for User Safety" in Chapter 5). Because mountain bikers are such a large segment of the bicycling population, you should consider accommodating them through the development of mountain bike parks along your multi-use trail. Mountain bikers can then use your trail to access these parks, designed for their exclusive use, that include rugged terrain and challenging obstacles. Contact your local mountain biking organization, if one exists, or the International Mountain Bicycling Organization (IMBA). Many organizations are willing to offer technical advice and volunteer labor for the construction and maintenance of such parks.

Equestrians

It is increasingly difficult in many areas of the country, particularly urban centers, for equestrians to find places to ride. Some multi-use trail corridors are wide enough to accommodate equestrian use, but many trails prohibit the activity, fearing conflicts with other users and damage to the trail surface. If a trail is properly designed and developed to include equestrians, however, problems will be minimal.

Hard surfaces like asphalt and concrete are undesirable for equestrians because they can injure horses' hooves. Granular stone may also present problems because loose aggregate can get stuck in hooves. Dirt or stabilized dirt is a preferred surface. If you are considering a hard surface, you should plan to include a softer, separate 5-foot-wide tread for horses (Figure 3.7). Although equestrians prefer a separate tread, a cleared shoulder will suffice if necessary. Equestrian organizations may prefer to develop their own trail within the corridor where sufficient width exists; work with them to accomplish this.

If you plan to develop a single tread that will accommodate numerous users, including equestrians, make sure the sub-base and sub-grade of your trail are firm and properly prepared. Horses are unlikely to damage a trail surface unless the sub-base is poorly prepared, since the surface is merely a reflection of what lies beneath.

Figure 3.7. Equestrian meandering along the Gateway Trail in Minnesota.

Vertical clearance for equestrians should be at least 10 feet (Figure 3.8), with a horizontal clearance of at least 5 feet. Low-hanging tree limbs should be cut flush with the trunk (Figure 3.9). Leaves, branches, and other protrusions that could injure the horse or rider, or damage gear, should be removed; and within the tread, large rocks, stumps, and other debris should be

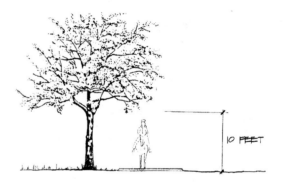

Figure 3.8. Vertical clearance for equestrians.

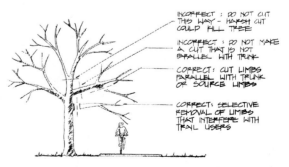

Figure 3.9. Proper tree pruning for clearance.

cleared. Sight distances for equestrians, who usually travel between 4 and 6 miles per hour, should be at least 100 feet.

Signs indicating that equestrians have the right-of-way on a multi-use trail should be included in your design plan. Signs that quickly and clearly indicate right-of-way protocol can help educate other trail users about equestrians and encourage a share-the-trail ethic. Additional signs encouraging bicyclists to give a clear voice warning before passing also minimizes potential conflict between user groups.

It is recommended that you provide support facilities for horses and their riders. Parking and staging areas are particularly critical and require a substantial amount of space. (See "Trail Support Facilities" later in this chapter). In addition to rest rooms and drinking fountains for equestrians, water for horses is also needed along the trail. Hitching posts should be installed at rest stops, picnic areas, and rest rooms so that horses can be tied off the trail while their riders take a break.

For horseback riders, a water crossing is preferred to a high, narrow, and potentially scary bridge. Horses easily negotiate steep slopes and graveled streambeds, although situations that might cause erosion or stream siltation should be avoided. If a water crossing is not practical, provide mounting blocks or space at the ends of bridges and tunnels so riders can dismount and lead their horses. A large, firmly placed log located off the trail will suffice, but a more elaborate design could be used. Work with eques-

trian groups to develop such facilities according to their needs.

Cross-Country Skiers

Many multi-use trails that are used for bicycling, walking, and horseback riding during warm months are ideal for cross-country skiing during winter months (Figure 3.10). With a little preparation (and minimal maintenance), a multi-use trail can easily become a cross-country ski trail. Six inches of snow on the trail offers excellent cross-country skiing without damage to the trail or to ski equipment.

A one-way trail used exclusively for cross-country skiing should be at least 4 feet wide; a two-way trail requires at least 7 feet. Clear the trail of shrubs, debris, and vines at least 2 feet on each side of the tread, and provide an over-

Figure 3.10. Cross-country skiers along Minnesota's Root River Trail.

head clearance of at least 7 feet above the average snow level.

Local retailers of cross-country ski equipment may be interested in promoting cross-country skiing on the trail by providing equipment rentals and skiing lessons. If cross-country skiing is popular in your area, you may actually consider grooming your trail (setting a track for the skis) during the snow season. Grooming creates a consistently packed snow surface so the skier can move more easily. If your trail is a long-distance trail frequented by cross-country skiers, consider developing "warming shelters" along the way. These simple structures provide a fireplace and small shelter, suitable for camping in cold climates.

Snowmobilers

While some multi-use trails are designated snowmobiling trails during the winter months, snowmobilers have transformed many others into de facto snowmobiling trails (Figure 3.11). In fact, many of these routes are used to access existing snowmobile trails. Multi-use trails can be converted into snowmobile trails with as little as 6 inches of snow, without causing much damage to the trail surface. Note, however, that snowmobiles can damage a trail tread if snow cover is inadequate. Signage at trailheads should advise snowmobilers of snow-depth requirements.

You should keep in mind several design requirements if snowmobiling is a potential use

Figure 3.11. Snowmobilers enjoy the Tuscobia State Trail in Wisconsin.

of your trail. For one-way snowmobile traffic, the trail tread should be at least 8 feet wide (10 is preferred); for two-way traffic, it should be at least 10 feet wide (14 is preferred). The trail should be free of branches and debris for at least 2 feet on either side of the trail and at least 10 feet above the expected snow base.

Horizontal sight distances should be 400 feet because of the high speeds that snowmobiles can attain. If this sight distance cannot be achieved, post caution signs at least 100 feet in advance of any problem area to encourage snowmobilers to slow down. Try to provide a 100-foot turning radius if possible.

Make sure any bridges or tunnels are wide enough to accommodate snowmobiles. They need at least an 8-foot-wide clearance and a minimum carrying capacity of 5 tons. Intersections can be dangerous areas for snowmobilers, so the approach grade should be 5 percent or

less, and the intersection should be cleared to double the trail width if possible.

Conflicts can easily erupt between cross-country skiers and snowmobilers, particularly because of the noise and difference in speed. Many believe that the two uses are incompatible, although some multi-use trails have been developed to accommodate both user groups. If both groups want to use the trail, educating them about trail user etiquette is a must. Signs are critical, and speed limits for snowmobilers may be appropriate.

Some trail managers have developed creative solutions to addressing the conflict between these two user groups. Minnesota's Luce Line Trail allows snowmobilers on half of the 60-mile-long trail and cross-country skiers on the other half. Other managers have set up a system whereby skiers and snowmobilers have access to the trail on alternate days. If you anticipate conflicts between these two users, develop creative solutions during the design phase rather than after the trail is open.

In-line Skaters

In-line skating, or "rollerblading," has become an increasingly popular activity on trails, especially in urban areas. Multi-use trails that accommodate pedestrians and bicyclists are likely to attract in-line skaters as well. In some areas, conflicts have arisen among in-line skaters and other user groups due to the high speeds of skaters. Signage and education programs can

Figure 3.12. Many multi-use trails attract in-line skaters.

help to make trails used by in-line skaters safer for all user groups (Figure 3.12).

In-line skaters require the same trail widths as bicyclists (10 feet minimum) and the same horizontal clearances as pedestrians (7 feet). Harder surfaces are better for accommodating in-line skaters. Amenities for skaters are the same as those for bicyclists, although benches to change into and out of skates will be appreciated at trailheads and along the trail where skaters can use them as rest areas.

Other Users

During your design phase, you should also consider other users, including people who want fishing access, skateboarders, dogsledders, and others. Try to involve them in your design process and encourage them to identify their special needs. Consider how well your trail will be able to accommodate baby strollers, people with pets, birdwatchers, and other occasional, often slower, users. In the end, you may not be able to accommodate every use, but you should consider all the possibilities before making crucial design decisions about trail surface material and facilities.

Making Your Trail Accessible

Your multi-use trail design should be accessible—free of barriers and obstructions and usable by people in wheelchairs (Figures 3.13 and 3.14). This is extremely important because 54 million Americans with permanent disabilities (one-fifth of the population, according to a 1994 census) may want to enjoy a trail experience with other people, rather than have a separate, "special" facility.

The primary sources of information for developing accessible standards for all buildings and facilities are the *Uniform Federal Accessibility Standards* (UFAS) and the *Americans with Disabilities Act Accessibility Guidelines* (ADAAG). You should also be familiar with the policies set forth in the Americans with Disabilities Act (ADA). These guidelines were estab-

Figures 3.13 and 3.14. People using wheelchairs along the Washington and Old Dominion Railroad Regional Park.

lished to ensure the civil rights of people with disabilities, and they apply to any newly built or altered structure, such as a parking lot, museum, or rest room. Get copies of all these documents, and consult any state and local codes before constructing your trail. The best source of available, up-to-date information on

federal accessibility guidelines is the U.S. Architectural and Transportation Barriers Compliance Board, also known as the Access Board. They can be reached at www.access-board.gov or by calling 1-800-USA-ABLE. This report contains a table comparing the trail design standards contained in the ADAAG and those in the AASHTO guide for bicycle facilities. In most cases, the design specifications contained in the AASHTO guide exceed those in the ADAAG.

Since 1993, a committee formed by the Access Board has been working to develop uniform national guidelines to address accessibility issues for trails and other outdoor resources (since this issue is not specifically addressed in ADAAG). These draft guidelines are due to be released in 2000 as a Notice of Proposed Rulemaking (NPRM) and should be finalized within a few years as a part of the ADA. The draft NPRM represents the best available information on the subject. This report is available at www.access-board.gov/pubs/outdoor-rec-rpt.htm.

A recent comprehensive study of accessibility design guidelines and practices that should be consulted is *Designing Sidewalks and Trails for Access, Parts I and II,* published by the Federal Highway Administration (FHWA). Part I of the series was published in 1999, and provides a review of existing guidelines and practices. Part II is scheduled to be published by 2001, and will contain recommended accessible designs for sidewalks and trails.

Five feet is the minimum width to accommodate a wide range of users with disabilities, and your trail is likely to be double this width. Hard surfaces, such as asphalt and concrete, make a trail most accessible. Compacted crushed stone also works well, provided that the stone's diameter is less than 3/8 inch. Loose gravel is not recommended because it can pose problems for people using wheelchairs or walking aids.

An accessible trail gradient should not exceed 5 percent. If it does, build a ramp (not stairs) to accommodate all users. Although *UFAS* recommends a maximum ramp grade of 8 percent, a 6 percent maximum is strongly recommended. Ramps, which should have a level landing for every 30 inches of vertical rise, must have a hard, slip-resistant surface (Figure 3.15). Install

32-inch-high hand railings on ramps and on bridges.[1]

An accessible trail calls for a rest area every 200 to 300 feet, preferably cleared, with a bench. If installing numerous benches is not possible, plan to post (at trail access points) the distance between rest stops. Signage at trailheads should also include other accessibility information, including distances to important destinations, trail grade profiles, tread information, degree of difficulty, temperature and altitude information, location of drinking water and rest areas, and emergency information. Users will then know the challenges, available amenities, and distances before they set off on the trail.

At trail access areas, provide at least one accessible parking space. (For actual dimensions,

see "Trail Support Facilities" later in this chapter). Also, if you plan to develop any barriers along the trail, such as bollards or gates to prevent motorized access, provide at least a 32-inch-wide clearance for wheelchairs. Be sure to install accessible trail support facilities, including restrooms, drinking fountains, and picnic tables. The more accessible your trail, the more users can enjoy it.

Recommended Tread Widths for Multi-Use Trails

Multi-use trails, by definition, should accommodate various users simultaneously, although this can be difficult given the diverse needs of each user group. Accommodating a range of users within a single trail depends on trail width, trail surface, and speed of trail users.

The width of a trail depends on the land available within the boundaries of your project and may also depend on the sensitivity of the natural resources in the area. For example, if an abandoned railroad bed is built up several feet above the surrounding grade, there is little opportunity for separated treads immediately adjacent to the railroad bed. Similarly, it may be wise to minimize clearing of a streamside area, wetland, or forest where building a wider trail corridor will adversely impact the setting.

Many trail planners and designers recognize the AASHTO bicycle facilities design guidelines as national standards for multi-use trail widths. AASHTO recommends a minimum 10-foot

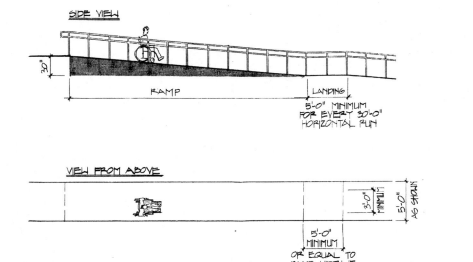

Figure 3.15. Accessible ramp.

---

[1] Continental Bridge, *How to Buy a Bridge* (Alexandria, MN: Continental Bridge, 1991), 8.

width for bicycle trails, but some paths need to be wider to handle the ultimate volume of users. Consider the number of people who are likely to use your trail. Urban areas may receive very heavy traffic, and significant traffic will occur in many suburban areas as well as in some rural areas. Where "significant" trail traffic is anticipated (100 trail users per hour during peak periods), the width of a two-way, single-tread path should be at least 12 feet (Figure 3.16). In urban areas, where "heavy" trail traffic is anticipated (300 users per hour during peak periods), the width of a two-way path should be at least 14 feet.

The types of users who will use the trail add another layer of complexity. See Table 3.1 for the multi-use trail widths needed to accommodate a wide variety of user groups in various settings.

Under certain conditions it may be advisable to provide separate, parallel facilities for bicyclists and other users. When separating users, you need to decide what configuration will work best within your corridor: one primary, hard-surfaced tread primarily for bicyclists and other wheeled users, with a single shoulder for pedestrians and possibly equestrians; one main tread with a shoulder on each side; or two completely separate treads, segregated from each other by a few feet or by vegetation. Two treads can separate faster users requiring hard surfaces (such as bicyclists and in-line skaters) from walkers, runners, and equestrians, who prefer softer surfaces. During winter months, the two treads separate snowmobilers from cross-country skiers.

A primary tread should be a minimum width of 10 feet in an urban or suburban area, 8 feet

Table 3.1. Multi-Use Trail Widths (in feet)

User Groups	Urban	Suburban	Rural
All nonmotorized users	14	12	10
All nonmotorized users, except bicyclists and in-line skaters	10	8	5
Nonmotorized users and snowmobilers	14	12	10

in a rural area. If using a single shoulder for pedestrians and equestrians, it should be at least 5 feet wide (Figure 3.17). (These widths are also appropriate when you are developing two separate treads.) For dual shoulders, you need a minimum of 2 feet on each side of the primary tread, with 2.5 feet preferred.

Sub-grade, Sub-base, and Trail Surface

It is easy to assume that the difference between a smooth trail and a bumpy one is the material used to surface the trail. This is rarely the case. If you were to saw vertically through the surface and into the soil mass several feet down, you would reveal the three components of well-built multi-use trails: the sub-grade, the sub-base, and the trail surface (Figure 3.18).

The sub-grade is the native soil mass of the

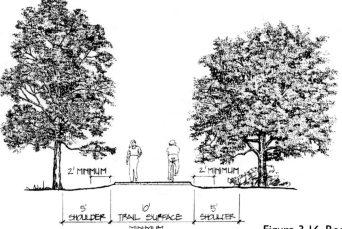

2' MINIMUM   2' MINIMUM

5' SHOULDER | 10' TRAIL SURFACE MINIMUM | 5' SHOULDER

Figure 3.16. Recommended single-tread width.

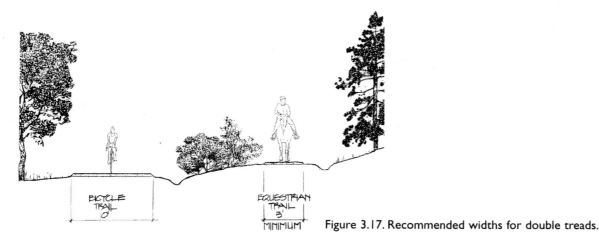

Figure 3.17. Recommended widths for double treads.

landscape; the sub-base is a human-made layer of stone and rock constructed on top of the sub-grade; and the trail surface is the material installed on top of the sub-base. Working together as a unit, the structural qualities of these three components determine the strength and quality of a trail. If you properly evaluate, design, and construct these layers, your trail surface will be smooth and should last for many years.

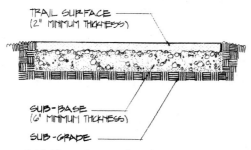

Figure 3.18. Three layers of trail composition.

Ground Surface Concerns

As you plan the precise layout of your multi-use trail, examine the condition of the ground surface, especially the vegetation growing within or immediately adjacent to the corridor. Vegetation should be cleared and stumps and roots removed along each edge of the trail for at least 5 feet from the edge (Figure 3.19). This is recommended for several reasons: to prevent roots and later growth from eventually encroaching on the trail sub-grade, sub-base, or trail surface; to maintain clear sight lines along the edge of the trail; and to permit access by trail construction equipment and emergency vehicles. Smaller shrubs, ground covers, and grasses will eventually grow back in the cleared area. They should be carefully maintained to stabilize exposed soils (see "Landscaping" later in this chapter).

The Sub-grade

The sub-grade is the trail's foundation. To be suitable for trail development, the sub-grade must be able to accommodate the trail's intended uses without overly expensive or severe alterations. The suitability and structural properties of the sub-grade will determine how the sub-base and trail surface must be designed and constructed.

Depending on its length, your trail may traverse a number of different landscapes, and, therefore, you may encounter several types of sub-grade. A highly suitable sub-grade has moderate slopes, good drainage, and firm, dry soils. In other words, topography, soils, and drainage are key factors in evaluating the sub-grade.

TOPOGRAPHY. Topography—the shape of the land—can be defined as flat, gently rolling, hilly, or mountainous. If you have conducted a physical assessment of your corridor (see "Site Considerations: Inventory and Assessment" in Chapter 1), then you know the longitudinal slopes and cross slopes throughout your trail corridor. Table 3.2 lists ranges of longitudinal and cross slopes acceptable for specific trail user groups. Fortunately, few rail corridors or canals ever reach longitudinal slopes greater than 3 percent, so most of these multi-use trails can accommodate virtually all users.

SOILS. Soil composition is the most important factor in determining the sub-grade's structural

NATURAL VEGETATION | VEGETATION CLEARANCE 5' | TRAIL | VEGETATION CLEARANCE 5' | NATURAL VEGETATION

Figure 3.19. Vegetation clearance for trail preparation.

Table 3.2. Trail User Slope Requirements

Trail User	Average Speed (mph)	Longitudinal Slope	Cross Slope
Pedestrian	3–7	No restriction	4% maximum
Person in wheelchair	3–7	3% preferred; 5% maximum	2% maximum
Bicyclist	8–10	3% preferred; 8% maximum	2–4%
Equestrian	5–15	10% maximum	4% maximum
Skier	2–8	3% preferred; 5% maximum	2% preferred

suitability. The best foundation for a multi-use trail is firm and well-drained soil. Characteristics such as drainage, vegetation type, and composition are visually obvious, but others must be evaluated through scientific and engineering tests.

In addition to the structural suitability of your sub-grade soil, you will want to evaluate the following four soil qualities:

1. *Susceptibility to freezing:* This is important because your trail can be damaged during cold winter months if the water in the soil freezes and pushes the fine-grained soil particles toward the surface. Known as frost heave, it will cause large lumps or mounds in the surface. You can prevent this problem by replacing fine-grain soil with coarser material, such as a graded aggregate stone.

2. *Permeability:* This is the soil's ability to drain. Finer-grained or heavy clay soils will not drain as well as coarse-grained soils that contain more air pockets. Poorly drained soils will cause the trail surface to develop water ponds that can remain for more than a day. Replace poorly drained soils with a coarser material.

3. *Bearing strength:* This is the soil's ability to bear a specified load. Saturated soils cannot support as much weight as well-drained, moist soils. Low bearing strength can cause the surface of your trail to rut under normal or heavy usage. If your trail will be on a former rail bed, then the railroad company probably solved this problem. If not, the solution is to modify soil composition to obtain good compaction and permeability.

4. *Shrink and swell:* This is the soil contraction and expansion caused by water and temperature. A change in soil volume most often occurs with "expansive soils." Expansion and contraction of the soil mass can cause the surface of your trail to crack like an eggshell. Prevent this by replacing expansive soils with a coarser, better-draining material.

To evaluate the four soil qualities, contact your local Natural Resource Conservation Service (www.nrcs.usda.gov) and ask them to test the soils and provide you with a complete description of the types located along the trail corridor. In most states, this service is free.

DRAINAGE. Proper drainage is defined as the efficient removal of excess water from the trail cross section. Proper drainage of surface and subsurface waters is the most important consideration in trail design, construction, and management. Improper drainage will have the greatest detrimental impact on the surface and sub-grade of a trail.

Proper drainage serves many functions: it prevents erosion of the sub-grade and sub-base by accommodating surface water flow; it mitigates the effects of flooding by providing areas where floodwaters can be absorbed naturally; it maintains or improves the water quality of adjacent or perpendicular streams; it maintains areas where surface waters can slowly percolate through the soil mass to recharge aquifers; and it helps ensure that wildlife is not permanently disturbed by trail development.

There are two types of drainage flow: surface water runoff and subsurface water runoff. Surface runoff is water that moves on top of the ground, creating rills, troughs, and intermittent creeks and eventually draining into streams, rivers, and lakes. Subsurface runoff is water that moves through the soil horizontally or vertically, depending on the soil type and its permeability.

The trail designer must ensure that the trail does not interfere with proper on-site and off-site surface and subsurface runoff. On-site runoff typically results from rainfall. The design objective is to maintain the water-flow level that existed before the corridor was developed. Off-site runoff, usually in the form of adjacent or

intersecting streams, should not be altered or obstructed. These are the two fundamental principles that will lead to successful management of drainage along your multi-use trail.

Three basic drainage methods are employed to mitigate surface water runoff: an open system, a closed system, or a combination system. An open system uses swales (shallow drainage channels running adjacent to the trail), ditches, and sheet flow, combined with on-site detention ponds that absorb excess water flow (Figure 3.20). Sheet flow allows the water to disperse evenly over the trail and surrounding landscape, preventing ruts and water channels on the trail surface. Use the open drainage system wherever possible—it provides the most natural and cost-effective approach to mitigating surface water drainage. A closed system uses underground structures such as catch basins, drain inlets, culverts, or underground piping and outlet structures to contain excess water flow (Figure 3.21). In a combination system, flows are divided and directed to different systems based on conditions at the site (Figure 3.22).

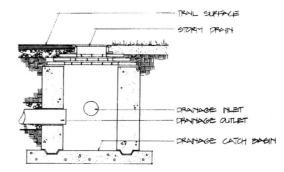

Figure 3.21. Closed urban drainage system.

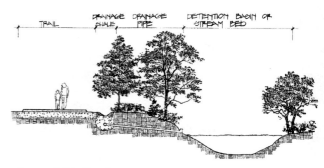

Figure 3.22. Combination drainage system drain pipe with standpipe exit.

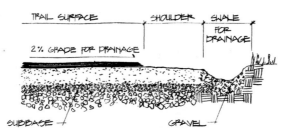

Figure 3.20. Open drainage system.

Three underground drainage techniques mitigate subsurface water runoff:

1. Installing piping to carry excess water away from the subsurface of the trail cross section (Figure 3.23)
2. Constructing French drains, trenches filled with permeable material that collect water and route it toward a creek or stream (Figure 3.24)

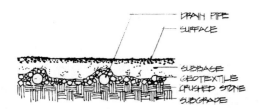

Figure 3.23. Underground piping drainage system.

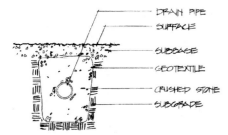

Figure 3.24. French drain.

3. Creating sloped and contoured underground drainage channels, where subsurface water is encouraged to flow through the trail cross section unimpeded (Figure 3.25)

Work with professional landscape architects, engineers, or your local Natural Resource Conservation Service for cost-effective and successful solutions to any drainage concerns throughout the trail design process. By no means should you underestimate the value of proper drainage systems in the design, development, and management of your trail.

WETLANDS. Wetlands are a unique condition of the sub-grade and surface areas of the soil

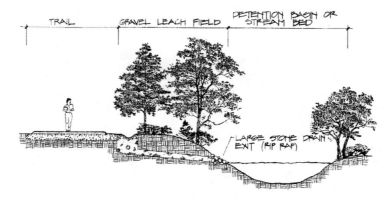

Figure 3.25. Sloped underground drainage—gravel leach field with riprap.

mass—a result of topography, soils, and drainage. Because they are a valuable natural resource, and because they are protected by federal law (Section 404 of the Clean Water Act P.L. 92-50), it is best to avoid developing trails through wetlands. If you must route a trail through a wetland, the best way to accommodate trail users is by constructing boardwalks, observation decks, bridges, or some other elevated structure. Observation decks and interpretive overlooks may, however, be appropriate only at the edges.

The use of impermeable surfaces, fill material, and other construction through wetlands is prohibited without a permit from the U.S. Army Corps of Engineers. If you don't know whether wetlands exist in your corridor, or if you need assistance in selecting an appropriate trail surface through a wetland, contact a local environmental or design professional with wetlands expertise, your local Natural Resource

Conservation Service, the Army Corps of Engineers, the U.S. Fish and Wildlife Service, or your state's wildlife agency.

The Sub-base

The sub-base lies between the sub-grade and the trail surface and serves as a secondary, built foundation for the trail surface. The purpose of the sub-base is to transfer and distribute the weight from the trail surface to the sub-grade. The sub-base serves a vital drainage function, preventing water from migrating up from the sub-grade into the trail's surface. It also allows natural cross drainage to flow through the trail cross section.

The sub-base is usually a graded aggregate stone (gravel), which provides bearing strength and improves drainage. You can select from a variety of stones; your choice depends on local conditions and availability. The thickness of the sub-base is dependent on the condition of your sub-grade. Know the sub-grade's characteristics before determining the sub-base's thickness. As a general rule, the sub-base should be 4 to 8 inches thick. Four inches is sufficient if the sub-grade is in excellent condition; up to 8 inches may be necessary if the sub-grade is of poor quality.

The sub-base can be placed either by hand or by machine and should be compacted with a mechanical roller that weighs at least as much as the trail's anticipated design load (see page 67). The sub-base surface should be smooth and level because the trail surface will be only as firm, smooth, and resilient as the sub-base and sub-grade.

It is *critical* that the sub-base remain intact for the trail's life span if the surface and structural qualities of the trail are to fulfill their design function. Three factors—ballast, design load, and geotextiles—dictate the design and required depth of the sub-base and determine how you should maintain the integrity of this layer during the projected life of your trail.

BALLAST. A term used mostly by railroad workers, ballast refers to the layer of crushed rock used to elevate a railroad bed above the surrounding natural grade to provide proper drainage, a level surface for the ties and rails, structural stability for the track, and ease in maintaining the rail bed. Ballast retarded the growth of native vegetation and absorbed the shock from heavy loads. Railroad companies

Figure 3.26. Ballast surface.

used different materials for ballast, ranging from cinders to gravel to fist-sized rocks (Figure 3.26).

If your trail corridor is on an abandoned rail corridor, evaluate the condition and type of ballast still present; railroads sometimes remove ballast when a line is abandoned. If the ballast is gone, evaluate the foundation soils and design your sub-grade and sub-base appropriately to support your multi-use trail.

A common question relating to ballast is, should it be kept in place, or should some of it be removed? The answer depends on the rail bed's condition and the surrounding natural landscape. Remember that the sub-base transfers weight from the surface to the sub-grade and improves drainage. If you remove ballast, you are removing a valuable component of the road bed cross section. Meanwhile, keep in mind that rail beds supported loads of 30,000 pounds per wheel, at speeds of 50 miles per hour—significantly heavier loads and greater speeds than your trail will need to support.

Occasionally, some reduction in ballast depth may be called for, but before embarking on an arbitrary reduction, employ the services of a structural or geotechnical engineer. This person can evaluate the existing ballast sub-base and recommend the amount of ballast that can be removed without compromising your trail's structural integrity. Do not dispose of excess ballast, as it does have some market value and selling it could cover some of your development costs. Alternatively, it may be possible to process the ballast using a portable crusher to create suitable aggregate or granular stone for your trail surface. In working with ballast, bear in mind the possibility that contaminants could be present from materials that may have fallen off rail cars. Check with an environmental specialist.

Another potential concern is "track tie memory," the imprint left by the railroad cross ties on the ballast. Only some rail corridors are affected by it, particularly those with soft soils.

To find out if you need to deal with track tie memory, examine the rail bed where the cross ties have been removed. If you believe your corridor has track tie memory, the top layer of ballast will need to be removed. The remaining ballast then needs to be regraded, recompacted, and then reconstructed to an elevation that can support the trail's design load. The use of geotextiles, discussed later in this chapter, will prevent track tie memory from appearing in the trail's surface.

Figure 3.27 illustrates the role that ballast can play in the development of a trail with a hard surface. If your budget is limited, however, graded ballast can serve as your trail surface (depending on the diameter of the stones); if you opt to upgrade the surface in the future, it can be layered on top of the ballast.

DESIGN LOAD. The trail's design load is another factor influencing depth of the sub-base. Design load is the *maximum weight* that the trail can carry at any point along its length. Your trail should be accessible by emergency vehicles, such as police cars and ambulances. Also, if you share your corridor with a utility company, the trail may be used by heavy trucks for maintenance and emergency repairs. Therefore, your minimum design load based on static wheel load (at each axle) should be 5,000 pounds, and the minimum design load based on gross vehicle weight should be at least 12,000 pounds. The maximum speed for vehicles equaling the weight of your design load should be 15 miles per hour.

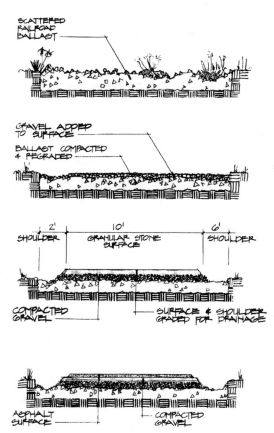

Figure 3.27. Role of ballast in asphalt trail preparation.

The design load is derived by evaluating and computing the combined structural properties of the sub-grade, sub-base, and surface as one unit. Determining the design load gives you the required depth of these components of the trail cross section. For example, if the sub-grade is well drained, with a high bearing strength, it will not need modification, and can sustain a thinner sub-base and surface. If the sub-grade is poorly drained, with a low bearing strength, it will need modification, and the sub-base and surface will need to be thicker to absorb and distribute the loads from trail use. Work with an engineer to make this determination and to define the proper design load.

GEOTEXTILES. Use of geotextiles may help reduce sub-base depth and promote trail structural stability. Geotextiles are fabric mats that increase the strength of the trail cross section, especially in areas where soft or unstable soils are present. Geotextiles reinforce structural qualities of the sub-grade and sub-base, help prevent weed growth through the trail surface, and improve drainage.

Most often used between the sub-grade and sub-base, geotextiles maintain the integrity of the sub-base by preventing it from migrating into the sub-grade (Figure 3.28). Migration, the downward movement of the sub-base into the subgrade, can create voids below the trail surface, resulting in trail tread damage. Geotextiles keep the sub-base intact, ensuring the strength and long life of the trail cross section. In some cases, this may allow a reduction in the thickness of your sub-base material.

Geotextile fabrics are of two types: woven and nonwoven. Fabric selection depends on your trail type and local soil and drainage conditions. A geotechnical engineer or land-

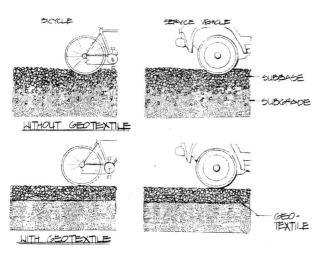

Figure 3.28. Role of geotextiles.

scape architect can help you select an appropriate fabric.

The Trail Surface

Many surface types are available to complete your multi-use trail—for example, granular stone, asphalt, concrete, soil cement, resin-based stabilized material, wood chips, and natural surface.

Surface materials are either soft or hard, defined by the material's ability to absorb or repel moisture. Hard surfaces include soil cement, crushed stone, asphalt, resin-based stabilized material, and concrete. Soft surfaces include natural earth and wood chips.

Many single-use trails throughout the country, particularly hiking and equestrian trails, have soft surfaces. These surfaces often do not hold up well under heavy use or varying weather conditions, and therefore are not ideal for multi-use trails, particularly those with substantial use. Hard-surfaced materials are more practical for multi-use trails, particularly in urban and suburban areas. They are more expensive to purchase and install but require less maintenance and can withstand frequent use. Hard surfaces also accommodate the widest range of trail users. Keep in mind that some hard surfaces are softer than others.

Trail surfacing can be used to encourage or discourage use. If you want to encourage as many users as possible, choose one of the hardest surfaces. If you want to limit use to a few groups, select a softer surface. You can also control the speed of trail travel by the surface type you select. The softer the surface, the slower the speeds.

When designing trails for use by people with wheelchairs, make sure that the surface is firm and stable. This does not necessarily mean that it must be concrete or asphalt. Other, more pervious surfaces, such as crushed stone, can accommodate wheelchair use, as long as they remain firm and stable. You can help to ensure stability by adding soil stabilizers to gravel or dirt surfaces, or by substitution. For example, trails made from wood chips are not accessible, but trails made from engineered wood fiber materials can be. (If you are uncertain about the suitability of your trail surface, check with the manufacturer to see if it has passed ASTM standards for stability, referencing code #F1951.)

Consider a variety of factors when selecting a surface: availability of the surface material, cost to purchase the material and install it, life expectancy, accessibility, costs of maintaining the surface, and user acceptance and satisfaction.

Remember that you can always upgrade the surface later. If you are dealing with a former railroad corridor and want an asphalt surface but cannot afford it at this point, open the trail with the existing ballast in place if it is suitable for anticipated users and upgrade it in the future. Dozens of high-quality trail facilities have been developed this way. After a trail is open (even with a modest surface), the support for it quickly expands and public pressure builds to develop a higher-quality facility.

The Cannon Valley Trail in southeastern Minnesota began as a crushed stone trail but was later upgraded to asphalt to accommodate commuting cyclists and attract touring cyclists. The Northern Central Rail-Trail in Maryland, on the other hand, opened with crushed limestone, with plans to pave it later with asphalt. However, the adjacent landowners and local users liked the surface so much (in part because it deterred in-line skating and fast-paced bicyclists) that the agency decided not to change it.

HARD SURFACES. Following is a detailed description of hard trail surfaces, ranging from the softest to the hardest. These surfaces are the most appropriate if you will have only one trail tread. If you plan to have two parallel treads, the following surfaces should be used on the primary (i.e., wider) tread. The cost estimates cited, which can vary significantly around the country, are in year 2000 dollars. They are for a 10-foot-wide trail and cover sub-base preparation and labor costs.

Soil Cement. Used in some areas where stone is not readily available and the price of asphalt is prohibitive, soil cement is a mixture of pulverized native soil and measured amounts of Portland cement (Figure 3.29). This mixture is usually created at the project site. It should be spread approximately 4 inches thick on a pre-

Figure 3.29. **Soil cement surface.**

pared sub-grade immediately after the mixture has been formed. It is then rolled and compacted to a very dense surface by machinery.

Soil cement will support most user groups; however, bicyclists and horseback riders will have the greatest impact on the surface. Results with this surface have been mixed: It can crack into large chunks with significant temperature changes or heavy use. Soil cement is inexpensive to install, costing approximately $60,000 to $100,000 per mile for a 10-foot-wide trail, but it may not be the best long-term option.

Drainage is very important to the upkeep of this surface. To prevent water erosion, you can permit sheet flow on longitudinal slopes of 4 percent and less. If the slope is steeper, however, you should crown the trail tread (make the middle slightly higher than the edges) and route the water into side ditches. Soil cement surfaces will last longer if installed on a well-prepared sub-grade and sub-base, although you will need to control vegetation and make spot repairs. The surface can be placed on longitudinal slopes of up to 8 percent and cross slopes not exceeding 2 percent.

Granular Stone. This is a very popular surface for multi-use trails because it accommodates a wide variety of trail users and can be compacted into a firm surface (Figure 3.30). You can choose from a variety of stones including limestone, sandstone, and crushed rock. These stones can be crushed to a very fine material and densely compacted to hold up extremely well

Figure 3.30. **Granular stone surface.**

under heavy use (see Box 3.1, "Top Ten Tips for Constructing Crusher Fines Trails"). This surface is also compatible with the natural environment and complements the aesthetic appeal of surrounding landscapes and historic transportation corridors.

If this surface is finely crushed and properly packed, it can accommodate virtually every trail user, from joggers to bicyclists to equestrians. It also works well for people using wheelchairs as long as the stone diameter is less than $3/8$ inch. Mixing stone dust with the stones is preferred, because the dust can act as a binding agent, decreasing the "marble" effect of gravel. It is not suitable for in-line or roller skaters or skateboarders, however. For an ideal surface, spread the granular stone into a layer at least 4 inches thick over a prepared sub-grade, and compact it with a motor grader.

The use of granular stone is increasing because of its moderate price. Depending on availability and proximity to the trail, crushed limestone or sandstone costs approximately $80,000 to $120,000 per mile for a 10-foot-wide trail. Maintenance is minimal. Stones should be replenished (and the surface regraded) about every seven to ten years, although spot repairs and grading will be necessary in the interim.

Be aware that stones from different quarries can vary significantly; for example, stones from two limestone quarries within the same state may have noticeably different compositions. This difference can affect how firmly the surface will compact and how well it will wear under heavy use. If possible, visit more than one quarry before selecting the stone for your surface.

It is critical to realize that fine-grained stones will retain moisture and thus vegetation may sprout within the surface. Use geotextiles to help prevent this problem. Heavy use of the trail also serves as preventive maintenance. Drainage can sheet flow across the surface, or the trail bed can be crowned so that surface water is routed into side ditches. Longitudinal slopes should not

---

Box 3.1. Top Ten Tips for Constructing Crusher Fines Trails

Crusher fines are a type of stone surface appropriate as a base material or surface material for multi-use trails. These tips come from Brian Muller, a planning manager and landscape architect for the Highlands Ranch Metro District, Parks and Open Space Program, in Highlands Ranch, Colorado. Brian obtained his experience with crusher fines trails by helping to build approximately 40 miles of trails in the Denver area, including the 19-mile Highline Canal Trail.

1. Know the material that is available in your area, have samples submitted to you, and compare them for:
   - **Color:** Depending on the rock mined in your area, colors may vary from light gray to brown, and even shades of pink and red. Colors may even differ among rock coming from the same mining pit.
   - **Gradation:** Gradation is critical for compacting and resistance to erosion. A good variation of aggregate sizes that are $3/8$ inch and less should provide an adequate, free-draining, firm-wearing course. Too much large aggregate will not compact, and the larger pieces will migrate to the trail edges. Too much small aggregate will soften with moisture and take on the qualities of mud.
   - **Density:** Heavier material is preferred because it will not move as easy as lighter material. This, again, relates to the ability to withstand erosion and remain in a compacted state. A simple test is to weigh an equal dry amount of each sample.
   - **Shape:** The type of rock will dictate the shape of aggregate pieces. Crusher fines are a small aggregate that remains after mining larger pieces of rock. If the pieces have thin or sharp points, they may harm bare feet or bicycle tires. Too round a particle could function like marbles and may cause skidding for runners or bicyclists.
2. Prepare a good sub-grade prior to laying material. The area to receive crusher fines should be excavated to a depth equal to the desired thickness of compacted material. In most cases, this will be between 4 and 6 inches. Make sure all organic material has been removed from the sub-grade bed and that the bed has been thoroughly compacted. This process is not unlike a preparation for concrete paving.
3. Prepare an adequate cross slope (or crown) on the finished trail surface so that puddles will not form. About $1/4$ inch per 1 foot should suffice. The continuous cross slope may be more

appropriate if the trail is benched into a slope, whereas a crowned condition may be best for flatter surfaces.

4. Try to design the trail so that it will not be in wet situations for long periods of time. Water is the universal solvent—crusher fines will degrade faster when exposed to water for longer periods of time. Keep irrigated areas away from this type of trail surface. If water is unavoidable, you might consider a change of surfacing (concrete or asphalt) in those areas that remain wet.

5. Keep all drainage contained in culverts, pipes, or adjacent swales so that trails will not erode. Water will want to run, in line, on a trail with any appreciable slope. Water will create small erosion channels that will be a constant maintenance concern. If the trail needs to slope in excess of 10 percent, you may want to consider an alternative surfacing so these areas will not erode. One compatible material that resists this condition while maintaining a similar appeal is recycled concrete screened to $3/8$ inch or less.

6. Keep vegetation in good condition along trail edges and try to avoid irrigation. A good dry-land grass allowed to grow high or mowed at a 6-inch height, as a maintained shoulder treatment, will confine the crusher fines but still allow drainage to pass through.

7. Trails that are 6 to 14 feet wide can be constructed with the use of an asphalt-spreading machine. This procedure saves an enormous amount of installation time. A uniform amount of fines can be placed over the sub-grade, rolled as a preliminary compacting measure, water applied, then roller compacted to complete the operation. This method also ensures uniformity in thickness and smooth horizontal curves.

8. Carefully consider the use of geotextile fabrics over the sub-grade prior to surfacing. Although fabrics deter the growth of weeds in the path, they can eventually cause problems in some areas, exposing worn or torn fabric that can trip users, if the surfacing is thin.

9. Crusher fines trails may eventually intersect other trails or hard-paved surfaces. These connections can be problematic due to loose material from the gravel trail spilling onto the hard surface. A trail user may slip and slide on this loose material. Plan a transaction pad constructed of a firm, textured material such as exposed aggregate concrete. Any loose material will collect in the rough texture, providing better traction for users.

10. Maintenance: Always keep a stockpile of material on-hand to fill eroded areas. Have the contractor provide this additional material when the trail is built, so the colors will match when you make repairs. Also, try to avoid snow plowing crusher fines trails because it may destroy the integrity of the trail. If you must plow, set the blade a few inches higher than the surface.

exceed 5 percent, and cross slopes should be limited to 2 percent.

Asphalt. Also known as "asphaltic concrete," this hard surface is very popular in a wide variety of trail settings and landscapes. It works particularly well on trails that are used for bicycle commuting or in-line skating. However, cross-country skiers may find that snow tends to melt more quickly on asphalt surfaces because the black pavement absorbs heat from the sun. In addition, equestrians generally cannot use an asphalt trail because it is hard on horses' hooves, and the hooves can leave imprints in hot weather. To avoid these limitations, you may want to construct a softer parallel tread along an asphalt trail or leave a wide enough shoulder for those who prefer a softer surface.

Asphalt is actually a "cement" comprised of tar and oils. In an asphaltic concrete surface a graded aggregate stone is mixed with asphalt (Figure 3.31). Small aggregate stones result in a smooth surface with few voids. Coarse grades of stones result in a rough, porous surface. When the proportion of asphalt cement is increased, the surface is smoother and less porous.

A flexible pavement, asphalt conforms to the contours of the sub-base and sub-grade. If your sub-grade and sub-base have been prepared properly, the surface will be smooth and level. Asphalt should be installed 2 inches thick and smoothed out with an asphalt machine and rollers.

At approximately $200,000 to $300,000 per

Stewart Watkins

vantages include possible environmental contamination and degradation when not "seasoned" by heavy traffic.

Concrete. The hardest of all trail surfaces, concrete is most often used in urban areas with severe climate changes, susceptibility to flooding, and anticipated heavy use. Like asphalt, it accommodates virtually all users, although a parallel path should be provided for equestrians and runners.

Although concrete is the most expensive surface, it lasts longer than any other—often twenty-five years or more. Approximate costs for concrete are $300,000 to $500,000 per mile for a 10-foot-wide trail. Concrete used for trail surfacing should be properly reinforced to prevent cracking where sub-grade conditions warrant. A wire or fabric mesh (which may be required where the heavy vehicles use the trail or there is the likelihood of frequent flooding with fast-moving water) is constructed over a well-prepared sub-base, and then from 4 inches to 6 inches of concrete are placed on top.

Concrete can be shaped to fit most conditions, and it is the only surface that can be tailored at the time of installation—it can be colored with special pigments or scored with grooves in the surface. Such alterations are often used to indicate an upcoming intersection. It should be rough finished with a stiff broom to avoid slipperiness when wet (Figure 3.32). Joints should be saw cut (not trowelled) to avoid

Greenways Inc.

Figure 3.32. Concrete surface.

bumpiness. When properly installed, concrete will need virtually no maintenance.

Boardwalk. Boardwalks are wooden structures that serve as "small bridges," most often used to provide trail access across wetlands and other ecologically sensitive landscapes. Boardwalks contain foundation, framing, decking, and, sometimes, railings. Railings, which follow the same requirements as bridge railings, are required if the height of the top of the decking is more than 30 inches from the ground. Decking should be at least 2 inches thick. The foundation of a wood boardwalk is usually a pier or wood post. If a post is touching the ground or submerged in water, it must be chemically treated with wood preservatives to add necessary longevity and structural safety. Many of these chemicals are toxic to the

mile for a 10-foot-wide trail, asphalt is more expensive than crushed stone. It needs minor maintenance, such as crack patching, and has a life expectancy of seven to fifteen years. Asphalt is a flexible surface that needs regular use to remain pliable and resilient, and will actually last longer with heavy use.

Asphalt can be installed on virtually any slope, but cross slopes should not exceed 2 percent. Drainage should sheet flow across the trail. Contrary to what some may claim, asphalt pavement will not "bubble up" or float away under normal surface drainage flow. Extreme flooding, however, can ruin asphalt, just as it does almost all other trail surfaces (except concrete). Disad-

natural environment, so you should consider using recycled plastic or concrete posts as an alternative. Boardwalks should be used only where necessary, as they are the most expensive type of surfacing, costing approximately $1.5 million to $2 million per mile for a 10-foot-wide trail. They can also be slippery when wet, so you should sign the trail appropriately.

Resin-Based Soil or Aggregate Stabilization. There are resin-based products on the market that can be used as an alternative to asphalt where site or environmental conditions dictate. The resin is a derived tree product and it will bind aggregate or soil particles together, creating a usable trail surface. Advantages of resin-based products may be cost if the surface is stabilized soil, aesthetics if one wants a more natural colored surface, and less environmental impact from oils and tars in asphalt. You should check with a landscape architect or engineer when considering a resin-based product to determine site suitability, maintenance factors, and cost competitiveness.

SOFT SURFACES. The following surfaces can work well in some rural areas and on parallel treads, particularly for equestrians, runners, and walkers. However, they may not be well suited for a multi-use trail surface that is expected to accommodate a high volume of many different uses.

Natural Surface. Natural surfaces include existing soil and vegetation (Figure 3.33). The trail

Figure 3.33. Natural surface.

bed will require less preparation than harder surfaces, but you will need to remove rocks, tree roots, and other obstructions from the subgrade. Maintenance will consist of fixing drainage problems, repairing eroded areas and removing new vegetation. Natural surfacing costs approximately $50,000 to $70,000 per mile to construct. The cost may be substantially less if volunteers do the work.

A natural surface that is well drained and properly sloped will be the most enduring. Drainage can be dispersed in a sheet flow across the trail surface or collected in side ditches and routed to a crossing at a low point in the trail.

Longitudinal slopes can vary, but cross slopes should not exceed 2 percent.

Wood Chips. An attractive surface, wood chips blend extremely well with the natural environment (Figure 3.34). Because hikers, runners, and equestrians like this soft, spongy surface, it works well as a parallel tread next to asphalt or concrete. However, this surface decomposes rapidly under prolonged exposure to sun, heat, and humidity; does not accomodate wheelchair use; and requires almost constant maintenance to keep the width consistent. Minimum thickness at the time of installation should be no less than 3 inches, and the entire surface needs replace-

Figure 3.34. Wood chip surface.

ment at least every two years. Wood chips are often available at no cost (or a nominal cost) from commercial tree-trimming services.

Wood chips may wash off a prepared sub-base under normal rainfall and do not allow cross drainage. The surface should not be installed on longitudinal slopes that exceed 5 percent, and cross slopes should be limited to 2 percent. Wood chip surfacing costs approximately $65,000 to $85,000 per mile to construct. The cost may be substantially less if volunteers do the work.

RECYCLED MATERIALS. As interest in recycling increases, recycled materials are being used in trail construction. Car tires, recycled asphalt, crushed glass, plastic, Styrofoam, and pottery are some of the materials being recycled as trail surfacing, benches, and signs. The recycled products industry continues to expand, with new products and new manufacturers emerging. If you are interested in using a recycled product, conduct some research into how it is made, if it has been tested for longevity, and if it is safe and practical for use in trail development.

Availability of Surfaces and Local Character

When selecting a surface, keep in mind how easily you can get the material, and look for materials that are unique to your region of the country. If you are building a trail in Indiana, for example, you may want to surface it with

Table 3.3. Trail Surface Synopsis

Surface Material (cost per mile) (longevity)	Advantages	Disadvantages
Soil cement, $60,000–$100,000, medium	Uses natural materials, more durable than native soils, smoother surface, low cost, accommodates multiple use.	Surface wears unevenly, not a stable all-weather surface, erodes, difficult to achieve correct mix.
Granular stone, $80,000–$120,000, medium-long (7–10 yrs)	Soft but firm surface, natural material, moderate cost, accommodates multiple use.	Surface can rut or erode with heavy rainfall, regular maintenance needed to keep consistent surface, replenishing stones may be a long-term expense, not for areas prone to flooding or steep slopes.
Asphalt, $200,000–$300,000, medium-long (7–15 yrs)	Hard surface, supports most types of use, all-weather, accommodates most users simultaneously, smooth surface to comply with ADA guidelines, low maintenance.	High installation cost, costly to repair, not a natural surface, freeze/thaw can crack surface, heavy construction vehicles need access.
Concrete, $300,000–$500,000, long-term (20 yrs plus)	Hardest surface, easy to form to site conditions, supports multiple use, lowest maintenance, resists freeze/thaw, best cold weather surface, most resistant to flooding.	High installation cost, costly to repair, not a natural-looking surface, construction vehicles will need access to the trail corridor.
Boardwalk, $1.5–$2 million, medium-long	Necessary in wet or ecologically sensitive areas, natural-looking surface, low maintenance, supports multiple use.	High installation cost, costly to repair, can be slippery when wet.
Resin-stabilized, cost varies depending on type of application, medium-long depending on type of application	Aesthetics, and less environmental impact, possible cost savings if soil used, can be applied by volunteers.	Need to determine site suitability and durability, may be more costly in some cases.
Native soil, $50,000–$70,000, short to long depending on local use and conditions	Natural material, lowest cost, low maintenance, can be altered for future improvements, easiest for volunteers to build and maintain.	Dusty, ruts when wet, not an all-weather surface, can be uneven and bumpy, limited use, possibly not accessible.

Surface Material (cost per mile) (longevity)	Advantages	Disadvantages
Wood chips, $65,000–$85,000, short-term (1–3 years)	Soft, spongy surface good for walking, moderate cost, natural material.	Decomposes under high temperature and moisture, requires constant replenishment, not typically accessible, limited availability, not appropriate for floodprone areas.
Recycled materials, cost and life vary	Good use of recyclable materials, surface can vary depending on materials.	Design appropriateness and availability vary.

limestone because it is easy and inexpensive to obtain. This choice would also highlight one of the region's natural resources and make the trail experience more memorable.

Designing Trails in Challenging Areas

As our cities and towns continue to grow, trail planners and designers are facing new challenges in locating continuous undeveloped corridors for trails. Many old railroad and canal lines, as well as utility corridors, are located near environmentally contaminated sites or active rail lines. Other corridors have been bisected by development, forcing trail planners to route users onto roadways and construct trails in difficult landscapes, in order to ensure continuous trail facilities. Designing trails in these challenging areas can be difficult, but is often possible if you are creative.

Floodprone Areas

If a section of your trail is located in an area that frequently floods, proper trail surfacing and streambank repair may be needed. Concrete is the best surface for a floodprone area, and has even been used to develop trails located on the shores of streams and rivers. Remember that floating debris can substantially damage railings, bridges, and other trail structures, so construct as few of these as possible in floodprone areas.

If your trail is located close to a stream or river, you should make sure that the banks are stable before constructing the trail. If not, your trail could be undercut by eroding floodwaters. Traditionally, engineers have used riprap (large stones), culverts, and walls to divert the flow of streams and rivers in order to protect developed areas. Although these techniques may be necessary under extreme circumstances, natural engineering techniques, known as soil bioengineering, should be used whenever possible to stabilize streambanks (Figures 3.35 and 3.36).

Before

After

Figures 3.35 and 3.36. Bolin Creek Greenway, located in Chapel Hill, North Carolina, incorporated stream restoration into the trail's development. These photos illustrate the stream during and after trail construction.

Environmentally Contaminated Sites

If you suspect your trail corridor is located near areas that could be contaminated, you should conduct an official assessment to examine the extent of the problem (see "Environmental Contamination Issues" in Chapter 1). In many cases, the future use of contaminated property directly affects the necessary level of cleanup. For example, areas to be used as playgrounds need to adhere to higher standards than areas to be used as parking lots. Work with environmental professionals to find feasible ways to mitigate contaminated areas, if possible. In some cases, the best solution is to route a trail away from contaminated areas (see "Gaps in Corridor Continuity" in this chapter).

Rails-with-Trails

Trails that have been developed adjacent to active railroad lines are called rails-with-trails (RWTs). Although these facilities are more difficult to develop than traditional trails due to safety and liability concerns expressed by railroad companies, they may offer significant opportunities for trail corridors in urban environments. In 2000, the Rails-to-Trails Conservancy (RTC) published *Rails-with-Trails: Sharing Corridors for Transportation and Recreation*, a study of sixty-one existing facilities in twenty states. The study included trails along industrial lines, mainline trains, and mass transit lines located in urban, suburban, and rural settings.

All rails-with-trails are separated from active rail lines through some type of barrier—either distance (from 10 feet to 100 feet), grade separation, vegetation, ditches, or fencing. The type of barrier used depends on the frequency and speed of rail traffic, as well as the preference of the railroad company. If you are considering developing a rail-with-trail as part of your trail facility, consult the appropriate railroad company and design the trail to maximize user safety. Be prepared for some resistance from the railroad company to the idea, and use the RTC study as a resource (Figure 3.37). Significant safety, security, liability, design, and operational concerns about RWTs exist for railroad operators, railroad customers, and trail users. The USDOT is developing a Rails-with-Trails Best Practices Report to document policy, design, and operational procedures for rails-with-trails.

Figure 3.37. Rail-with-trail in Toledo, Ohio.

This report is expected to be published in 2002.

Steep Slopes

If you are dealing with a trail corridor that is an old railroad, road, or canal, you may have problems with steep slopes where the corridor was built above the surrounding grade in order to maintain a minimal longitudinal slope. Utility corridor trail designers are very likely to encounter steep slopes in hilly areas, since a flat corridor is not usually required to run utility lines. You should consult a structural engineer to determine the feasibility of trail development along steep slopes and the amount of soil "cutting" and "filling" that will be required. Your design may need to incorporate retaining walls to stabilize slopes.

If steep slopes exist next to your trail's edge, railings may be necessary to ensure user safety. According to AASHTO, where a multi-use trail is adjacent to canals or ditches, or where adjacent slopes are steeper than 1:3, a minimum 5-foot separation from the edge of the trail pavement to the top of the slope is desirable. If this is not possible, a physical barrier, such as dense shrubbery, railings, or fences, will need to be provided (Figure 3.38).

Gaps in Corridor Continuity

Several factors can cause a corridor to become discontinuous—for example, encroachments by

David Burwell

Figure 3.38. This photo depicts the use of railings along trails where steep slopes exist.

Greenways Inc.

Figure 3.39. Bike lanes are separate travel lanes for bicyclists.

Steve Emmett-Mattox

Figure 3.40. A dramatic bridge along the Route of the Hiawatha in Idaho.

development, incompatible land uses, and disruptions in property ownership caused by landowner opposition to trail development. These gaps in continuity can be bridged through selecting alternate routes around these areas. Such routes can be off-road trails along streams, roadways, or other linear features. AASHTO guidelines discourage the development of trails along roadways, also known as sidepaths, because they can increase the potential for trail user/motorist conflicts. If you are considering sidepath development, consult AASHTO for information on proper design.

Gaps can also be bridged with on-road facilities—sidewalks and bikeways for pedestrians and bicyclists. Consult the AASHTO guidelines for detailed information regarding the design of bicycle-friendly streets, including the develop-

ment of bike lanes. Bike lanes are the preferred on-road bicycle facility for most cyclists because they provide travel lanes that are separate from those used by vehicle traffic (Figure 3.39).

Bridges and Railings for Multi-Use Trails

Bridges are among the most challenging elements of multi-use trail design and development because they require an understanding of physics, architecture, and engineering. At the same time, bridges can be some of the most interesting features of a multi-use trail—especially if they offer compelling views or if the structures themselves are historically or architecturally interesting (Figure 3.40). In any case, trail users tend to congregate on bridges.

The function of a bridge is to provide trail

users with safe passage over natural features such as streams and steep topographic conditions, and over such built features as active railroads, roadways, canals, and utility lines.

Safety should be the primary consideration in bridge design. Bridge safety is defined in terms of its design load, or the structural capacity of the bridge to support predictable forces and weights that the bridge is subject to during its projected life. Two types of design loads must be considered for every bridge type: the dead load and the live load.

The dead load is the total physical weight of the bridge, equal to the combined weight of all its structural components. The live load refers to the active forces and weights that the bridge is designed to support, including people, service vehicles, floodwaters, floating debris contained within floodwaters, wind, snow, and ice. An unplanned event (such as a tree that falls on a bridge during a storm) is not usually included in the calculation of the live load for trail bridges.

There are no standard bridge design codes written specifically for bridges on multi-use trails. As a general rule, multipurpose trail bridges should support a minimum design load of 12,500 pounds, or 6.25 tons. One source of information about dead and live loads for bridges is the *American Association of State Highway and Transportation Officials (AASHTO) Standard Specifications for Highway Bridges.* The information in the AASHTO manual can help in the identification and selection of bridge types. It also provides some guiding principles for the important features of bridge design and development. The AASHTO guidelines were developed for highway bridges, however, so the guidelines may result in an "overdesigned" (and unnecessarily costly) new bridge for a multi-use trail.[1]

For example, AASHTO recommends 85 pounds per square foot for uniform live load distribution on bridges, which may be impractical on long, clear-span bridges. Under these guidelines, a bridge 120 feet by 10 feet will support 102,000 pounds of live load—equivalent to 510 people weighing 200 pounds each. For bridges longer than 50 feet, a uniform live load of 60 pounds per square foot should provide a safe and serviceable structure. Nevertheless, specific design and construction specifications will vary for each bridge and can be determined only after all site-specific criteria are known. Always consult a structural engineer before completing bridge design plans, before making alterations or additions to an existing bridge, and prior to installing a new bridge.

If the Corridor Contains Bridges

If your corridor contains existing bridges (as is often the case with abandoned rail corridors and roadways), your first step is to have a structural engineer evaluate their integrity to ensure that they are capable of supporting your trail's design load. The engineer should visually examine each existing bridge and provide you with a certified written report describing the condition of key bridge components, including age, damage, decay, or structural degradation, fabrication and installation practices, and loading capacity. Once the analysis is complete, determine which structural components to retain or to remove.

If your bridge has architectural or engineering significance, you should have a local historian, an architect, or an engineer assess its historical significance. Check with your State Historic Preservation Officer to determine if the bridge has been identified as historic, making it eligible for the National Register of Historic Places. Verify important information such as construction date, architectural or structural style, original designer or engineer, and original building contractor, as well as unique features of the bridge.

You can also obtain information about a bridge's history from the *Historic American Engineering Record,* available through the National Park Service or the Library of Congress in Washington, D.C. If your bridge has historic value, you may want to restore substandard components to their original condition.

BRIDGE DECKING. The surface installed on a bridge to make it usable for trail purposes is called decking. A key part of the bridge's structure, decking serves as a surface for trail users to walk or ride on and also distributes the live load. If your bridge does not have decking suitable for trail use, you will need to install durable, nonslip decking.

To accommodate bicycles, horses, and snowmobiles, use 4-inch-thick, pressure-treated planks to deck the bridge. If your bridge will serve pedestrians only, 2-inch planks will suffice. Planks should be laid perpendicular to the beams of the superstructure (Figure 3.41). In some cases, such as abandoned rail corridors that still have ties in place, decking can be laid at a 45-degree angle to the superstructure. Wood decking should be nailed to the superstructure, with gaps of $1/8$ inch to $1/4$ inch between planks to allow for drainage—gaps any wider would be dangerous, especially for bicy-

---

[1] Continental Bridge, *How to Buy a Bridge* (Alexandria, MN: Continental Bridge, 1991), 8.

Figure 3.41. Cyclists ride over the bridge along the Gateway Trail in Minnesota.

clists and wheelchair users. People using canes could get cane tips caught in large gaps. Some trail agencies have found concrete decking superior to wood planking because it is less slippery, more durable, and cost competitive. It consists usually of concrete poured over corrugated metal decking.

BRIDGE RAILINGS. Railings are another important structural and safety component of bridges and other places where hazardous drop-offs exist. Railings are made of posts and rails or

possibly posts and mesh. The vertical posts are usually attached to the bridge deck or superstructure or mounted along the trail edge and spaced evenly no more than 6 feet apart. In the case of a bridge, they may provide an essential transfer of load or weight from the trail to the superstructure of the bridge. The horizontal rails or mesh are usually attached to the posts.

AASHTO guidelines recommend that posts and railings support an outward transverse, or vertical load, of 50 pounds per linear foot of rail height. This load is applicable up to 5 feet above the surface of the deck and is dependent on the spacing of the posts.

The height of your railing depends on the anticipated users of the bridge or trail. A pedestrian railing should be at least 42 inches above the surface or the bridge decking. Railings for bicyclists must be 54 inches high. For equestrians, post signs encouraging them to walk their horses across any bridge for safety reasons, or, where possible, provide a low-water crossing, or ford. Railings can be constructed from wood, metal, wire, concrete, steel cable, metal alloys, plastic, or rope.

At a minimum, most multi-use trail railing should have a top rail, a middle rail, and a bottom rail. Avoid vertical or "picket"-style railings because they may catch a bicycle wheel. The middle railing should be 33 to 36 inches from the deck surface for pedestrian and bicycle use. And the middle railing should be no wider than 1.5 inches so it can serve as a handrail. The underside of the bottom railing should be

Figure 3.42. Bridge railing dimensions.

installed no higher than 15 inches from the deck surface. The maximum vertical opening between railings should not exceed 15 inches, and you should check with local codes for minimum specifications. For bridge railing dimensions, see Figure 3.42.

If drop-offs are hazardous, especially to children using the trail, adhere to local, state, and federal building codes that restrict passage of a 4-inch sphere. Also be sure that the design will not enable a child to fall through or become trapped in between openings in the railing. A mesh rather than bar-type railing may be more cost effective and functional.

BRIDGE APPROACHES. The approach to a bridge is often neglected in bridge design. Bridge approaches have two basic requirements: approach railings that facilitate safe passage onto the bridge, and an approach width that accommodates potential congestion near the bridge. Avoid sharp turns prior to bridge approaches.

Approach railings should be constructed in the same manner as bridge railings, but the posts should be installed in the ground, rather than attached to the superstructure. The approach railings should extend at least 15 feet from each end of the bridge and should be flared out to funnel trail traffic onto the bridge.

Because bridges span different landscapes, they often cause trail users to slow down, contemplate the crossing, and congregate on the bridge deck. The result is congestion. Therefore, sight lines onto the bridge should be free of obstructions, and the approach to the bridge should be wider than the trail to accommodate potential congestion on and near the bridge. Some railroad bridges were designed with outcroppings where people could safely stand when a train passed. If possible, retain or create these outcroppings as a way for people to pause on the bridge without interfering with through traffic.

If the Bridge Has Been Removed but Footings Remain

If your corridor contained a bridge that has been removed, it is possible that the superstructure has been removed but the footings remain intact. What should you do?

First, have a structural engineer conduct a thorough evaluation of the remaining footings, piers, or foundations. By evaluating the size and type of footings as well as the site's soil and geology, the engineer will be able to determine the structural capacity and integrity of the footings. Remember that your design load should support at least 12,500 pounds. Most likely, this is significantly less than the design load for any previous use, such as train or car travel.

After evaluating the footings, a qualified engineer can complete the design and installation of the bridge superstructure. The superstructure is the framework of the bridge, which includes the beams, joists, cross bracing, trestles, trusses, and arches. The superstructure transfers loads from the decking and handrailing to the footings. The specific type of superstructure you should reconstruct varies with the site. It depends on the length of the span, the design load, and other features of the site such as height above the stream or road and construction access to the site. Superstructures can be made of wood, metal, concrete, high-strength metal alloys, steel cable, and rope. The superstructure can be prefabricated off-site, assembled and lifted into place at the crossing, or it can be constructed at the site.

PREFABRICATED BRIDGES. Prefabricated ("prefab") bridges are constructed off-site by a bridge manufacturer, loaded onto a transport vehicle, delivered to the site, assembled near the crossing, and lifted onto appropriate footings by a crane (Figure 3.43). Constructed from wood, steel, high-strength metal alloys, or concrete, prefab bridges have several advantages—low

Figure 3.43. Installation of a prefabricated bridge along the Monon Trail in Indiana.

cost, minimal disturbance to the project site, and, usually, simple installation that requires minimal skill and expertise. In addition, the bridge can be manufactured in advance of other construction.

The only component of bridge construction that is generally not part of the bridge manufacturer's responsibility is the installation of bridge footings. However, most prefab bridge manufacturers will supply required drawings and specifications detailing how the bridge attaches to the footings, which you may need to have reconstructed or replaced, depending on the results of the engineering analysis.

ADAPTIVE REUSE OF BRIDGES. Old bridges, no longer sufficient to carry modern highway traffic, sometimes are available for adaptive reuse on trails. They often have a scale and character

If No Bridge Exists

If the superstructure and footings of an old bridge are gone, or if there was no bridge to begin with, the first step will be to determine if an alternative crossing is feasible. Evaluate the corridor on both sides of the former bridge site to determine the feasibility of an alternative crossing. With luck, this will be only an interim solution until you are able to reconstruct the bridge.

It may be necessary to develop a permanent alternative crossing. Find out if any existing roads can facilitate a crossing. In this case, work with a local or state department of transportation to come up with an acceptable crossing (see "Road Crossings" later in this chapter). If there are no roads, you may need to work out an access agreement with adjacent landowners. Or it may be necessary to purchase additional land to install a crossing that is shorter, safer, and more economical in the long run than a constructed bridge would be.

If a new bridge is needed, begin by working with a geotechnical and structural engineer to evaluate the load-bearing abilities of the soils at the crossing. Once you have determined that, have a structural engineer design the appropriate footings for your bridge.

Evaluate several different footing designs, including spread footings, pile-driven supports, and piers (Figures 3.45–3.47). Make your decision based on cost, design style, and environmental compatibility. Once you have completed the footings for your bridge, you are then ready

Figure 3.44. Developers of the Fox River Trail in Illinois added a trail bridge underneath an active train line.

John Hazelton

not found in new or prefabricated bridges. Designed for heavy loads, old bridges often need little upgrading for trail use. At the Fox River Trail in northeastern Illinois, for example, developers creatively adapted an existing bridge to meet their needs for a river crossing (Figure 3.44).

Funding for bridge relocation and site preparation engineering work (design of piers and abutments) is available from the Historic Bridge Program within the Federal Highway Administration of the U.S. Department of Transportation. Also, conduct some research on the Internet in order to find new or used bridges at reasonable costs. Many bridge companies advertise on the Internet, and will send you catalogs of their products.

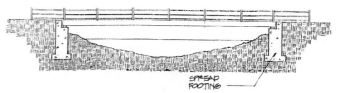

Figure 3.45. Trail bridge—spread footings.

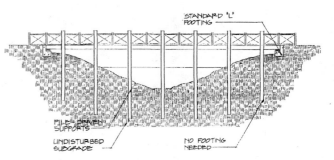

Figure 3.46. Trail bridge—pile-driven supports.

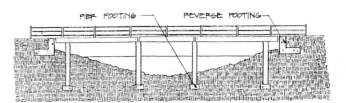

Figure 3.47. Trail bridge—pier footings.

to construct the superstructure, decking, and railings that are appropriate for your multi-use trail.

Remember that whenever you are crossing a roadway or body of water, you will need to work closely with the local department of trans-

Figure 3.48. A pedestrian overpass provides safe passage across a major highway in northern Virginia.

portation and the Army Corps of Engineers to obtain permission prior to construction (Figure 3.48).

Tunnels

Tunnels are among the most striking physical features of a trail and one of the most memorable aspects of a trail experience. If your multiuse trail corridor is in a hilly or mountainous region, there is a good chance you have one or more tunnels. A tunnel can present challenging structural, design, and management questions. Yet over the long term, many historic railroad tunnels have become, in effect, the signatures of their trails.

Is Your Tunnel Structurally Sound?

If your corridor includes a tunnel, your first step is to have the structural soundness investigated. It is best to consult a geotechnical engineer, but a mining engineer or civil engineer is also suitable. The engineer should undertake a visual inspection of the tunnel and provide you with a written report. The report should address the tunnel's apparent condition; what work, if any, needs to be done to make the tunnel safe for trail use; and how much that work is likely to cost.

Every tunnel was individually created to meet a particular need and to serve a particular site, so some tunnels were lined and others were not. If the tunnel was bored out of strong and stable rock, it is probably unlined. If it was drilled through weaker rock that tends to crumble, the tunnel was likely lined with wood, reinforced concrete, plain concrete, steel, or possibly bricks. The liners generally do not hold up the tunnel's walls but prevent loose pieces of rock from falling off the ceiling (or crown) and sidewalls.

Unlined tunnels can be sound-tested for structural stability by using a forklift truck and a handheld steel bar. Stable rock will yield a characteristic ring. But if a piece of rock gives a distinctive dull response, it is judged loose and is mechanically removed. For example, inspection of the three-quarter-mile-long Tunnel Number Three on Wisconsin's Elroy-Sparta Trail, which takes a week, is carried out every other year.

Schedule regular inspections for your tunnels, preferably during periods of low use because tunnels will be closed to the public during inspection. Use a qualified professional to conduct such tests.

Lined tunnels cannot be sound-tested. The liner obstructs the sound; it also hides from view much or all of the geologic activity within the tunnel. Thus, the investigating engineer must look for liner cracking, bulges, flaking (in the case of concrete liners), seepage, movement, rotting wooden timbers, and other signs of trouble. Again, use a qualified professional to conduct such tests.

If these problems exist, the solutions include bolting, injecting "shotcrete" or another type of mortar mix to fill voids in the liner, adding permanent liner material to hold the rock, and installing netting. For most trails, adding liner material is the best solution. Although this reduces the inside tunnel clearance, the clearance in most tunnels is sufficiently high for trail users, including equestrians. Reduced clearance poses a problem only if there is a chance that the corridor will return to its original use—for example, as a railroad. Before adding liner material to a tunnel, make sure that reduced clearance will not preclude any future use.

The portion of the tunnel most vulnerable to damage is the entranceway, or portal. Portals take the full brunt of the elements—erosion, freezing and thawing, falling tree limbs, rain and snow, and sometimes vandalism. Because they are frequently built with one side against a hill and the other over the edge of a valley, they are particularly susceptible to uneven ground movement. Often, portals are walls that extend out of the tunnel, so the footings of those walls should be checked for their structural strength.

In cold climates, some railroad companies installed huge wooden doors at a tunnel's opening. The doors were swung shut between trains to protect against winter winds, maintaining the natural 50-degree temperature of the ground. Such doors can be beneficial for a multi-use trail as well. On the Elroy-Sparta Trail, for example, the doors have been refabricated (Figure 3.49) and are locked shut from mid-November through mid-April. They reduce the freeze-and-thaw cracking within the

tunnel, especially at the portals. (The state of Wisconsin has built a steep alternative route for snowmobilers and skiers to get around the tunnels.)

Water is another potential problem in tunnels. As with any other segment of trail, proper drainage is critical and can be accomplished either by digging ditches at the sides of the trail or by adding a layer of well-drained ballast in the center of the tunnel and raising the trail above any standing water.

Solving Structural Problems

Most railroad tunnels were constructed as a "last resort," to provide passage in inaccessible terrain. Thus, it is far superior to utilize a tunnel than to reroute around it. If your tunnel has severe structural problems, however, you have four possible courses of action: raise the money to get the tunnel fixed; shut the tunnel with lockable gates but allow groups through periodically, preceding each tour with a certified safety inspection; issue permits to use the tunnel; or seal the tunnel shut.

If you seal the tunnel, you can do so with thick wood, steel, or concrete, or, preferably, you can install strong jail-like bars that allow users to peek into the tunnel and at least see what a major tunnel is like. (An interpretive sign would work well here, too.) Ideally, the long-term plan would be to unseal the tunnel, repair it, and incorporate it into your trail.

If You Need a New Tunnel

Most trails built on former railroad and canal corridors contain tunnels, where needed, that were built long ago. Occasionally, though, the need arises for a new tunnel, particularly in places where a highway department has taken out a bridge or trestle over an abandoned railroad track and replaced it with soil and rock fill. Trails built within utility corridors may need new tunnels as well, to route users under roadways.

A new tunnel should be as beautiful as those once constructed by the railroads, but with today's costs, achieving that ideal is unlikely. Most new tunnels are constructed with large corrugated metal culverts or precast concrete culverts (Figure 3.50). The hole is cut with standard soft-dirt tunneling equipment to accom-

Figure 3.49. One of three tunnels along Wisconsin's Elroy-Sparta Trail.

Rails-to-Trails Conservancy

Figure 3.50. Along Idaho's Wood River Trail, a concrete culvert provides passage under a highway.

Jonathan Stoke

modate the culverts, which are made in several sizes.

The tunnel's vertical clearance should be at least 10 feet and the width of the tunnel must be at least as wide as your trail, including the 2-foot-wide clear shoulder space on each side. Therefore, the tunnel should be no less than 10 feet wide and preferably 14 feet wide.

If you opt to use the less expensive corrugated metal culvert, attempt to improve the appearance of this utilitarian structure by angling each protruding surface down to the ground and facing each with rocks.

TYPES OF ROADWAY CROSSINGS

Grade-Separated
- Overpasses
- Underpasses

At-Grade
- Unsignalized
- Signalized

Special Considerations for Tunnels

Tunnels should have a source of light, not only for safety and security but also because the underground geology and construction techniques of historic bridges are interesting to users. In fact, tunnels are prime locations for interpretive signs and even for narrated tours. Unfortunately, however, tunnels in rural locations are often far from economical sources of electricity.

If possible, install lights in your tunnel or underpass. Lighting should consist of several low-wattage lights contained within wire cages, installed at least 10 feet above the floor to discourage vandalism. Lights should be kept on at all times and regularly maintained.

Many tunnels are short enough that, even in the center, some daylight is visible. Other tunnels, because of length and curvature, are literally blacker than the darkest night. If this is the case with yours, make every effort to publicize the fact that flashlights are necessary, and arrange to sell flashlights at convenient locations on or near the trail.

Trail managers usually post signs at the portals of dark tunnels requiring bicyclists and equestrians to dismount and walk through. This is prudent, considering the possibility of collisions or scrapes against tunnel walls.

Road Crossings

Streets and roads typically are classified in a hierarchical system that determines which street has priority at intersections. The street with the higher traffic volume usually has priority. For example, users of residential streets stop at intersections with arterials, and public roads usually have priority over private roads and driveways. This consistency is critical to road safety since it provides predictability for road users.

The same principles should be applied to trail intersections with public and private streets. Where a trail crosses a high-volume public street, the street will have the right-of-way. Trail users will stop and yield to traffic on the public street.

In some cases, however, a trail may have substantially more volume than a residential street, in which case the trail users should have the right-of-way. A trail should have the right-of-way when it crosses a private street or driveway, requiring road and driveway users to stop or yield to trail traffic. Avoid making exceptions, as they will create confusion and compromise safety.

Trail Crossings at Grade

When a trail crosses a road, you need to decide whether an at-grade crossing will suffice or whether a grade-separated crossing (bridge or tunnel) is necessary. The type of road crossing is extremely site-specific, so determining how to cross should be made on a case-by-case basis.

A safe at-grade crossing has either light traffic or a traffic signal that trail users can activate. If neither of these exists, you need to work with a traffic or transportation engineer to evaluate the intersection's characteristics, including current traffic volumes and times of peak vehicle travel, speed of travel, sight lines to and at the intersection, unique features of the intersection that pose problems or offer opportunities for a safe crossing, and the anticipated number of trail users likely to pass through the intersection.

Once this information has been evaluated, your engineer should perform what is known as a gap analysis. This is a determination of the times during each day when the roadway is most heavily traveled, and the times when vehicle traffic is lowest. (This can also vary by season, such as "beach traffic" in the summer months.) Understanding the gaps in traffic will help you determine the safest type of crossing. Perhaps the intersection can be made safe by

adding a crosswalk and some "Trail Crossing" signs on the road. Or you may decide that a traffic signal is vital. In that case, you will need to investigate with your local or state transportation agency the possibility of installing a special pedestrian signal light at the intersection to facilitate a safe crossing. Unless you can provide "warrants"—demonstrated pedestrian traffic or accident history—it can sometimes be difficult to convince a transportation department to install pedestrian-activated traffic signals.

Trails should cross public streets as close as possible to an intersection (if one exists), in the same place a crosswalk would normally be placed. This creates a predictable movement for trail users and motorists who are used to pedestrians crossing at crosswalks. It also allows the stop bar for the motorist to be placed behind the crosswalk, thus reducing the likelihood of cars blocking the trail as they sit waiting to proceed. If trail users are crossing at an existing intersection, make sure that there are curb cuts, crosswalks, and pedestrian signals installed for their use (Figure 3.51).

If your trail crosses a street with curbs, the curb cuts should be the same width as the trail (e.g., a 10-foot-wide trail should have a 10-foot curb cut). Consider providing a median refuge area for bicyclists and pedestrians when crossing roadways that are wider than three lanes. Keep in mind that the volume of users on your trail will probably grow over time, thus necessitating more sophisticated types of road crossings in the future.

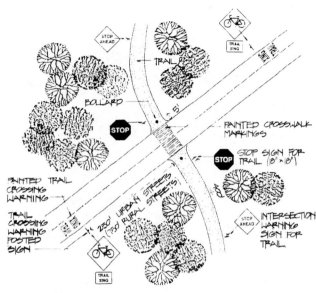

Figure 3.51. Typical road/trail intersection.

CONTROLLING ACCESS ONTO THE TRAIL. Bollards are a commonly used method of controlling motor vehicle access to multi-use trails. An important question to ask is whether a bollard is necessary to restrict unauthorized vehicles since they can pose a hazard to trail users and make it difficult for maintenance and emergency vehicles to access the trail. If you determine that a traffic barrier is necessary, ensure that barriers are well marked and visible to bicyclists, day or night (usually by installing reflectors or reflector tape). Explore the use of "soft," flexible materials for bollards. Bollards must be at least 3 feet tall and should be placed at least 10 feet from the intersection. This will allow trail users to

Figure 3.52. Typical bollards on a multi-use trail.

cross the intersection before negotiating the barrier posts (Figure 3.52).

One bollard is generally sufficient to indicate that a path is not open to motorized vehicles. The post should be placed in the center of the trail tread. Where more than one post is necessary, a 5-foot spacing is used to permit passage of bicycle trailers, adult tricycles, and wheelchairs. Always use one or three bollards, never two. Two bollards, both placed in the paved portion of a trail, will channel trail users into the center of the trail, causing possible head-on collisions. Bollards should be designed to be removable or hinged to permit entrance by emergency and service vehicles. In addition, it may also be desirable to remove the posts in the winter if snowmobilers will be using the trails. Figure 3.53 shows a typical bollard design.

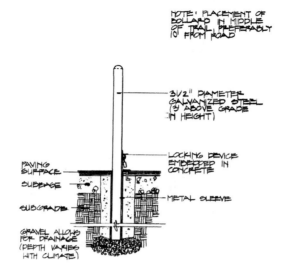

NOTE: PLACEMENT OF BOLLARD IN MIDDLE OF TRAIL, PREFERABLY 10' FROM ROAD

3 1/2" DIAMETER GALVANIZED STEEL (3' ABOVE GRADE IN HEIGHT)

PAVING SURFACE

SUBBASE

SUBGRADE

LOCKING DEVICE EMBEDDED IN CONCRETE

METAL SLEEVE

GRAVEL ALLOWS FOR DRAINAGE (DEPTH VARIES WITH CLIMATE)

Figure 3.53. Bollard detail.

Once your trail is established, the need to prevent access may decrease. Many trail managers discover that after a few years unauthorized vehicle access is no longer a problem, so they remove the bollards at all but their most problematic intersections.

An alternative method of restricting entry of motor vehicles is to split the entryway into two 5-foot sections separated by low landscaping. Emergency vehicles can still enter if necessary by straddling the landscaping. Other, more restrictive methods of preventing motor vehicle access are generally not acceptable since they create a hazard for nighttime trail users and deny access to trail users in wheelchairs and bike carts as well as those who cannot lift a bike over a barrier.

STOPPING TRAIL USERS AT INTERSECTIONS. Obstructions such as numerous bollards, fences, rumble strips, and speed bumps should not be used at intersections to force trail users to slow down or stop. The hazard they create is greater than the problem they are trying to solve. On an asphalt path, an 18-inch concrete strip (a pad, not a speed bump) can be placed across the trail, 30 feet from the intersection, to create a change in pavement texture and color that alerts the trail user to an upcoming intersection. A centerline should be painted on the final 150 feet of the approach to alert users (especially bicyclists) to look up and concentrate on safely navigating the intersection. Stop signs should be posted approximately 4 to 5 feet from the roadway, giving cyclists enough time to come to a complete stop. Finally, a detectable surface should be provided across the full width of the trail for a distance of 2 feet from the roadway edge.

STOPPING SIGHT DISTANCES. Multi-use trail intersections and approaches should be on relatively flat grades. Stopping sight distances at intersections should be checked, and adequate warning should be given to permit trail users to stop before reaching the intersection, especially on downgrades. According to AASHTO guidelines, for bicycles, the distance required to reach a full controlled stop is a function of the bicyclist's perception and brake reaction time, the initial speed of the bicycle, the coefficient of friction between the tires and the pavement, and the bicycle's braking ability. Consult the AASHTO guide for detailed information on minimum stopping sight distances for curves along your trail.

Trail Crossings Above and Below Grade

Crossings above grade (pedestrian overpasses) and below grade (tunnels) have their advantages and disadvantages. In terms of personal security, above-grade crossings are less threatening and are perceived by the user as safer than below-grade crossings. However, above-grade crossings can be unsightly and require long access ramps. Spiral ramps can invite improper use by roller skaters and skateboarders, and they are difficult to build to the recommended AASHTO bicycle design speed of 20 miles per hour. Moreover, trail users frequently ignore above-grade crossings, finding it quicker to simply cross the street and avoid the long climb up the access ramp.

Going under a roadway usually involves the installation of a pedestrian tunnel. If your trail borders a stream you may be able to convert an existing drainage structure to a crossing. You should evaluate, with the help of a hydrologist and a structural engineer, the feasibility of using existing structures for pedestrian passage. The big disadvantage of below-grade crossings is that they can feel threatening and may collect trash and graffiti. They will also have to be designed so they do not flood during heavy rainfalls. On the plus side, they work well for bicyclists, who pick up speed on the downhill ramp and have

enough momentum to climb up the opposite side easily. Proper design will ensure that your below-grade crossing will be used if built. Trail users prefer a well-lit, open, wide, and short crossing under a roadway.

For crossings at freeways and other high-speed, high-volume arterials, a grade-separated structure—either an overpass or an underpass—may be the only possible or practical treatment. On a new structure, according to AASHTO guidelines, the minimum clear width should be 10 to 20 percent wider than the paved multi-use path, and the desirable clear width on both sides of the surfaced path should be 2 feet. This provides the minimum safe horizontal clearance from the railing on a bridge or the wall of a tunnel. It also provides needed maneuvering space to avoid conflicts with pedestrians and bicyclists who may be stopped on a bridge or inside a tunnel. This horizontal clearance also allows emergency vehicles to gain access to the trail on either side of the overpass or underpass.

The preferred minimum vertical clearance for a new multi-use trail bridge or tunnel is 10 feet. The absolute minimum is 8 feet, although this will not suffice if equestrians will be among your trail's users, and some emergency vehicles may have difficulty passing through an 8-foot clearance. Provide the maximum amount of vertical clearance feasible, especially for tunnels and underpasses, as narrower spaces can make these places darker and more "closed-in," causing trail users to feel less secure about using them.

In the event that neither a tunnel nor a

bridge is possible, investigate the possibility of routing trail users for a short distance to an alternative crossing off the trail: to a traffic signal, a bridge that crosses the road, or a tunnel beneath the road. If you choose an alternative crossing, be sure that the route is safe and accessible, and posted with signs providing clear directions to trail users. Remember that trail users, especially pedestrians, will usually tend to take the shortest route, even if that means crossing a road at midblock. Discourage this unsafe activity through placing fences or dense vegetation along the trail at the location of a potential cut-through.

Railroad Crossings

For safety reasons, trails should cross railroad tracks at a right angle to the rails. The more the crossing deviates from this angle, the greater the potential for a bicyclist's front wheel to be trapped in the rail flangeway, thereby causing loss of steering control. It is also important that the trail approach be at the same elevation as the rails.

Consideration should be given to the materials of the crossing surface and to the flangeway depth and width. If the crossing angle is less than 45 degrees, consider widening the trail to give bicyclists and other users adequate room to cross the tracks at a right angle. Where this is not possible, compressible flangeway fillers, which are commercially available, can enhance trail user safety while allowing trains to continue

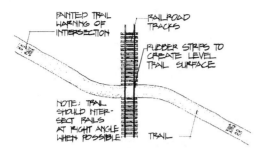

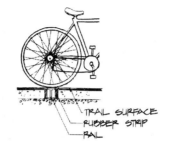

Figure 3.54. Trail/railroad intersection.

operating (Figure 3.54). Place railroad crossing warning signs and pavement markings on the trail. Consult the railroad company and state public utility commission during the design phase of your trail to obtain permission for a crossing.

Signs for Multi-Use Trails

Signs play an important role in trail design. They give directions and offer needed information along trails, as well as providing safety tips. When developing signs for your trail, take time to think about how they influence perceptions of the landscape and how they can shape a trail user's expectation of what is around the next bend.

Types of Signs

The primary role of trail signs is to aid and instruct users along the linear route. There are four types: regulatory, warning, informational, and educational.

REGULATORY SIGNS. In general, regulatory signs give operational requirements of the trail and are used for traffic control. Regulatory signs include stop and yield signs, right-of-way signs, speed limit signs, and exclusion signs. These are normally erected where the specific regulation applies.

WARNING SIGNS. These signs point out existing or potentially hazardous conditions on or near the trail and caution users to reduce speed or dismount a bicycle or horse for safety reasons. Warning signs are typically used near intersections, bridges, crossings, and tunnels; they indicate significant grade changes, upcoming traffic-control devices, and changes in surface conditions.

INFORMATIONAL SIGNS. Used to provide trailside information to orient trail users geographi-

cally, informational signs often point out nearby support facilities (including water, rest rooms, and emergency phones) and local points of interest. Informational signs include distance markers (Figure 3.55) as well as kiosks along the trail that orient users to their surroundings using maps. These maps should include connecting trails, designated on-street bike routes, connecting sidewalks, local parks and schools,

Figure 3.55. Mile marker 41.5 along Virginia's Washington and Old Dominion Railroad Regional Park Trail.

and mass transit stations as well as consumer information such as the location of a nearby bike shop. Informational signs can also include an assessment of the difficulty level of a trail.

Some informational signs are temporary signs offering public information. Such signs—announcing concert dates, festivals, lectures, and meetings—are most effective when clustered together in a central location. They are an important part of a community's involvement in the trail's use. Temporary signs also include information about trail closures, construction, or other short-term conditions. Although temporary signs are secondary to the design of permanent trail signs, bulletin boards or informational kiosks for their display should be erected in visible locations. Without adequate space for temporary signs, unwanted posters and fliers may spring up in inappropriate places along the trail.

EDUCATIONAL SIGNS. Educational signs point out areas of interest that make the trail unique, including natural and historic features. Consider highlighting historically significant points by calling attention to sites of important political or social events or the location of historic architecture and bridges along the path (see "Understanding the History of Your Trail" in this chapter). If appropriate, provide interpretive information on industrial relics such as bridges, canal locks, signaling devices, and switching stations. Also consider interpreting modern conditions, such as a local manufacturing facility or

ethnic neighborhoods. Research the natural and human history of your rail or canal corridor for ideas.

Planners in several areas are enriching the trail experience by incorporating local history. For example, signs along the Little Miami Scenic State Park Trail in southwestern Ohio point out a group of Native American burial mounds. And the citizens working to create the Farmington Canal Greenway in Cheshire, Connecticut, researched the history of Italian immigrant laborers who built the stone bridges dominating one section of trail.

Ecologically significant areas along the trail can also be interpreted. Native plant groupings, local animal habitats, or unusual geological features are all of interest. Signs should also point out particularly sensitive terrain and suggest appropriate trail etiquette. Educating the public about flora, fauna, and special terrain can be more effective than setting up barriers and "Do Not Enter" signs. Making your trail a place for environmental education and providing informative signs generate a new purpose for the trail, one beyond transportation or recreation.

Use of Standard Signs

Trails are transportation corridors, and therefore recognizable transportation signs should be adapted for trail use. The U.S. Department of Transportation's Federal Highway Administration (FHWA) has outlined the size, shape, and color criteria for signs in the *Manual on Uni-*

form Traffic Control Devices (MUTCD). Standard shapes and colors should be used for trail signs where feasible. Minimum sizes of signs for bicycle facilities are provided in the *MUTCD*. See http://mutcd.fhwa.dot.gov.

Standard Sign Shapes

Figure 3.56 illustrates the standard sign shapes and sizes listed below:

- The octagon is reserved exclusively for the stop sign.
- The equilateral triangle, with one point downward, is reserved exclusively for the yield sign.
- The circle gives advanced warning of a railroad crossing.
- The diamond shape is used only to warn of existing or possible hazards either on or adjacent to the trail.

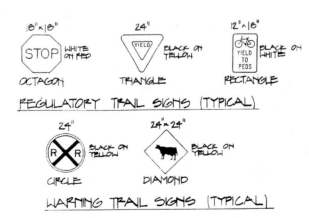

Figure 3.56. Standard trail signs.

- The rectangle, with the longer dimension vertical, is for regulatory signs (except stop and yield signs).
- The rectangle, with longer dimension horizontal, is for directional information signs.

Standard Sign Colors

- *Red:* Background for stop signs, do-not-enter messages, and parking prohibition signs. Red is also used for the prohibitory symbol (circular outline and diagonal bar).
- *Black:* Background color on one-way signs, and the message on white, yellow, or orange signs.
- *White:* Background color for regulatory signs (except stop signs) where white is used for the message. White is the message color on blue, brown, and green signs, as well as stop signs.
- *Orange:* Background color for construction and maintenance signs.
- *Yellow:* Background for warning signs (except where orange is specified) and school signs.
- *Fluorescent Yellow-Green:* Background for pedestrian, bicycle, and school warning signs.
- *Blue:* Background for services guidance.
- *Green:* Background color for directional guidance and permitted movements.
- *Brown:* Background color for recreational and cultural interest guidance.

Standards for guidance signs include the Sign Symbol system, a standardized set of pictographs developed by the American Institute for Graphic Arts for the U.S. Department of Transportation. These symbols—legible at a greater distance than text would be and understandable to people who do not read English—can be used to supplement text signs.

Design Guidelines for Trail Signs

Although trails should borrow the conventions of highway signs, it is not necessary to erect large highway signs on your trail. Large highway signs are made so that drivers of high-speed vehicles can recognize them in seconds. The scale of trails is much smaller, and speeds much slower, so smaller signs are appropriate for your trail.

Intended to help users negotiate their way along a trail, signs should be clearly readable and easy to understand. Legibility is determined by visibility, user comprehension, sign shape, color contrast, text character height, and proportion. Information on a sign should be concise and direct; lettering styles should be simple and bold.

The effective viewing distance for multi-use trail signs is between 20 and 150 feet. Effective text height for most trail signs is between 3 and 6 inches. Guidelines for letter size suggest 1 inch of capital-letter height per 30 feet of required viewing distance, or 1 inch of lowercase letter height per 50 feet of viewing distance. Large lettering, which mandates large signs, would be out of scale and character for pedestrian-scaled systems.

Color, contrast, and shape can be useful for transmitting messages quickly, but only if the meaning is easily understood. Symbols or logos should not be too abstract and should not be the exclusive means of communication. As a rule, use text and symbols together for the clearest message. Also, minimize negative messages on signs because they are more prone to vandalism and theft.

Use contrasting colors with light images on dark backgrounds to make signs easy to read, especially from long distances. But don't use color as the sole means of communication—nearly 12 percent of the population is color blind. Instead, use regularity in sign design. Similar shapes and sizes as well as consistent symbols, lettering styles, and color schemes help users quickly understand and utilize a trail's sign system.

Sign Sizes and Placement

Trail stop signs should measure 18 by 18 inches, trail yield signs should be 24 by 24 inches, and regulatory signs should be 12 by 18 inches, as required by the *MUTCD*. Various dimensions may be used for recreational and cultural-interest signs.

Where you place signs along your trail is extremely important (Figure 3.57); improperly placed signs may present an obstacle or hazard to trail users. Place signs in a clear area, where they will not be obscured by parked cars, vegetation, or buildings. Place post-mounted signs at least 3 feet off the edge of the trail. Signs should be raised between 4 and 5 feet off the ground.

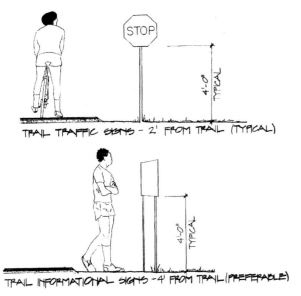

Figure 3.57. Typical placement of trail signs.

Place non-traffic-oriented signs, such as information boards or educational signs, at least 4 feet off the sides of pathways. The greater distance allows groups of pedestrians, people using wheelchairs, and bicyclists to get completely out of the path of travel to read the signs, minimizing disruptions on the trail.

Placing signs within sight-distance limits and required stopping distances is critical, particularly for regulatory and warning signs. Adequate time to read and respond to traffic signs must be calculated into your sign layouts.

For a bicyclist traveling 20 miles per hour, the viewing distance for stop signs should be between 100 and 125 feet. To prepare riders or pedestrians, warning signs should be placed 125 to 150 feet in both directions from the conditions they address. And stop signs where the trail intersects with roads should be visible from at least 200 feet. Warning signs for intersections should be placed no fewer than 400 feet from crossing points.

Location Principles for Signs

- Do not group regulatory or warning signs together. Make them clear, concise, and easy to read.
- Keep at least 75 feet between signs to allow users time to read and react to the messages.
- Group informational signs together, especially at trailheads, rest areas, and trail facility locations. Bulletin boards or kiosks work well for this (Figure 3.58).

Figure 3.58. An attractive kiosk displaying trail information along the New River Trail State Park in Virginia.

- Avoid placing signs where they may detract from natural surroundings and diminish the trail experience. Do not place a sign so that it diminishes a scenic vista or minimizes the dangers of a hazardous area.
- Balance the need for signs and their functions with the impact they have on the overall aesthetic appeal of the trail.

Pavement Markings

Pavement markings are commonly used to reinforce signs along multi-use trails, but they should not replace signs altogether. Striping is the most common form of pavement markings, although warning and regulatory messages are sometimes used. However, use pavement markings sparingly and only where necessary to attract additional attention to a possible problem area since signs painted on pavement often increase the danger of sideslipping and can make stopping difficult. Do not use pavement signs at critical turning and stopping points. Never use them as an exclusive signing method in areas where snow, sand, or leaf buildup is a problem, or where excessive wear is likely, because the signs may be obscured. Figure 3.59 demonstrates an effective use of pavement markings.

If you do opt for stenciled pavement markings, they should be white for best visibility. (The exception to this is a yellow centerline that you may opt to use to separate heavy trail traffic.) The height of letters (or arrows) on the

Figure 3.59. Pavement markings warn trail users to stop ahead.

pavement should be between 3 and 4 feet. Pavement signs you may consider include "Stop," "Yield," "Slow," "Bike Lane" and "Pedestrian Lane." Messages should be placed at the beginning of your trail, before roadway intersections, or near intersections with trail facilities.

Materials

You should take into account several factors when choosing materials for a sign system: budget, aesthetics, durability, and maintenance costs.

• Plastics (especially acrylics, polycarbonates, butyrates, polypropylenes, and laminates) are widely available and adaptable to many fabrication processes. Select plastics based on color, appearance, impact resistance, durability, and suitability for certain fabrication techniques. Many plastics expand and contract with temperature changes.

• Fiberglass (fiber-reinforced polyester) is durable, impact resistant, and easily formed into customized shapes. Graphics and colors are often applied to the surface and sealed under coatings that improve finish and color-fastness. Fiberglass is available in opaque or translucent forms and is sometimes used for internally lit signs.

• Wood usually requires special treatment to protect against decay. Solid woods (especially cypress and redwood) are typically used for carved signs. High-density plywoods are widely used for sign faces and are relatively inexpensive. They are made with various exterior-rated adhesives and finishes, and all edges must be sealed. Vandals can easily damage wood signs.

• Aluminum is widely available, is lightweight, and does not rust. But it requires specialized welding skills and equipment. Laminated products with aluminum faces and plastic or wood cores are also available. Some aluminums require a painted or anodized finish to protect against pitting.

• Steel is relatively economical, is available in many forms, and is easy to cut, form, weld, or rivet. However, steel requires galvanizing or special finishes to inhibit rust. Specialized alloys of steel (including stainless steel) offer increased strength and corrosion resistance but at a higher cost.

• Brass and bronze are often used for cast signs or cut letters. They can be allowed to develop an oxidized patina, or they can be sealed with lacquers. Both metals are quite durable but are comparatively expensive.

• Stone is extremely durable, but is hard to work with and expensive. If graphics are to be used on the sign, they generally will be sandblasted or carved into the stone. Some types of stones are susceptible to damage or discoloring from airborne pollutants.

• Fabrics (including nylon, cotton, and other synthetics) are used for awnings, banners, and flags. Translucent fabrics can be backlit to highlight text or graphics, and awning fabrics can be treated to improve durability and resistance to fading and dirt. Exterior banners suffer wind damage and fading and must be replaced periodically. Interior banners are durable but may require periodic removal for cleaning.

• Recycled materials can also be used for signs. Recycled aluminum from beverage cans, recycled plastics from bottles, and recycled steel are all durable materials that should be considered. Recycled materials can be more economical than other materials and offer another concept for interpretation. The Swift Creek Recycled Greenway in Cary, North Carolina, used signs made from recycled materials to teach trail users about the recycling process and the use of these materials in trail development.

Using Signs to Make Trails Unique

In addition to serving important functions, signs can help define your trail's image. Signs, especially informational signs, offer you a chance to establish a dominant image or visual tone along a trail. By repeating logos or other forms along the trail's length you can create a sense of continuity and consistency.

Both the U.S. Forest Service and the National Park Service have developed well-recognized sign systems. Their white or yellow letters on a maroonish brown background generally connote conservation and the outdoors. Both include sign types for roadways and trails that are instantly recognizable.

You could also highlight the people who built the historic structures, especially since canal and railroad construction represents one of the most dramatic periods of U.S. immigration and labor history. A multi-use trail lends itself to educational displays documenting the struggles and history of the corridor's creators. You may also want interpretive signs relating to Native Americans who may have once inhabited the area.

Developing a trail-specific logo is one way to highlight the uniqueness of a trail and its landscape. You can generate a logo by abstracting or simplifying an image, picture, or symbol into a

Figure 3.60. Trail logo examples.

graphic element. But keep your logo simple so it can be easily reproduced in different sizes. Dominant landscape elements—mountain peaks, rivers, valleys—are all potential logo sources, as are footprints, bicycle tires, and other trail-evoking images. The first letter of your trail's name, the seal of your town or city, or an anagram of a local trail organization can also serve as logo models. Many trails have developed interesting logos (Figure 3.60).

Repetition of logos and certain signs reinforces the image and uniqueness of a trail. Placing signs at regular intervals keeps the trail's identity in the trail user's mind. Distance markers at half-mile intervals, for example, are not only popular among trail users gauging their

progress, but also excellent ways to reinforce a trail theme. In addition, markers can facilitate quick response to medical emergencies. Interesting distance markers can be placed along the sides of trails or on the trail surface.

Similarly, informational signs can have logos included on them as part of their borders or color schemes. The Washington and Old Dominion Railroad Regional Park has developed a "Share the Trail" campaign, which includes numerous signs (printed with the campaign's logo) along the trail. Trail logos can be affixed to benches, drinking fountains, gates, rest-room doors, trash cans, and fences, serving the dual purpose of identifying the facility as trail property and advertising the trail system to users.

Temporary signs also provide opportunities for displaying logos. Fabric banners or flags for annual events such as road races, benefit events, and seasonal openings can be placed at entrances, at exits, and along special sections of the trail. Place a logo on any temporary signs posted on trail kiosks to reinforce trail identity.

Trail Support Facilities

The types of facilities your trail will need—and their placement along the trail—depend on several factors: the setting and proposed uses of the trail, the trail's intensity of use, the level of servicing or maintenance that the facilities need, and the utility or infrastructure requirements of the facilities. Whatever the location, user

TRAIL SUPPORT FACILITIES

- Parking areas
- Rest rooms
- Drinking fountains
- Benches
- Shelters
- Bicycle racks
- Picnic areas
- Fitness courses
- Emergency telephones
- Trash receptacles
- Signage systems

groups, and desired activities along the trail, you must plan for trail facilities from the start. Even if you cannot afford to develop all facilities at the outset, know the types of facilities that you and your community ultimately want. Keep in mind that some facilities will need upgrading as the trail's use increases. Don't forget that your trail support facilities should also be accessible— all parking areas, fountains, tables, benches, and rest rooms should adhere to applicable accessibility standards (see "Making Your Trail Accessible" in this chapter).

Group your trail amenities together when possible. Grouping makes them recognizable from a distance and saves space along the trail's edge. Clustering complex features such as rest rooms, drinking fountains, and telephones also minimizes construction costs and the visual disturbance of the landscape along the trail corridor.

Consider establishing both minor and major trailheads. Minor ones include sitting areas, shade shelters, picnic areas, and informational or interpretive signs. These facilities are the least complicated to locate and accommodate. Your sitting and picnic areas could consist of commercially manufactured benches and tables, or they could be as simple as big logs or boulders arranged for sitting. Secure signs, furniture, and trash receptacles by bolting them to buried footings. A minor trailhead should require little maintenance over its lifetime.

Major trailhead facilities will likely include rest rooms, a drinking fountain, a phone, a recycling drop-off point, an air pump for bicycles,

and possibly even vending machines for snacks and drinks. Locate major trailheads near more heavily used access points. Rest rooms and drinking fountains can be difficult to accommodate because they need running water, buried pipes, and access to sewage lines. However, simple, self-composting toilets are also an option. When designing either major or minor trailheads, allow flexibility for change over time.

The following text and illustrations below demonstrate a range of options for the design, materials, and placement of facilities along your multi-use trail. The components, configurations, and dimensions are not absolutes—they should serve only as guidelines.

Facilities at Access Points

When planning support facilities for a multi-use trail system, start with the trail's access points. What facilities will be located at these points? The answer is important because a trail user's first and last impressions are formed when entering and exiting the trail.

Think of access points as opportunities to link the trail with the surrounding community, including destinations and points of departure known to the entire community, not just trail users. Where possible, locate access points in developed areas— next to public parks, shopping centers, or residential developments. Many public amenities, including rest rooms, telephone booths, parking areas, and refreshment facilities, will already be in place. When located in developed areas, access points tend to be safer because of their frequent public use. These locations are also more accessible to emergency help and maintenance.

Access points should link the trail to as many systems of transportation as possible. The proximity of trails to ample parking lots, on-road bikeways, sidewalks, bus stops, light rail stops, and train stations allows users to make convenient connections to the trail, thereby assuring its success as a true public amenity.

Access points, which need to be accessible to everyone, should follow a hierarchy. Rather than designing all access points similarly, decide which locations will serve as major access points, or trailheads, and which will be minor ones. The difference will be the number of facilities and amount of parking at each point. Major access points should be established near commercial developments and transportation nodes, making them highly accessible to the surrounding communities (Figure 3.61). Minor access

Figure 3.61. Xenia Station, Ohio, is a major access point where four trails converge.

Figure 3.62. Minor trail access point.

points should be simple pedestrian and bicycle entrances at locally known spots, such as parks and residential developments (Figure 3.62), and in effect, every street crossing serves as an access point. Also consider access points from the trail to nearby rivers and streams.

Parking Areas

The primary design consideration for a parking area is simplicity; parking areas should never be complex or designed to test a driver's patience. A parking area should also be designed in harmony with its surroundings and be a functional space with an easy-to-understand circulation system. The lot should have clearly marked spaces and a safe entrance and exit coordinated with traffic flows from adjacent roadways.

For efficient land use, parking lots should have 300 to 350 square feet for each car space required. Use this number to calculate the size

and capacity of an efficient parking facility. The minimum area required to park a standard-sized car is about 144 square feet, or a rectangle 18 feet long and 8 feet wide. Compact cars require about 113 square feet, or a rectangle 15 feet long and 7 1/2 feet wide. The larger-sized space should be used as a minimum for unsupervised or unregulated lots.

Parking spaces for the disabled occupy between 234 and 270 square feet, with 13-by-18- or even 15-by-18-foot spaces. Accessible spaces usually require a 9-foot width with a 5-foot access aisle on one side of the space (or between two accessible spaces). Provide at least one accessible space in every lot. In general, the *Uniform Federal Accessibility Standards (UFAS)* recommends one accessible space for every twenty-five spaces. Before beginning any lot design, consult the "Americans with Disabilities Act Accessibility Guidelines," as well as local codes for all required parking dimensions.

You need to provide several significantly large spaces if equestrian use of your trail is planned. Ideally, these spaces should be about 45 feet long—35 feet to accommodate the vehicle and trailer, and an additional 10 feet for unloading the horses. Spaces should be 15 feet wide, which will allow horses to be tied to the trailer, where tack and feed are stored. Another option is to install picket posts about 10 feet behind the trailer parking. Equestrians can tie ropes between the posts and tie the horses to the ropes, thus eliminating the need to secure the horses to nearby trees (Figure 3.63).

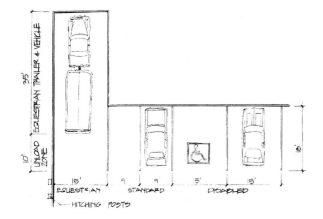

Figure 3.63. Recommended dimensions of parking stalls.

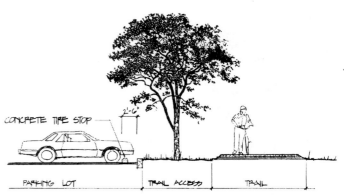

Figure 3.64. Trail section at a parking lot.

To minimize conflict with adjacent street traffic, you should clearly define the parking lot's entrance and exit. Separate entrance and exit points work best along heavily traveled roads. Entrances and exits should be offset from street intersections by at least 50 feet. Single-lane parking lot entrances and exits should be 12 feet wide, and double-lane entrances should be 24 feet wide. Turning radii at entrance and exit points should be at least 15 feet, with a 5-foot minimum turning radius for getting into individual spaces.

A parking lot's layout and orientation are important if the lot is to function smoothly and safely. Lots can be laid out with either one-way or two-way circulation aisles, depending on the circumstances of the site. In general, orient parking lot aisles so they are perpendicular to the major destination of the site (Figure 3.64). This orientation minimizes the number of times

pedestrians must cross the vehicular traveling aisles.

The design of aisle widths depends on the orientation of the parking spaces along the aisle. The standard 90-degree orientation between spaces and aisles, which works only with two-way traffic flows, requires a minimum of 22 feet, preferably 24 feet. Angled orientations, which work only with one-way circulation, require 18 feet at 60 degrees and 12 feet at 45 degrees (Figure 3.65).

Your parking lot should be paved if you are planning on year-round use. Grading should provide adequate drainage and the surface should abate dust. Parking lots should never exceed a 5 percent slope in any direction because too steep a pitch will make opening and closing car doors hazardous, and, on icy surfaces, cars can potentially slide under their own weight even after parked. Crushed stone surfac-

ing is adequate if proper drainage is provided. More rigid surfaces, such as concrete and asphalt, generally last longer, are easy to maintain, and withstand plowing in the winter. These surfaces (just like a trail surface) require adequate subsurface drainage if they are to last. Base your decision about surface material on climate and cost and on environmentally sound practices (i.e., planning for lot runoff, etc.). Also, if you plan equestrian use, it is best to provide a softer surface in the area where horses will be standing prior to entering the trail.

Rest Rooms

Aside from parking lots, rest rooms are probably the most expensive and complex facilities for a multi-use trail. They need utility connections for running water and sewage (unless you install a portable or self-composting type), and they

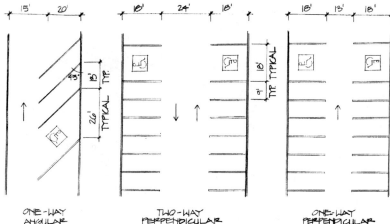

ONE-WAY
ANGULAR

TWO-WAY
PERPENDICULAR

ONE-WAY
PERPENDICULAR

Figure 3.65. Parking lot configurations.

require considerable maintenance and service. Rest rooms must also meet local ordinance standards and accessibility codes. The number of stalls will vary, depending on the predicted level of trail use. These and other requirements should be considered during the early stages of design.

Full-service rest rooms that include running water and flushing toilets must be located near existing utilities and should be easily accessible to cleaning and servicing personnel. If existing utilities, such as sewage lines, are inconveniently located, consider portable toilets with holding tanks, a septic system, or composting toilets. The feasibility of these alternatives, however, depends on local codes, the characteristics of the site, the level of anticipated use, and the level of maintenance and security (particularly in urban areas) that can be provided. Toilet facilities

should be visually buffered and separated from adjacent residences, businesses, picnic and rest areas, and other incompatible uses.

The space required for rest-room facilities depends on the number of toilets to be provided at each station. Toilet stalls for the disabled must allow sufficient room for maneuvering a wheelchair. As a rule, at least one toilet must be accessible to wheelchairs. Therefore, if only one stall is provided, it should be a wheelchair-accessible unisex toilet. If single men's and women's toilets are provided, both must meet accessibility codes. Approximately 50 to 60 square feet should be allotted for each accessible toilet stall, including the toilet area, aisle space, and sink area.

Standard toilet facilities for a single stall require a minimum space of 3 feet by 9 feet, 6 inches with a sink, and 3 by 8 feet without a

sink. Wheelchair-accessible single-stall toilets require a minimum of 5 by 10 feet with a sink, and 5 by 8 feet without a sink. In wheelchair-accessible stalls, grab bars should be located 30 inches from the floor. The height of toilet seats should be between 17 and 19 inches above the floor. The minimum doorway width (for rest-room and stall entrances) is 32 inches, preferably 36, and the doors should open outward.

As shown in Figure 3.66, any rest room needs at least one mirror, one sink, and one towel dispenser, all of which should be usable by people in wheelchairs: Tops of sinks should be no higher than 34 inches from the floor; pipes and valves below the sink should be covered to prevent the user's legs from being burned or scratched. Towel bars, soap dispensers, and shelves should be no higher than 42 inches from the floor. The bottoms of mirrors should be located at the same height. Even better is a full-length mirror that accommodates everyone, including children. Floors should be even and level, extending to the outside without steps, lips, or barriers.

For cleaning ease, rest-room interiors should be finished with concrete, tiles, fiberglass, or metal. Adequate light and ventilation should be provided either naturally or mechanically. Provide a floor drain in case of toilet overflow. And, if possible, include a secure area that protects mechanical systems and provides storage for paper and cleaning supplies. Finally, make provisions for locking and securing the facility at night or during the off-season.

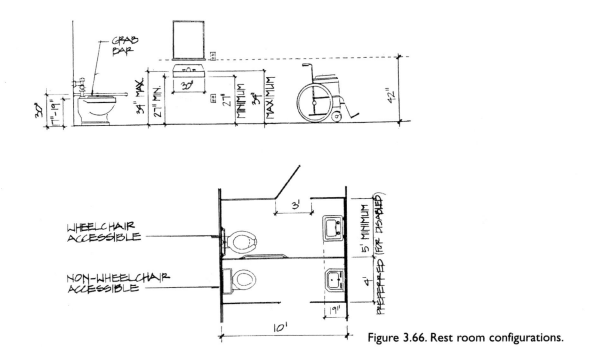

Figure 3.66. Rest room configurations.

Figure 3.67. Along Indianapolis's Monon Rail-Trail, a water fountain made from limestone blocks salvaged from the old Kessler Boulevard railroad bridge provides refreshments to people, pets, and plants. The fountain drains into an irrigation system.

Drinking Fountains

Drinking fountains also require access to water utilities and disposal lines. Consider installing drinking fountains near rest rooms to get the most out of utility access and improvements. But in locations where there is no access to water, consider providing bottled water dispensers or drink vending machines, and post signs at trail entrances to let users know that they should bring their own water.

The design of drinking fountains must incorporate the needs of all potential users. Spigot heights for adults should be 42 inches above the ground. Heights for disabled users should be no higher than 36 inches, with at least 27 inches below the basin to allow wheelchairs to pull up to the fountain. To accommodate all needs, provide both standard- and accessible-height spigots and install steps to the side of the standard spout for children to use. If you are providing a separate spigot for children, it should be about 30 inches from the ground.

An additional spigot at the base allows people to fill water bottles and basins for uses other than drinking. If possible, provide for both hand and foot operation. You should locate fountains at least 4 feet off circulation pathways. The surface around the fountain should be accessible and well drained and should slope away from the direction of the trail. If a non-porous pavement is used, such as asphalt or concrete, provide a nearby drain (Figure 3.67). As with any outdoor public amenity, sturdiness is important. The best materials for drinking fountains are cast iron and pre-cast concrete.

Benches

When designing or purchasing a bench, consider user comfort, simplicity of form and detail, ease of maintenance, durability of finish, and resistance to vandalism. Some benches are simply "slab-type," meaning they have neither arms nor backs; others are double-backed; and some are seating walls.

Figure 3.68. Bench dimensions.

Benches can be made from a variety of materials. Simple, rustic benches can be made from flattopped boulders or split-faced logs. Weather-resistant materials include treated wood, painted metal, recycled plastic, and concrete. Whatever you choose, make sure that the seat and back are well drained, preferably by a cross pitch or slats, not just holes or perforations on a flat surface. Be sure the bench is securely anchored to the ground, so that it will not overturn. (People often use benches in curious ways—they sit on the backs, stretch against them, and employ them as workbenches for bicycle repair.)

Locate benches where they offer a good view or shelter from seasonal winds and the sun. Benches should highlight the trail's variety, taking advantage of sunlight or shade (Figure 3.69). Place some in quiet areas and others in busier spots.

Typically, a bench's seat is located between 16 and 20 inches above the ground, with handrails on the end between 6 and 12 inches above the seat. The depth of a bench seat ranges from 18 inches to 20 inches. Usually a width of 24 to 30 inches is allotted per person. A comfortable three-seater bench would measure between 72 and 90 inches wide. Bench backs are usually 15 to 18 inches high and are set from 3 inches to 9 inches above the seat (Figure 3.68).

Bench seats are not set parallel to the ground but are generally tilted back between 8 and 15 degrees for greater comfort. This tilted position also allows for the drainage of rain and snow. To keep a seat free of standing water requires a minimum tilt of one-eighth to one-quarter inch for every 12 inches of seat width (a slope between 1 and 2 percent). A slight angling of the bench back, between 5 and 15 degrees, allows for a relaxing resting position.

Figure 3.69. A well-placed bench along the Oil Creek State Park Trail in Pennsylvania.

Benches and other furniture should be placed away from pedestrian and bicycle circulation paths, at least 3 feet from the trail edge, to allow adequate room for people's outstretched legs, walking sticks, and canes.

Hard pavement or a gravel bed may be laid 1 foot beyond the outside dimensions of a bench to ensure that puddling will not occur where people put their feet. As with any pavement or gravel area, grade the bench site to allow water to drain away from the bench and the trail. A slope of at least 2 percent should be maintained in these areas.

Provide wheelchair access alongside benches, at least a 30-by-48-inch area for adequate maneuvering. If benches are next to each other (either side by side or face to face), allow 4 feet between them. A distance of 1 foot between benches and amenities such as trash receptacles, utility poles, and sign posts is adequate. A distance of at least 4 feet between such facilities as rest rooms, phone booths, and drinking fountains allows easy circulation.

Shelters

Shelters with roofs and protected seating areas will be well received by users, particularly on long multi-use trails. Shelters protect users from sun, wind, rain, lightning, and snow while providing a pleasant place to rest.

Shelters should be located at least 3 feet, preferably 5 feet, from the trail's edge. The measurement of this setback should be taken from the point of the shelter nearest the trail. Shelters should never interfere with safe movement of trail traffic. When determining where to place a shelter, think about the location of existing and proposed utility systems, including fire hydrants, power and telephone lines, below-grade utilities such as water and sewer lines, other underground conduits, and existing and proposed plantings.

Existing objects such as trees, shrubs, utility poles, signs, and other natural and built obstructions should not substantially interfere with visibility into or out of the shelter. To ensure that shelters are perceived as safe, locate them as close as possible to the trail, clustering them with other trail facilities such as pay phones, parking areas, drinking fountains, and rest rooms. Shelters should also be positioned to provide maximum protection from prevailing winds.

The exterior walls of shelters range from 10 feet to 16 feet in length and are from 5 feet to 8 feet wide. The interior height should be between 7 feet and 8 feet, 6 inches. The roof should be sloped to permit adequate drainage and, where necessary, to prevent the buildup of snow. If wind is a problem, windscreens should be provided along the front of the shelter. When a windscreen is used, entrances should be located at either end of the shelter. The windscreen's entry and exit openings should be unobstructed and at least 36 inches wide. In addition, shelters should meet structural wind and snow loading requirements for their location. Check local building codes for requirements.

Bicycle Racks

You need to consider three criteria when choosing bicycle racks for your multi-use trail: the locations, how the racks secure the bicycles, and the dimensions of the bicycles likely to be used on the trail. Bike racks should be located as close as possible to destinations without interfering with traffic flow. Bike storage areas or racks set more than 50 feet away from a destination encourage bicyclists to seek out the nearest utility post, bench, or tree instead. Locate bike racks in areas where visual supervision is likely and where lighting and shelter are available.

There are several ways to secure a bicycle: Put it into enclosed storage; lock it to a rack, post, or other stationary object; or make it inoperable by weaving a chain and lock through the frame and wheels.

The first two methods are the most effective. Among the various options available, coin-operated or leased lockers provide the greatest security and eliminate the need for bicyclists to carry locks and chains. But lockers are bulky and costly to install and maintain, and may only be necessary where commuters want to leave their bike for a full day. The stationary rack or post is more affordable. Racks and stanchions that allow cyclists to lock both the wheels and the frame reduce casual theft. Bike racks must secure the entire bicycle frame. Don't use bike racks that only provide support at one wheel. Because they can't support the bicycle frame, they leave the bicycle vulnerable to wheel damage because it is easily tipped over. Racks or

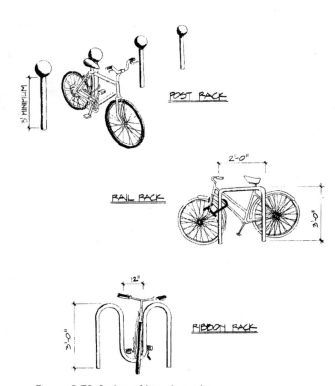

Figure 3.70. Styles of bicycle racks.

Picnic Areas

Locate picnic areas where they provide for the maximum comfort and enjoyment of users. Picnic areas should not be located near potentially hazardous areas—for example, areas with low-hanging branches or poisonous or thorny plants. Because of their relatively large size and high level of activity, picnic areas should be set back sufficiently from circulation pathways so they will not interfere with activities on the trail.

Typically, picnic areas consist of picnic tables and benches, but you can also include cooking facilities, rest rooms, trash receptacles, and drinking fountains. The simplest picnic facility includes just enough room for a picnic table with attached benches. As a general rule, this requires about 168 square feet, a rectangle measuring 12 by 14 feet. A picnic table and bench unit usually measures 6 by 8 feet, and a circulation space of 48 inches for wheelchair access should be maintained on all sides of the unit. All tables should be accessible to wheelchairs and so should be situated on level, free-draining ground with a fairly hard, compacted surface. Tabletops should be between 30 and 34 inches high, with a 29-inch clearance at either end to allow for wheelchair access (Figure 3.71).

Most picnic table units are made of wood, but metal, hard plastic, and concrete are viable alternatives. If you are building or selecting a wood unit, remember that wood decays easily and should be treated. Painting or staining will prevent rotting, but naturally weather-resistant and decay-resistant woods such as redwood,

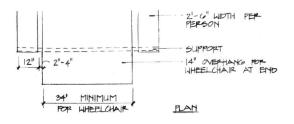

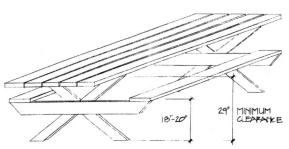

Figure 3.71. Typical dimensions of a picnic table.

cedar, or cypress are preferable. The use of treated woods should be considered cautiously, as the additives used are often irritating to the skin and can be carcinogenic.

Fitness Courses

Fitness courses, also known as exercise courses, obstacle courses, and par-courses, are popular additions to a multi-use trail. A fitness course consists of a circuit or loop divided at intervals by stations, each equipped with apparatus and directions for specific exercises. A fitness system

stanchions should be high enough that excessive cable or chain lengths are not needed to secure both frame and wheels.

A bicycle rack should allow 2 feet of space between bicycles, so that cyclists can move their bicycles into and out of the racks with minimum effort and damage. A rack should accommodate a bicycle length of 5 feet, 6 inches and a height of 42 inches. The examples in Figure 3.70 illustrate some possible options.

leads users through a progressive routine that includes warm-up, strengthening, aerobic, and cool-down exercises. Since the stations generate activity, they should be located away from trail traffic. The areas where stations are located should be level, free draining, and clear of obstacles such as landscaping, boulders, or steep drop-offs. Wood chips, gravel, or coarse sand should be used to prevent excessive wear on the ground underneath the course and to avoid puddling; more rigid surfaces such as asphalt or concrete can lead to injuries.

The fitness course usually includes equipment of two or three different sizes to provide varying levels of difficulty and to accommodate different-sized users. The first stop on the fitness course should outline the entire circuit and explain the different types of exercises. Signs at the remaining stations should be numbered and labeled with their specific routines, and each should include text and an illustration describing the exercise to be performed. To obtain equipment and plans for a fitness course that is appropriate for your particular trail, contact commercial manufacturers. Figure 3.72 shows typical fitness equipment and signs near a trail.

Wildlife and Multi-Use Trails

Regardless of whether your trail's setting is urban, rural, or wilderness, it will most likely run through some kind of environment that plants and animals require for survival. The

Figure 3.72. Fitness cluster on the Northern Central Railroad Trail in Maryland.

nature and condition of this corridor as wildlife and plant habitat will depend on a number of factors—geographic location, climate, corridor width, species living in the corridor, previous use of the corridor, and the kinds of adjacent land uses.

A corridor running through the Rocky Mountains will be quite different from one crossing the prairie, and both will differ from one traversing coastal lowlands. In the case of prairie, rail lines and other corridors can serve as ecological threads of remnant prairie holding together a delicate network that was once a grassland "sea." In some midwestern areas, the only remaining "black soil" prairies lie along derelict rail lines. Similarly, abandoned corridors through forests, wetlands, and even cities can be

home to important plant and animal communities. A rail-trail corridor in the wilds of Montana may traverse big game habitat. One skirting the edges of the Carolina coast might pass through important tidal wetlands. In urban areas, the edges of rail, canal, and utility corridors may offer viable habitat because the immediate edges of such corridors tend to remain undeveloped. A trail planner needs to understand the trail's effect on wildlife and plants and how to develop a trail that will enhance, not hinder, habitat.

Understanding Habitat

Understanding what constitutes habitat will assure a sensitive design process that matches the trail to its setting. This calls for visualizing your trail corridor as habitat—some creature's home—comprised of water, food, territory, shelter, and a place to breed and bear young. Each factor must be present for a healthy habitat.

WATER. A key component for almost all habitats, water is vital for drinking, bathing, and sustaining plants that provide food and cover. Consider how your trail will affect not only surface water (rivers, lakes, and wetlands), but also the vital unseen water system in aquifers and water tables beneath the ground. Will trail construction alter or block water flow, introduce contaminants, or inhibit subterranean water systems?

FOOD. A healthy habitat includes species ranging from microorganisms to plants to vertebrates. Most species depend on the survival of others in the food chain. Healthy habitats also have proper predator-prey relationships that keep populations in check. Will trail development affect any food sources or population balances?

TERRITORY/SHELTER. Most animals need a defined territory and migration routes in which to move, get to water, forage for food, and find mates. Many animals are sensitive to intrusion by people, invasive species, or feral pets. Most creatures need shelter or a place of cover. Some plants may need special growing conditions, including appropriate soil makeup and moisture and sun exposure. Will your trail and its users disrupt territory, disturb sensitive species, or introduce or disrupt vital wildlife movement patterns?

BREEDING AND BEARING YOUNG. Animals need undisturbed places to mate, build nests, and raise their young. Again, some species are sensitive to intrusion. Will your trail affect important breeding areas?

The Impact of Trails on Sensitive Environments

A corridor's previous use, be it a railway, canal, or utility line, has had an impact on wildlife. Grading and construction activities altered drainage patterns, excavation and filling changed soil conditions, vegetation removal and herbicide application affected growing conditions, and human presence may have driven some species away. However, some corridors may have protected a special habitat, such as prairie in the Midwest.

Trails are a relatively benign component in the environment, but a trail and its users may alter it nevertheless. The trail surface, coupled with groomed edges, can result in a 10- to 20-foot-wide swath of land altered with surfacing and vegetation removal. While this may seem insignificant, the total habitat loss over several trail miles is noteworthy. Even a swath as narrow as 10 feet occupies more than an acre of land per trail mile—a significant landmass, especially if it traverses a sensitive area such as wetlands. Other components, such as parking areas and bridges, may impact habitat either by their use or during the construction process (see Box 3.2).

After the trail opens, people will use it and some may wander off the path, disturbing wildlife. Some sensitive species are disturbed by the mere presence of people and pets on the trail. Trail construction or use may also introduce opportunistic or invasive plants, including noxious weeds. The trail's impact on nearby wildlife and plant communities, therefore, can be significantly wider than the 10- to 20-foot swath. It can range up to several hundred feet or more on either side of the trail, depending on the sensitivity of the species in the area and the amount of buffering between the trail and surrounding habitat.

The width and significance of this impact zone also may vary by season. For example, a certain habitat may be occupied by wintering bald eagles between November and March but not occupied by sensitive species during the balance of the year. Also, many big game species, like bighorn sheep, may be more sensitive to stress during the winter and early spring months than at other times. Early in the planning process, you should have conducted an assessment of your corridor (see "Site Considerations: Inventory and Assessment" in Chapter 1). As you conduct the design phase, you need to review your findings, evaluate potential impacts on wildlife, and select design options that minimize or mitigate those impacts. You should also contact your state wildlife agency to identify any federal, state, or local wildlife and plant preservation regulations. If you think your trail may have a negative impact on wildlife or if there are regulatory issues, consult a local ecologist for techniques that will minimize impact.

Planning and Design Techniques to Minimize Impact

Strive to make your trail "wildlife friendly." Use the following tips to ensure that your multi-use trail is a good neighbor to nearby animals and plants:

- Think in terms of corridor rather than trail. Always consider the swath of impact—approximately 100 feet on each side of the trail's alignment.

Box 3.2. Top Ten Tips for Sustainable Trail Construction

Although many trail developers consider ecological effects as projects are planned and designed, trail construction techniques should also strive to minimize environmental impact. These tips come from Kim Sorvig of Santa Fe, New Mexico, co-author of *Sustainable Landscape Construction: A Guide to Green Building Outdoors* (Island Press, 2000; co-author William Thompson). The book provides further details behind the methods of, and reasons for, sustainable trail construction.

1. **Survey:** While you need to know your site conditions, try to avoid survey damage. Use Global Positioning or other methods that minimize clearing during survey.
2. **Tools:** Use hand tools because they are flexible and protect the site better than power equipment. If power equipment is essential, favor hand-carried power tools, or small low-ground-pressure machinery. This applies to materials delivery as well.
3. **Work area:** Carefully designate and limit construction work areas, and don't park or stockpile outside them. Note protected site features on plans, and fence them in the field *before* work begins.
4. **Vegetation:** Follow up-to-date tree protection and planting standards; avoid disturbing tree roots. Remove invasive nonnative plants if possible.
5. **Grading:** Design trails to minimize grading, and follow existing contours as much as possible. Where crossing contours, be especially careful with stormwater runoff. Resist pressures to "over-build" the trail.
6. **Stormwater:** Prevent runoff and erosion as much as possible. Use biotechnical slope stabilization ("living retaining structures"). Infiltrate stormwater near where it falls into the ground.
7. **Porous surfacing:** Use porous trail surfacing wherever possible, including porous concrete, porous asphalt, cellular containment, grass- and gravel-pavers, and soft mulchlike surfaces. Never harden surfaces more than function demands.
8. **Materials:** Use recycled materials and local products, in order to minimize transportation to the site. Avoid PVC (polyvinyl chloride) plastics and conventional wood preservatives.
9. **Life cycle:** Analyze life-cycle costs (both monetary and energy) during trail design; plan for sustainable, resource-efficient maintenance.
10. **Lighting and Noise:** Add the minimum necessary artificial lighting, and try to avoid spillover or glare. Similarly, design the trail not to add noise to its environment.

- Design trails to discourage unwanted diversions off the trail surface, particularly shortcuts through sensitive areas. This can be accomplished with grading, plantings, and, if necessary, signs discouraging "cutoffs" from the trail.
- Using grading or vegetation, provide buffer zones between the trail edge and potentially sensitive areas such as stream edges or wetlands (Figure 3.73).
- Direct the trail away from areas of critical or sensitive habitat. Leave a buffer zone between any critical area and the trail edge. In some cases, you may need to close your trail during critical times.
- Develop interpretive vistas and observation points for viewing wildlife where appropriate. You can point out or describe nesting areas, mating activities, wildlife food sources, medicinal values of certain local plants, and other interesting wildlife information. Be aware, however, that if their presence is made public, some sensitive species may be more jeopardized by overzealous viewers.
- Provide informational and interpretive signs as well as leaflets that make the public aware of wildlife values along the trail corridor. Let people know that there may be sensitive wildlife and vegetation species. Ask them to stay on the trail and to avoid disturbing plants and animals. Phrase requests in positive terms such as "Please tread lightly and help protect this precious natural resource" rather than "Do not disturb wildlife."

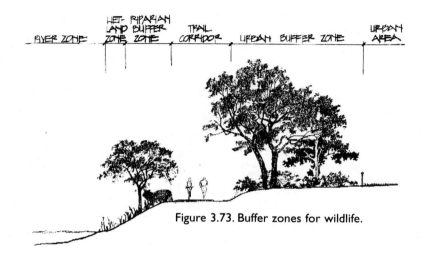

RIVER ZONE   WET-LAND ZONE   RIPARIAN BUFFER ZONE   TRAIL CORRIDOR   URBAN BUFFER ZONE   URBAN AREA

Figure 3.73. Buffer zones for wildlife.

landscapes and rich experiences for the trail user. But in other situations, significant work is needed to give the trail a personality of its own.

To create a successful trail experience you must consider the perspective of the user. "Since landscape is usually experienced by a moving observer," author Kevin Lynch writes, "it is not the single view that is important as much as the cumulative effect of a sequence of views."[2] Trails are multidimensional, with things to see, hear, smell, feel, and even taste along the way. Users will also have emotional, intellectual, and spiritual reactions to a trail experience. You need to keep all of this in mind as you plan your trail's landscape.

Early in the trail planning process, you should have conducted a physical inventory of the route (see "Site Considerations: Inventory and Assessment" in Chapter 1). Much of the information you collected then will be used to develop a landscaping plan.

In developing your landscaping plan, you must factor in the costs of both installation and maintenance. Landscaping is not a one-time cost, but an ongoing commitment. You also need to think of possible constraints in landscaping your trail. If your trail is in a dry area, will irrigation be necessary, or can you use drought-resistant plants to avoid irrigation costs? What types of soil are located there, and what is the soil's condition? Are toxins that might affect future landscape plantings present in the area? Can disturbed areas be made suitable for landscaping without compromising the quality of the surrounding environment?

- Include wildlife and habitat protection as a key component of the trail corridor's maintenance and management program once the trail is open—and be sure to budget accordingly in advance.

- If the corridor traverses sensitive areas, choose a trail surface that has minimal environmental impact. In general, water-permeable surfaces such as granular stone are preferable to impermeable surfaces like asphalt and concrete.

- Minimize vegetation removal and soil erosion in your trail design. Special designs may be needed in certain areas. For example, laying boardwalk is preferable to building a filled causeway through a wetland.

- Locate high-activity areas such as trailheads, parking lots, visitor centers, and rest rooms away from sensitive areas.

- Promote the preservation (or restoration) of natural and native landscape along the trail edges. Avoid turf grass, exotic species, and invasive plantings. In some cases, significant healthy habitat may remain in your trail corridor. In other cases, the habitat may have been disturbed by the previous uses. Recognize that not all species—for example, noxious or invasive weeds—are good for the habitat. Emphasize plant material that provides the habitat's basics—food and shelter—for the wildlife species you want to encourage.

Landscaping

What does it take to create a great trail experience? It helps to start with a beautiful trail corridor. Fortunately, many corridors offer exceptional

[2] Kevin Lynch, *Site Planning* (Cambridge, MA: MIT Press, 1973), 202.

Ongoing maintenance is a major factor in a multi-use trail's landscape plan. Even "natural" landscape along a trail requires maintenance, if only to manage weeds and remove overhanging tree limbs. Therefore, you need to make a realistic assessment of your financial ability to maintain different types of landscaping improvements.

After assessing your landscape opportunities and constraints, you are ready to prepare a landscape plan that addresses the following items. You may want to seek the assistance of a landscape architect who has experience in planning public spaces.

The Trail Edge

You need to address what will be planted along the trail's edges. Urban trails should include a mowed shoulder (at least 2 feet wide) on each side of the trail. This groomed look offers better visibility and a "lane" for joggers, equestrians, and others who prefer not to use the trail surface, especially if it is paved. Trees and large shrubs should be set back at least 5 feet from the trail's edge to reduce possible damage to the trail from root growth. Keep in mind that a tree's root system usually equals the width of its branches.

The Role of Plants and Trees

When developing your landscaping plan, consider the various roles that plants and trees can play along your multi-use trail.

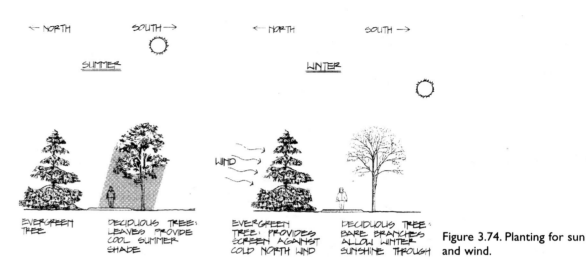

Figure 3.74. Planting for sun and wind.

TREES AND LARGE SHRUBS. The use of different varieties of trees and shrubs can create shade and define spaces visually. Large plants also can direct trail traffic if they are planted to form corridors. In addition, trees and shrubs serve as screening for adjacent property, help block the wind, and frame important views.

Visualize the corridor in each of the seasons and try to offer attractive settings year-round through careful selection of a variety of species. Select plant and tree species that are native to your area and suitable for your climate zone, especially in a drought-prone area. Also, try to avoid trees with invasive roots.

Keep in mind the effects of tree type and placement. Evergreens on the south side of the trail, for example, may promote ice buildup in winter, while a row of evergreens on the north side can help block cold winter winds. A row of trees in the right location can serve as a "snow fence," reducing snow buildup on the trail. Deciduous trees are appropriate on the south side of a trail. They provide cooling shade during summer, but they drop their leaves in winter, letting sunlight warm the trail (Figure 3.74).

Trees and shrubs play an important role in creating spaces and breaking up monotony along the trail corridor. Plant them in clusters and groves rather than in single straight lines. For planting detail, see Figure 3.75. If a more formal look is desired in some areas, consider planting trees in double rows on each side of the trail, in a staggered pattern, to create a more exciting passageway. In some areas, groups of trees might be planted close to the trail and others farther away to create outdoor "rooms" and meadows.

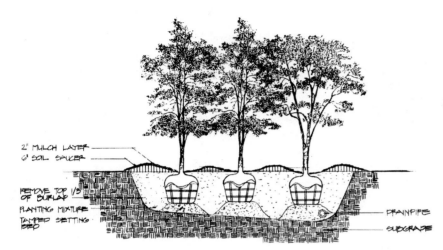

2" MULCH LAYER
6" SOIL SAUCER

REMOVE TOP 1/3
OF BURLAP
PLANTING MIXTURE
TAMPED SETTING
BED

DRAINPIPE

SUBGRADE

Figure 3.75. Tree planting detail.

UNDERSTORY. Formed by small shrubs and various woody plants, the understory adds visual interest to the landscape and helps crowd out weeds. The understory should include a variety of species and groupings, among them plants that provide food and shelter for birds, mammals, and other wildlife. The understory can also include special small plants of interest that slower-traveling trail users will enjoy. In urban areas, dense understory should be avoided to promote better visibility, which in turn will increase personal safety.

GROUND COVER. Different types of ground covers—grasses, wildflowers, vines, and other surface plantings—can form the "floor" or "carpet" of your corridor. Ground cover can also provide food and cover for wildlife. Your maintenance plan should include provisions for some mowing in the corridor, especially on the trail shoulders and around rest areas. Selective mowing can help shape ground cover and create a groomed look without the use of formal landscaping. In dry climates, consider native soil, decomposed granite, or gravel "ground covers" to minimize maintenance and water consumption.

Safety and Security

Your landscape plan must address user safety and security. The design needs to create both genuine security as well as perceived security. Start with good visibility. Trail users should have at least 100 feet of both forward and rear visibility on a level grade. Sight distances are particularly important at approaches to tunnels, bridge underpasses, and intersections; the user should be able to see all the way through before entering the area.

Do not allow dense understory to grow next to the trail since it can create shadows or blind areas. Keep the trail edge groomed to create an open view and a maintained look. Ideally, dense understory growth should be cleared at least 5 feet back from the trail's edge.

Your design should provide occasional "escape routes"—ways to retreat from any problems. There should be no "box canyons," areas where the trail corridor is fully enclosed by dense vegetation, walls, backs of buildings, or other barriers. To minimize the sense of isolation, place your plantings to maintain visibility between the trail and adjoining residences, shops, and businesses. Trees and shrubs planted in groups can help break up the imposing look of long walls. Work with owners of adjoining buildings to pursue appealing landscaping.

Service and Access

Your plan should describe how the landscape will be serviced—how maintenance personnel will mow, trim, and care for plants, and what equipment will be used and when. Consult personnel to be sure there is adequate room to mow and groom around plants. If irrigation is required, determine where the water supply will come from and how the irrigation lines will be laid.

It is best to use a variety of plants that do not require chemical pest control or fertilization. Environmentally sensitive areas, and areas near drinking water reservoirs, may have restrictions on the use of chemicals. If that is the case in your corridor, be especially careful not to plant species that are prone to pests or require fertilizers.

Addressing Odor and Noise

Some multi-use trails pass by facilities such as stockyards and sewage plants that create unpleasant odors. While you probably cannot eliminate the problem, you may be able to diminish its effect. One option is to screen with fragrant plants such as evergreens. Another is to develop a series of interpretive signs to explain the source of the pungent smell. A sign explaining that the purpose of a sewage plant is to protect public health and water quality, for example, may help mitigate the public's reaction to the odor. Some odors can be interesting. For example, just north of Baltimore, a rail-trail passes near a spice factory. An interpretive sign could give special meaning to the mysterious aroma.

If a road is the primary source of noise, the problem will vary with traffic volume and speed. In some instances you may decide that a solid fence is necessary, although this may look rather unappealing. In addition, a solid fence could create security problems, especially in urban areas, as a trail user would have no "escape route" if a dangerous situation arose. More desirable is a landscaped buffer zone between the trail and the source of the noise.

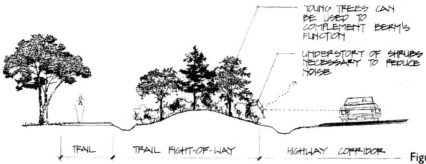

Figure 3.76. Noise-reduction berm.

Even a narrow band of vegetation—5 or 6 feet wide—will help. Although the actual noise-dampening effect of trees and shrubs may be marginal, the psychological effect is significant (Figure 3.76).

Timing and Spacing

Your landscape plan must anticipate the growth and maturity of plants over time. Trees take time to grow, and in the early years can look quite scruffy. Just after trail construction, when the ground is disturbed, weeds are likely to invade in full force. Therefore, plan to prepare disturbed areas and seed them as soon as possible after construction. Also schedule time to remove thorny and noxious weeds so that desirable plants can take over.

Make sure there is enough space between plants to allow for future growth, and be sure to plan (and budget) for plant mortality. It is not unusual to lose 10 to 20 percent of new plant-

ings, and other plants will eventually die of natural causes. Plant a variety of species and types to avoid a sudden die-off in the landscape as a result of age or disease.

Remember, too, that plants live in communities with other plants. Some live together better than others. Note each plant's special needs for sun, shade, room to grow, and other factors, and group compatible plants together.

Cost and Implementation

Costs of trail landscaping vary, depending on the region of the country, the preexisting landscape along the corridor, and the goals of your trail-building effort. Urban trails often require more landscaping than do rural trails.

Typical landscaping costs are difficult to gauge because prices vary widely. In general, trees that are one-half to 1 inch DBH (landscaping measurement equating to a stem's diameter at breast height) cost approximately $180 to

$270 each installed. Shrubs that are 1- to 5-gallon size range from $50 to $75 each. Contact your local Natural Resources Conservation Service or Extension Office to learn more about the appropriate types of landscaping required in your specific region of the country.

With a little resourcefulness, you can reduce these costs. Use volunteers for trail landscaping and maintenance—tree and shrub plantings are increasingly popular community projects. Get contributions from local businesses and service clubs. In Littleton, Colorado, a group called Volunteers for Outdoor Colorado planted more than 2,500 trees and shrubs along a trail in a single day as part of a three-year volunteer program called "10,000 Trees." Also, ask local nurseries to donate surplus stock as a tax write-off.

Develop an "Adopt-a-Trail" program for landscape maintenance. Dozens of individuals and groups help maintain the landscaping along the 44-mile Washington and Old Dominion Trail in northern Virginia. Boy Scouts, Girl Scouts, and senior citizens can make ideal tree and plant custodians if they are properly trained and monitored by professional maintenance personnel.

Finally, work with the resources you already have along the corridor. Can simple grooming, trimming, and spot plantings meet your trail's landscaping needs? Can you phase in projects over time? Trail landscaping offers many opportunities to be resourceful and creative.

Understanding the History of Your Trail

A wealth of resources is available to help you define and interpret the history of your multi-use trail, particularly if your trail is a former rail line. Museums, archives, your state Historic Preservation Office, people living near the right-of-way, and retired railroad employees can all help.

There are important questions to ask when researching your route's background: When and why was the canal or railroad built? Who traveled over it, and what goods were shipped over it? What kinds of trains or canals ran here? When and why was it abandoned? Answers to these questions and others will provide valuable insight into your trail's history.

Researching an Old Railroad

Because most rail lines have existed for many decades (the oldest began about 1825), it is unlikely that your line carried a single name or designation throughout its history. Mergers and takeovers resulted in frequent name changes in the East and Midwest, and to a lesser degree in the West. Knowing the names under which your line operated gives you several advantages. First, you'll be better equipped to conduct research. Railroads generated a great deal of paperwork, and knowing all the names under which your line operated will help you make specific research requests. Otherwise, you might have to

chip away at mountains of data that may not contain the information you want.

Second, knowing all the previous corporate names will be an important factor in choosing a name for your trail. Also learn what railroaders or local residents called the line, as it may differ from the actual corporate name. Third, using the right terminology can give you credibility with the community at large and with the rail history community.

If an active railroad abandoned your line, the company may be able to provide access to track charts, bridge drawings, and other engineering data. If the line was abandoned by a company that no longer exists, you will need to get your information from bankruptcy trustees (who can function as real estate firms for years after the railroad is gone), a museum, a university library, or a railroad history society. Some local historical societies maintain railroad records, particularly in areas where a railroad was a large employer or had regional offices.

If the line existed as a common-carrier (public use) railroad at the time the federal government ordered a national railroad-property-valuation survey (1915–1927), chances are very good that the National Archives' Suitland (Maryland) Reference Branch in suburban Washington, D.C., will yield some valuable information. These files contain mile-by-mile maps, photos, and many other kinds of data. Archivists there cannot conduct your research for you, so you must actually visit the center. If you live too far from the Washington, D.C., area, you might consider hiring a researcher to find the information for you.

Among the variety of forms issued by railroads, one especially helpful document is the track chart. It shows the track's alignment, number, locations, and degrees of curvature; steepness of grades; types of bridges; location and character of all structures (like wooden shelters and brick freight stations); sidings and yards; signals, tunnels, water tanks, and milepost designations; town populations; political subdivisions; and grade crossings.

Another resource, railroad-published maps, vary widely in their usefulness. Older ones show the names of every town that ever had a flag stop, but newer ones may be computer-generated and show only the locations at which customers existed at the time the map was compiled.

Books have been published on almost every facet of railroad history. These may help you find, for example, whether a U.S. president ever traveled over your line, or whether your route was part of the federal government's land-grant program to stimulate development and settlement.

Structures and Markers

If your property includes a railway station or shed, chances are good that it can be restored to its original appearance. Photographs and company records of standards for painting structures and trim are probably available to help you reconstruct the building's original appearance.

Large railroads had many stations to maintain, and so most found it simpler to build them to the same specifications and to use the same colors of paint on many buildings. As a result, it is fairly easy to find references to original colors and, in some cases, even paint chips. Railroad history groups often have or know where to find this information. These groups may also be able to supply diagrams for re-creating station signs, which are among the most evocative and easily constructed details you can fabricate.

Railroad history groups also may have access to graphic materials such as lettering stencils and railroad logos. Resources like these are invaluable because designing your trail signs with the same style of type and colors as those used by the railroad honors the heritage of what was there before and promotes continuity. Seek a professional preservationist's help if converting a building into a trail amenity is a possibility. He or she can determine how much of the original structure is left and whether it should be remodeled or restored (Figure 3.77).

Old canal and railroad structures opened for public use often serve as small museums. Collect any valuable items associated with the former use of your corridor. Try to convey to visitors the relationship between what they're seeing and why it's there.

Try to incorporate into your trail's design any small structures remaining within the corridor, such as distance markers and mileposts. They will remind trail users of the corridor's heritage and may add an interesting interpretive element to

Figure 3.77. The restored Yellow Springs Station along the Little Miami Scenic Trail in Ohio.

the trail. On Minnesota's Cannon Valley Trail, a concrete slab lies below mile marker 80, serving as a small memorial for a 1912 train wreck.

Rolling Stock

You may have the opportunity to obtain a piece of retired rolling stock such as a boxcar or caboose. You could use it for storage, for display, or even as an office. Make every effort to get a car that was used on your route or, at the very least, one formerly owned by the same railroad company of which your line was a part (or one owned by a former shipper on the line). Nothing will chill the cooperation of railroad history groups faster than a preservation project built around a piece of rolling stock having no relationship to its surroundings. Such a car might be viewed as a caricature.

Do your best to avoid removing a car's wheels and mounting the car on concrete blocks. Take the trouble to buy or seek the donation of a few ties and rail lengths to put the car on a short stretch of track so that it looks genuine (Figure 3.78).

Contact rail history groups to provide guidance in restoring a car to its original appearance. Some information is irretrievable if you're not careful about how you approach the restoration. Treat the car as if it were an archeological site: Don't rush into sandblasting it only to discover that you forgot to document its color, markings, and number, or failed to note whether different colors, mark-

Figure 3.78. In-line skaters pass by a preserved caboose along the Kokosing Gap Trail in Ohio.

ings, and numbers were hidden under a coat of paint. It is usually best to get professional preservation and restoration assistance.

Canal Structures

Historic canal corridors may contain remnants of the abandoned canal itself, including locks, gates, and associated buildings. Contact a local canal historical society for insight on the location of any such features. Many trails constructed on abandoned towpaths (paths used by mules to pull canal boats) highlight canal structures along the way with educational signage. A few trails include restored sections of a historic canal, complete with canal boat tours and staff dressed in period clothing (Figure 3.79).

Figure 3.79. Visitors may view the Paw Paw Tunnel (shown here in this historic photograph) as well as numerous aquaducts, culverts, locks, and other canal structures along the 184-mile C&O Canal.

Human Resources

Railroad and canal history groups can be a valuable resource for learning about your line's history. Some railroad groups are composed of several local constituencies (e.g., the Western New York Railway Historical Society), while others are devoted to a single railroad company (e.g., Friends of the East Broad Top). Still others are based on a common subject interest, such as depot photos or collectible artifacts such as lanterns or timetables. The two national rail history organizations find most of their strength in active local chapters. The National Railway Historical Society (www.nrhs.com), founded in 1935, is the largest, with 20,000 members and 150 chapters; and the Railway & Locomotive Historical Society (www.mp1.com/chapters. html), founded in 1921, is the oldest. The American Canal Society (www.canals.com/ACS/ acs.htm) works nationally to preserve and restore historic canals. Dozens of local affiliated canal societies can be contacted through this national organization.

To raise public interest and gain a higher profile, you might consider organizing events such as an oral history day, in which you encourage people to come and be videotaped as they recall stories of working on or traveling over your line. Or you could coordinate a show-and-tell day, encouraging people to come and display photos or other artifacts in their collections.

Local historical societies and railroad history groups can help you find people who worked for or used the railroad. Unions can be a resource for finding employees who worked on a line. Current union members may have worked on your route before it was abandoned, and union retirees may also have worked on the line. Unions often send their newsletters to retirees, so a notice in the newsletter from you, requesting contact with anyone who ever worked the line, may bring surprising results. Keep in mind that labor organizations are specialized. If you want to follow this path, you'll have to work through one union for the locomotive engineers, another for train crews (conductors and brakemen), another for switch tower operators, another for maintenance-of-way personnel, another for clerks, and yet another for shop workers.

Railroad museums can also be important resources. Two of the nation's largest are the California State Railroad Museum at Sacramento, and the Railroad Museum of Pennsylvania at Strasburg. These state-owned facilities serve as hosts for a semiannual preservation symposium, held in California in the spring and in Pennsylvania in the fall. Other railroad museums are operated privately or by trusts and foundations. Examples of institutions that are not exclusively devoted to railroad history but maintain railroad-related archival material include the Mercantile Library in St. Louis, the Smithsonian Institution in Washington, D.C., and the Hagley Museum in Wilmington, Delaware.

Making Your Trail Unique

Your multi-use trail will be an integral feature of your community, so its design should reflect the identity of its surroundings and should satisfy your community's needs. The following suggestions are designed to help you create a trail that highlights the uniqueness of your area.

Accommodate Users

A multi-use trail can also reflect its predominant users, adding to the trail's uniqueness. For example, if a demographic study of the trail's surrounding area shows a high concentration of older residents, you will want to develop your trail to accommodate them, possibly by building additional benches and other support facilities. If, however, you anticipate mainly young, fitness-conscious users, perhaps a self-guided fitness course adjacent to your trail is most appropriate. Offering extra features for a particular age-group—such as a small play area for children—will give your trail special character.

Emphasize Local Conditions

When local natural features, climate, flora, fauna, and local materials and culture are incorporated into trail design, the result is a trail that is a memorable reflection of your area. Refer to the notes that you made during your initial assessment of the trail corridor (see "Site Considerations: Inventory and Assessment" in Chapter 1); it should highlight special features along the route.

NATURAL FEATURES. A trail should be skillfully incorporated into its surrounding natural features. For instance, the path could extend onto a hill to take advantage of a special vista or pass near rocky crags and rock formations. A marshy terrain could be a potential bird and wildlife preserve, and a flat plain will offer good views of sunrises and sunsets. The Appalachian Trail is a good example of how to emphasize local natural features. While following the ridgelines of mountains, trail users can view scenic landscapes reflecting local heritage and character, from old Virginia farms to Vermont villages. Examine the unique natural features of your trail corridor and investigate ways of highlighting them.

CLIMATE. Climate can also add to the distinctiveness of your trail. If your trail is in a hot, sunny desert area, shade will be one of its most important and desirable features. If appropriate to your region, you can plant trees for shade, or you can build rest stations. These can be "ramadas," simple wood-frame structures overlaid with branches or trellis structures covered with vines. A cold, snowy climate calls for the planting of evergreens. When placed strategically, they add color and act as wind shields for windy sections of the trail (see "Landscaping" earlier in this chapter). Responding to your region's climate in your design will increase the trail's usability.

FLORA.   Consider the most distinctive plant of your area. Maples? Hemlocks? Saguaro cactus? Readily available and easily identified by local people, native vegetation is a point of pride and should form the foundation of any trail design. In parts of the Northeast, for example, the autumnal show of fiery red, gold, and orange leaves is emblematic of the region's character (Figure 3.80). Similarly, the dramatic image of the saguaro dotting the desert has come to represent the Southwest (Figure 3.81).

There are endless possibilities. Consider plants that attract local bird populations or the commercially grown plants in fields around the trail. A cluster of lemon trees within a trail corridor linking urban and rural regions might be appropriate in California. The Baltimore and Annapolis Trail in suburban Maryland is dotted with patches of wildflowers to attract but-

Figure 3.80. Northeastern vegetation.

Figure 3.81. The vegetation of the Southwest is striking along this trail in Tucson, Arizona.

terflies to the trail. People so much enjoy seeing the butterflies fluttering about that they donate money specifically for wildflower plantings.

A multi-use trail could even offer fruit-bearing plants, such as blackberries, blueberries, or the nearly forgotten paw-paws. Local garden clubs could be tapped to help maintain the trail and to develop interpretive signs.

FAUNA.   Certain areas attract wildlife because of their proximity to water or forest cover. A local bird-watching organization could help create an environment along your trail that fosters the presence of birds. Talk with an ecologist at a local college or university about establishing or preserving wildlife along trail corridors. Also

consider plantings that provide food, shelter, and nesting areas for wildlife.

LOCAL MATERIALS.   When designing your trail, consider using local or regional materials to construct the trail's built elements, including the surface material, fences, bridges, and signs. If, for example, the trail winds through cuts in rock, the use of that crushed local stone will echo the topography of the site (of course, it must have the proper composition for a trail surface).

In York County, Pennsylvania, broken plates, cups, and saucers from a local dinnerware factory were crushed into fine stone and used as a subsurface material on a rail-trail. The Willard Munger State Trail in Minnesota is testing rubber asphalt (made from old tires) on a section of the rail-trail; and a $100,000 project in Portland, Oregon, has used rubber-modified asphaltic concrete on nearly 2 miles of paved strips. Ground glass has also been used to supplement asphalt pavement. Often added to asphalt in New York City streets and used in pathways in Boston, ground glass not only extends the surface's use but also gives the street a pleasing mica-like sparkle at night.

Familiarize yourself with local factories and companies dealing in materials such as stone, plastic, wood, and metal. You may be able to obtain materials for a reduced price in exchange for free publicity, or some companies may even donate materials as a contribution to the community. Even if these materials must be purchased, money stays in the local community, and the trail displays something produced in the area.

LOCAL HISTORY AND CULTURE. Incorporating local history and culture into a trail project can provide a memorable experience for many trail users.

Incorporating historic sites and structures—canal locks, railroad depots, and historic buildings—into the trail also will enrich trail users' experiences (see "Understanding the History of Your Trail" earlier in this chapter). The Farmington Canal Greenway in Connecticut has designed a pedestrian bridge over a busy street to highlight the tradition of New England's covered wooden bridges. The Delaware and Raritan Canal State Park Trail is surfaced with crushed stone, representative of the condition of the former towpath along the historic canal.

Figure 3.82. This memorable "cow" grazing along a rail-trail in England is an interesting way to recycle former railroad parts.

You might also consider asking local artists and designers to create artworks based on local history (see Case Study 9). In England, old railroad equipment is converted into sculpture and placed along rail-trails (Figure 3.82). Not only

are these sculptures memorable, but they also remind trail users of the route's history. In Washington State, a collection of folk windmills and whirligigs built by local artists is displayed next to an electric power substation in a local park, juxtaposing the modern power station against a much older method of generating power. Consider seeking a grant from a local or national arts organization. City and state arts councils and the National Endowment for the Arts offer funds encouraging the use of local talent for innovative projects.

These guidelines are only starting points. Allow regional characteristics and local history to guide you through the design process. In every aspect of design, consider different ways of using available local resources to give your trail some interesting local flavor.

CASE STUDY 7

Resolving Conflicts between Cyclists and Equestrians

Multi-use trails have become popular transportation and recreation facilities for equestrians, cyclists, walkers, runners, and in-line skaters alike. As the amount of public land decreases, the need for multi-use trails will grow and so will the need to find solutions to possible

user conflicts. Equestrians and mountain bicyclists are only two of the various user groups that find themselves at odds over shared-use paths. Equestrians are largely concerned by the possibility of horses being startled by cyclists. Accidents involving horses and cyclists have

been known to cause injuries and even a few horse fatalities. Cyclists can add to conflicts by being either inconsiderate of equestrians or unaware of how best to approach a horse. Inexperienced horse riders or poorly trained horses can also contribute to conflicts.

Michael Kelley of the International Mountain Bike Association (IMBA) believes that trail user conflicts can almost always be solved with a proactive approach. He speaks to trail advocates around the country about resolving horse-cyclist conflicts with education and joint experience. Dramatic evidence of this comes from the peninsula south of San Francisco. Imagine this scene: A well-intentioned equestrian sees a pack of horses coming toward him with cyclists not far behind. He rushes forward to warn them about the bikes and is met with the reply, "That's okay, they're with us." This is the annual ROMP n' STOMP ride in California. ROMP (Responsible Organized Mountain Pedalers) meets for an annual picnic and joint trail ride with equestrians. They ride the same trails, to the same destinations, in mixed groups. The experience provides an opportunity for both cyclists and equestrians to learn about the other's sport and how to share the trail.

Barrie Freeman, an equestrian and mountain biker who has helped organize several ROMP n' STOMPs, explained the process of creating an event. Usually, an off-road cycling group creates a subcommittee to work in concert with an equestrian group to plan the event. In addition to the ride, a bar-b-que, door prizes, entertainment, as well as an opportunity to exchange mounts and to work with horses to help desensitize them to bicycles (both under controlled conditions) are all planned as part of the day's activities. All participants are required to sign a Release of Liability or Hold Harmless Agreement. Prior to the ride, trail etiquette and safety concerns are discussed with participants. A leader and drag rider are chosen in advance to answer questions along the way and help ensure that the ride proceeds safely.

Realizing that not everyone will participate in events such as the ROMP n' STOMP, Kelley also suggests initiating trail patrols to help ease tensions and educate users. According to Kelley, combined patrols, which involve all user groups, can be very effective. Patrollers receive training, often including CPR and first aid instruction, and may work with public safety departments. They act as a peer group, giving advice on proper trail behavior and being role models. Several patrols already exist around the country, including those in New York, New Jersey, Colorado, and California. To find out more about mountain bike trail patrols, visit the IMBA Web site at www.greatoutdoors.com/imba/.

CASE STUDY 8
Cross Florida Greenway Overpass at I-75

The Cross Florida Greenway, a 110-mile linear park with a series of land and water trails, was converted from the 1940s barge canal system stretching from Yankeetown, on the Gulf of Mexico, to Palatka, Florida. The greenway corridor is bisected by Interstate 75, a six-lane highway, just south of Ocala National Forest, presenting a dilemma for travelers. To connect the greenway, the Florida Department of Transportation and the Department of Environmental Protection cooperatively built a 1,000-foot "land bridge" over Interstate 75 that allows bicyclists, hikers, equestrians, disabled users, emergency vehicles, and migrating animals to safely cross the busy road. The land bridge, the first of its kind in the United States, illustrates how creative solutions can be applied to common parks, trail, and greenway design problems.

Designed by the firm of Daniel, Mann, Johnson and Mendenhall, the structure incorporates very unique features. The 59-foot-wide structure consists of a 16.5-foot Florida shellstone multi-use trail along its center with a gathering area, leaving approximately 31 feet for earth berms and planting areas. Native Marion County field-stone is incorporated into the walls and decorative pillars leading into the gathering area. The walls and fencing separate users from vehicular traffic, serving as important control barriers for both humans and wildlife.

Special design elements using native soils and vegetation enhance the trail experience for people and are intended to entice animals to use the corridor to cross the highway. Native Chandler

series sand, a layer of topsoil, and native trees and shrubs promote a sandhill habitat. The re-creation of the native landscape with a built-in irrigation system will foster seed stock growth for the future generations of vegetation. On either side of the bridge, 18-foot wide vegetation planters screen the view and noise of the highway.

An important and innovative feature of the structure will be the use of Florida U-beams. This project will be the first bridge constructed in the state to feature these new beams. The center pier of the bridge also incorporates two

"V"-shaped columns with a "triangular" opening in the center that will provide the structure with an aesthetic feature uncommon to most pier designs.

The land bridge is a critical segment in Florida's emerging statewide system of greenways and trails. It exemplifies how modern ingenuity can help piece together the multitude of fragmented habitats that dot the landscape.

CASE STUDY 9
Enhancing Your Trail with Art

In California, a cluster of brightly painted aluminum oranges adorns the Ventura River Trail. At the York County Heritage Trail in Pennsylvania, users will be welcomed to the trail by a life-size horse and hiker sculpture molded from used bicycle parts. And in Wormley, England, a large Roman-style sculpture stands at the intersection of the Bristol to Bath Cycle Path and the old Roman Road outside the city (Figure 3.83). The sculpture, which incorporates a water fountain, illustrates how art on trails can creatively and uniquely celebrate community and local culture.

Figure 3.83. This sculpture/water fountain of a Roman engineer stands along the Bristol to Bath Trail in England.

An art-on-trails program initiated in 1995 by the nonprofit trails group Sustrans (which stands for sustainable transportation) has resulted in nearly 1,000 pieces of art—varying from benches and water fountains to monuments and trail markers—along 2,500 miles of trail. The pieces celebrate nature, culture, community, and history. Katy Hallet, lead artist for the United Kingdom–based organization, attributes the popularity of the program to the ability of art to reflect the distinctive characteristics of the communities through which the trails pass.

Consider the following advice, adapted from

Sustrans Arts Coordinators guidelines, when establishing your own trail arts program:

1. **Partnerships:** Work with a wide range of partners who can fund the project, commission the artwork, or get involved in the project's creation—for example, historical societies, government officials, voluntary organizations, and private companies. Adopt a flexible approach and facilitate a consensus among them. Appoint a regional arts coordinator to facilitate community consultation, ensure flexibility, and increase participation between the artist and all interested parties, including traditionally underrepresented groups.

2. **Type of Art, Selection, and Contract:** Art may be functional (e.g., benches and drinking fountains), landscape oriented (e.g., landscaping routes, earthworks), or landmarks, gateways, and mileposts. Choose an artist once funding is secured. The contracts should include terms and conditions, schedule of work, and the names of the ultimate owner. Once signed, the project can begin.

3. **Site Selection:** Involve project partners in the site selection. Seek advice from relevant agencies with regard to environmental and historical concerns surrounding the site selection. It is important to make utilitarian art accessible for people with disabilities.

4. **Budget Proposal and Funding:** Account for artist fees, management costs, marketing, and other installation costs. Sustrans's proposals include an agreed-upon budget, partners, site, type of artwork, artist, community involvement, any equal opportunity issues, and creation and installation, monitoring and evaluation, and marketing and maintenance costs.

5. **Publicity and Marketing:** Create a publicity and marketing plan in consultation with project partners. Review the plan as the project progresses.

6. **Monitor and Evaluate:** Success of projects may be evaluated in terms of community participation, long-term benefits, economic benefits, and increased use of the trail.

4

Building Your Trail

At this point, assume that you've completed a master plan and, perhaps, a preliminary design for your trail corridor or a system of trails in your community. You are now ready to move forward with the implementation of all of these ideas. Before long, you'll probably break ground on your project. Transitioning from the completion of a trail plan to the construction of your trail involves some major tasks:

- Securing the necessary land, or right-of-way, for your trail and related improvements. A variety of methods can be used to acquire title or rights to property discussed in this chapter.

- Securing any required local, state, or federal permits or approvals.

- Completing final designs and construction bidding documents as discussed in Chapter 3. (This assumes you have completed preliminary design.)

- Raising the funds necessary to pay for land acquisition, design, and construction of the trail. These might come from federal, state, or local public sources, or from the private sector. In addition, partnerships between the public and private sectors are a relatively new way of building trails that can successfully generate funding and support for a trail project.

Creating an Implementation Plan

The first step is to formulate an implementation plan. To do this, start by expanding the above list of tasks with specific items. Identify which properties need to be acquired. List the permits and approvals needed. Break out the steps to be taken from the master plan through preliminary design to the preparation of bid documents. Prepare cost estimates for the professional services, land acquisition, and construction, and set a schedule that takes you from where you are today through construction and opening the trail. Identify potential funding sources and opportunities for partnerships between interested public and private agencies. Finally, and perhaps most important, identify who will be in charge of coordinating the trail development effort. Ideally, your implementation plan should be recorded in a written document that includes a budget and timetable. The plan should be distributed to the key partners and stakeholders and regularly updated with progress reports.

In assessing plan objectives, the cost estimates, the availability of funds, the difficulty of acquiring right-of-way, and other factors, it will make sense to prepare a phasing scheme to include in your implementation plan. If your project is a long-distance trail, or a system of trails, consider allocating staff and funding resources toward a pilot project. Your goal should be to concentrate your initial trail building efforts on building a section of trail, even if it is only a half-mile section, and to focus on quality, not necessarily quantity. Be sure, however, that the segment you build is logical—that it connects sensible destination points. You don't want to build a "trail to nowhere."

You should also include some of the ameni-ties. For example, if you have plans for 30 miles of trail connecting your city center to a park outside of town, phase your trail construction efforts so that a 3-mile segment of quality trail is completed with rest areas, benches, and signage. It might be best to locate the pilot project in an area of potential high use and visibility, such as in the city, instead of using those funds to build a bridge over a creek outside of town that does not provide connections. This technique will give the public, and potential donors, a pilot project that is used by local residents and shows a "hint of things to come," proving that community dollars are generating on-the-ground results (Figure 4.1). You can then extend the

Figure 4.1. This pilot project in Winston-Salem, North Carolina, generated additional support for trails.

trail segment by segment each year until it is done. If an unpaved surface is usable, you might add paving later if the type of project use demands it.

Be sure, however, that your improvements are solid and of good quality. Using community dollars to build facilities that are not initially used by the public or are viewed as "low quality" can be perceived as a misuse of funds, even if the trail is scheduled to be improved. High-quality pilot projects are especially important if the trail is the first to be built in a community—first impressions are lasting ones—and are likely to generate funding and support for expansion of the project. This does not necessary imply an extravagant or "gold-plated" project. The key is to build something that people will use, enjoy, praise, and demand more of the same.

Keep in mind that you may need to expand your project as the trail becomes more popular. Your trail should be a minimum of 10 feet wide with shoulders when it is first built—wider if you are in an urban area or anticipate heavy use. If you cannot afford a wider trail now, get wider easements for future expansion. Bridges and tunnels should be built to the ultimate future width of the trail because replacing them later will be extremely costly. Drainage culverts and basic grading should also be designed for the maximum future width if site conditions allow it.

Deciding which components to build to wider standards first will depend on the type of trail. A concrete trail is virtually impossible to upgrade safely once it is in place, because joints created where the new surface is attached are extremely hazardous for bicyclists. Widening an asphalt or crushed stone trail is not as difficult because the materials are less costly and can be blended. Note that different segments of the trail are likely to have different levels of use. It may be necessary to widen the trail only in certain areas where peak use occurs, such as through a downtown area or near a college campus.

Clearly, decisions about widening a trail now or later are based on case-by-case judgments that reflect economics, political considerations, user safety, and the ultimate goals of the project.

Strategies to Acquire Land

There are a variety of strategies that you can use to acquire right-of-way and associated lands for trails. Communities that have successfully acquired and protected trail corridors have found that combining several strategies is often the best way to preserve these resources. Local and state governments, nonprofit organizations, and landowners can all utilize the methods listed in this section. When considering each of the options and techniques, keep in mind that you should consult a real estate attorney for assistance in preparing and executing agreements for land and trails.

Make every possible effort to avoid condemning property for trails. Acquisition should involve only willing sellers or voluntary donors. Condemnation is a proven way of generating controversy and damaging publicity for a trail project.

Before you begin acquiring land, you will need to know the names of property owners along the trail corridor. See "Ownership and Land Use" in Chapter 1 for guidance on researching ownership along your trail. If you are working to build a trail within a utility corridor, remember that the utility company may not own surface rights or recreational access. In many cases, the land is leased to the utility (or the easement is limited to utility uses) and owned by adjacent landowners. If you are dealing with a railroad line and are unsure of its ownership status, consult *Secrets of Successful Rail-Trails*, a publication of the Rails-to-Trails Conservancy, for more information, or visit your local planning office.

If you are working to convert a rail line that has not yet been abandoned, contact the Rails-to-Trails Conservancy for information on railbanking. Railbanking is a method of protecting a rail corridor for interim use as a transportation facility (bicycles and feet instead of trains) until such time as it is once again used for rail purposes. This benefits trail developers by facilitating the transfer of the use of the corridor directly from the railroad to a trail agency or organization, regardless of ownership. Hundreds of miles of rail-trails have been acquired through railbanking, a strategy enacted by a federal law.

Landowner Benefactor Measures

DONATIONS. Before paying cash, always ask for donations. Experience has shown that up to 30 percent of adjacent property owners are willing to transfer property interest to their portions of railroad rights-of-way for trail development. The best way to solicit donations is to negotiate with landowners on an individual basis, making sure to explain all of the income tax deductions and tax credit benefits (donations of land for public recreation and conservation purposes are considered charitable gifts).

Donations can be an especially attractive option to landowners in areas that are rapidly developing, because of associated increases in property taxes. Some state and local governments offer additional incentives for donations of public land. For example, North Carolina offers a state income tax credit (up to $100,000 of 25 percent of fair market value for property that is donated for conservation purposes, including trails). Investigate any similar incentives offered by your state or local government.

If you are pursuing landowner donations, it is important to have legal advice to assist with the transaction, including, for example, tax lawyers who can advise you on potential tax benefits. The landowner should also be advised to consult his or her tax adviser and attorney. Be careful not to make representations about specific benefits without the advice of a specialist. As part of the conveyance arrangement, your agency might want to offer to cover costs of surveys, legal descriptions, legal fees, and appraisals associated with the donation, unless the donor is willing to absorb those costs. Organizations such as the Trust for Public Land may be able to

assist with land donations or direct you to the appropriate legal expertise in your area.

TRAIL EASEMENTS, LICENSES, AND REVOCABLE PERMITS. Easements, licenses, and revocable permits are ways to acquire the use of land for trail purposes without obtaining full ownership of the land. A trail easement is a legally binding agreement between a landowner and a private organization or public agency in which the landowner grants rights of public access, such as a trail, or forgoes development rights on the land, either for a specified period of time or permanently, for conservation purposes. An easement is a powerful way to protect trail corridors while maintaining land in private ownership. Easements may be donated, sold, or traded. Full title to the land is not purchased, only those rights granted in the easement agreement, so the easement purchase price is less than full title value.

Note that a conservation easement differs from a trail easement, but some easements grant both types of benefits. A conservation easement is oriented to the conservation of land resources, while a trail easement secures the right of public access and use. Be sure the grantors understand that a trail and use of the trail by the public is included in the conveyance.

A permanent or period-specific trail easement is attached to the title of the land, remaining in force when the property is sold or passed on to future generations of landowners. The agency or organization that accepts the easement is

responsible for monitoring the land at least annually to ensure that the terms of the easement are met. Because easements are enforceable, local, state, and federal governments can provide income tax incentives to encourage donations of easements for trails.

If an easement already exists along your trail corridor, for utilities, roads, or other purposes, investigate the terms of existing easement agreements to find out whether trail development could be considered an allowable use. Many trails are built within utility easements by modifying the existing agreement to permit trail development within the easement. Such a modification would require the permission of property owners.

Alternative partial conveyance techniques include licenses and revocable permits. A license grants access for a certain period of time with an option to renew. Some entities, such as railroads, may prefer to convey a license. Other entities may not have the legal capacity to convey an easement. Be sure, however, that the term is long enough to assure a meaningful trail. Some granting agencies that fund trails require a minimum number of years on a license. Try to secure at least a ninety-nine-year lease.

A revocable permit is similar to a license, but the grantor retains the right to withdraw rights of access under certain conditions such as the corridor returning to rail use. A revocable permit may also be a last resort technique to persuade reluctant landowners to allow a trail to be built through their property. In this instance, the landowner might retain the right to revoke access in the event the trail is not properly maintained or there are other problems such as vandalism.

LAND DEDICATION. Landowners and developers may dedicate corridors for trail use, typically accomplished when tracts are subdivided. Dedication for trails involves setting aside a portion of the parcel being developed, limiting the use of the dedicated portion to trail uses, and conveying the land to a government entity or nonprofit land trust organization. Many communities require developers to dedicate a specified percentage of land for recreational or conservation purposes when tracts are developed, and trails may qualify under this requirement. Other communities offer incentives for developers to provide trails and other amenities in exchange for certain exceptions from zoning ordinance requirements or an increase in development density that benefit the developer. In some cases, the trail corridor may be improved and maintained by a homeowners association.

Purchasing Land for Trails

FEE-SIMPLE PURCHASE. Fee-simple ownership means that you are purchasing full title to a property and all rights associated with it. Fee-simple purchase is the most costly method of acquiring land for trails, but is effective in achieving full ownership of a trail corridor. Negotiate with landowners on an individual

basis to generate interest in selling parcels of land.

BARGAIN SALE. A bargain sale occurs when landowners voluntarily sell land or an easement on land at a below-market value for trail purposes. The benefit of a bargain sale is that the landowner may be eligible to take charitable deductions from federal and state income taxes. The tax deductions would be based on the difference between the fair market value (as determined by appraisal) and the actual sale price of the land.

RIGHT OF FIRST REFUSAL. A right of first refusal provides the opportunity for you to match a purchase offer received by the landowner at a future time, if and when the owner decides to sell the property. The main disadvantage of the right of first refusal is the potentially higher future cost of the land when the landowner decides to sell. To avoid this problem, you may want to purchase an option of a right of first refusal with a clear understanding of the purchase price up front. An option of a right of first refusal can allow the buyer time to secure the exact funds necessary for the future land purchase.

LEASE PURCHASE. Some organizations and agencies have acquired right-of-way and open space lands through a lease purchase agreement. Through this method, the land is secured through a five-, ten-, or twenty-year lease, with

conveyance of ownership interest at the end of the lease term. A variation of this involves a lease with a donation of land at the end of the term. This allows both income and, ultimately, a tax break for the landowner.

In some cases, a third party, such as a land trust, may facilitate the transaction. The land would be sold, bargain-sold, or donated to a land trust that in turn would lease the land to the trails agency. This may be a way to defer costs if the trail entity cannot afford the purchase and does not have the capacity to borrow funds.

Compliance with Legislation and Permitting

As part of the process of developing construction documents, proper permitting must be obtained to ensure compliance with local, state, and federal laws. In most cases, permits will be required to construct a trail, particularly when it follows a waterway or is in an urban area. Most permits address environmental concerns, although permits frequently are required for construction activities such as installing an electrical conduit and plumbing.

Working through the maze of local, state, and federal requirements is complicated, but it need not be overwhelming. The key is to have a general understanding of the types of permits required and then to set up a process for identifying exactly what is required for a particular project.

For purposes of clarity and organization, think of regulatory legislation in four broad categories: environmental policy acts, which include requirements for environmental impact statements; shoreline and wetland regulations; permits and licenses; and construction regulations to which the contractor must adhere during construction.

Environmental Policy Acts (EPA)

An Environmental Policy Act (EPA) delineates when, where, and how an environmental impact statement (EIS) must be conducted. Most states and many cities and counties have adopted an environmental policy act based on the National Environmental Policy Act (NEPA), passed by Congress in 1970. NEPA applies to all projects using federal funds even if the funds are funneled through a state agency.

The primary purpose of EPA legislation is to disclose the environmental consequences of a proposed action, thus alerting the public, government agencies, and other decision makers of the risks involved. The law is intended to ensure that environmental values are considered before a proposed action is taken. EPA legislation, when applied to a project, will likely have one of three outcomes: The project will be declared categorically exempt; an environmental checklist will have to be completed; or the significance or nonsignificance of the impact must be determined.

CATEGORICALLY EXEMPT. Certain types of projects are deemed categorically exempt through

federal, state, and local EPA legislation. In other words, no further environmental documentation, including an EIS, is needed. In Washington State, for example, all bicycle lanes, paths, and facilities are categorically exempt, except when they are built over water or are on land classified as environmentally sensitive. Typically, an agency working on a trail project believed to be categorically exempt is required to fill out a standard form, which is submitted for approval to the local or state official responsible for administering the EPA law.

ENVIRONMENTAL CHECKLIST. If a project is not categorically exempt, an environmental checklist (ECL) must be completed. This standard "fill-in-the-blank" form requires a detailed description of construction and project impacts. Once completed, the checklist is submitted to the correct local or state official, who makes a "threshold determination," declaring the proposed project as having "significant" or "nonsignificant" environmental impacts. At the time the checklist is submitted, the lead agency is usually required to provide notice of the proposed project to allow for public comment.

DETERMINATION OF SIGNIFICANCE OR NON-SIGNIFICANCE. If it is determined that a proposal will probably have no significant adverse environmental impacts, the lead agency usually will be asked to prepare and issue a "determination of nonsignificance" (DNS), usually using a standard, pre-approved form. The DNS is then

filed with the appropriate state or local offices. Typically, there will be a public appeal period of fifteen to thirty days once the DNS is issued. If the project is "determined significant," an environmental impact statement must be drafted.

If you are required to prepare an environmental impact statement, you may want to consider contracting it out to a consultant. The EIS typically requires the following information:

- A detailed description of the proposed action, including information and technical data adequate to permit a careful assessment of environmental impact.

- Discussion of the probable impact on the environment, including any impact on ecological systems and any direct or indirect consequences that may result from the action.

- Any adverse environmental effects that cannot be avoided.

- Alternatives to the proposed action that may prevent some or all of the adverse environmental effects, including analysis of the environmental impacts of the alternatives and their costs.

- An assessment of the cumulative, long-term effects of the proposed action on the environment.

- Any irreversible commitment of resources that might result from the action or that would curtail beneficial use of the environment.

The EIS process begins with a scoping phase to identify potentially significant environmental impacts and issues that should be addressed in the study. Agency and public comment is taken during a subsequent time period (twenty-one days), which may include a public hearing. The next step is preparation of a draft environmental impact statement (DEIS). Once it is published, there is usually another comment period (thirty days) during which agency and public comment is encouraged. The last part of the process is to prepare a final environmental impact statement (FEIS), which responds to all comments received on the DEIS. This is issued within a specified time period (sixty days) from the end of the DEIS comment period. If substantial changes are made in the plan at any time prior to construction that may cause environmental impacts not addressed in the EIS, a supplemental environmental impact statement (SEIS) must be prepared.

Based upon the analysis in the FEIS or SEIS, the appropriate agency or department will issue its final decision approving, conditioning, or denying the project. Typically, a project may be denied only if the impacts are significantly adverse and cannot be mitigated. Once the final decision is issued, there is usually a time period (fifteen to thirty days) during which the decision can be appealed.

Projects on federal land (or those fully or partially funded with federal money) are subject to the requirements of the National Environmental Policy Act. The process, similar to that stated above, should be carried out by the lead federal agency.

Shoreline and Wetland Regulations

Many states, counties, and cities have adopted legislation to protect the vegetation, wildlife, water, and aquatic life of shorelines and wetlands. These laws vary greatly from one jurisdiction to another.

Shoreline and wetland protection laws typically include a purpose statement defining the intent of the legislation, as well as the procedures for obtaining the necessary permits. Also included may be shoreline and wetland overlay zoning and sensitive areas designation, each with its own specific development standards. Determining the need for shoreline and/or wetland permits typically occurs during the environmental review process. Most projects that do not require a full EIS are usually still required to secure shoreline permits. Permits are typically required for dredging, filling, and any other construction activity that may upset spawning and nesting patterns. Permits frequently require that certain construction activities be completed within a limited time period to minimize disruption to fish and wildlife. As with an EIS, most shoreline permits can be appealed within a specified time period (thirty days).

Permits and Licenses

In addition to the permits required by shoreline and wetland legislation, several local, state, and possibly federal permits and licenses may be required. The local agency or department that issues the master use permit (the umbrella permit covering all zoning and environmental permits) for a project will usually have a "punch" list of all permits and licenses that may be required for your project. Again, the specifics will vary from community to community. Possible required permits at the local and state levels can include the following:

- Land-use permit
- Shoring and excavation permit
- Drainage permit
- View protection certification of compliance
- Foundation permit
- Building permit
- Electrical permit
- Mechanical permit
- Street use permit
- Demolition permit
- Structural permit
- Sign permit
- Energy code approval
- Fire code inspection
- Plumbing permit
- Water permit
- Water quality certification
- Hydraulic permit
- Tidelands lease or easement
- Floodplain compliance permit

In addition, under the Clean Water Act, the U.S. Army Corps of Engineers requires permits for work in navigable waters and for filling or dredging in waters and wetlands determined to be under the jurisdiction of the federal government. "Jurisdictional" waters and wetlands are defined by federal law and administrative policies. If you are working in any stream, lake, marshland, or shore area, assume that you are dealing with jurisdictional waters and you will likely need a permit.

Commonly referred to as "404" permitting, the process involves review by appropriate Corps of Engineers officials, review by interested agencies such as the U.S. Environmental Protection Agency and appropriate local and state agencies such as state environmental protection and health departments. While the law and policies have been changing, the level of review may vary depending on the amount of impact your trail has. If the impact is deemed minor by the Corps—less than one-half acre or less than several hundred feet of shoreline (the actual amounts have been changing)—your project may be eligible for a "nationwide" permit that involves a simpler and speedier administrative approval.

If the impact is determined to be greater, or if the cumulative impact of your entire project is determined to be more significant, you may be asked to apply for an "individual" permit. This process requires a more detailed application, possibly a wetlands delineation study (that must be approved by the Corps), and a public review period (usually ninety days). You may also be

asked to mitigate or replace wetlands damaged by your project.

In addition to federal requirements, your state may have similar impact permit requirements. Begin by checking with the appropriate U.S. Army Corps of Engineers reviewing "Environmental Specialist." If possible, visit with them to discuss your plans or send a letter of enquiry describing your project, its location, and its anticipated impact on jurisdictional waters.

While the list of permits is long, it need not be overwhelming. Many of the permits are routinely issued once the master use permit is approved. Others are handled within the context of the environmental review process. The best approach is to find someone at the local level who knows the permit system and is willing to help guide you through the process.

Construction Regulations

During construction, the contractor will be required to have certain licenses, obtain certain permits, and abide by certain regulations. These should be spelled out in the contract that the contractor signs. While many tend to be "boiler-plate" requirements that appear in all contracts, it is critical to have professional help in developing the contract so as to avoid legal and quality control problems. Most local and state governments have standard forms of construction contracts that include the following:

- Requirements for maintaining traffic
- Barricade and sign requirements
- Procedures for shutting off gas and electric lines
- Dewatering plan
- Sewer license
- Site maintenance requirements
- Street cleaning requirements
- Air and noise pollution control
- Erosion and siltation control
- Materials specifications

In addition, contractors must meet federal, state, and local fair hiring and labor practices.

Funding Sources for Trail Development

A successful method of funding trail design, development, and management is to combine private sector funds with funds from local, state, and federal sources. The following funding sources represent some of the opportunities typically pursued by successful trail developers. Consider each of these sources as you look for ways to fund your trail-building effort.

Federal Sources of Funds

The largest source of federal funding for trails is authorized through federal surface transportation legislation codified in title 23 United States Code (U.S.C.). The Intermodal Surface Transportation Efficiency Act of 1991 (ISTEA) amended title 23 to provide the first broad eligibility for pedestrian and bicycle transportation facilities, including trails. ISTEA authorized millions of dollars for pedestrian and bicycle facilities and trails from 1992 to 1997. The Transportation Equity Act for the 21st Century (TEA-21), enacted in 1998, expanded the eligibility and funding for trails, and authorized many millions more for 1998 to 2003. Federal surface transportation funding beyond 2003 will require new authorizing legislation.

The Federal-Aid Highway Program provides federal financial assistance to the states to construct and improve the National Highway System, other major roads, bridges, bicycle and pedestrian facilities, and trails. Several of these programs can benefit multi-use trails. Trail projects will have to compete for funding with other eligible transportation projects.

SURFACE TRANSPORTATION PROGRAM (STP). STP funds may be used for pedestrian and bicycle facility construction or nonconstruction projects such as brochures, public service announcements, and route maps. Projects must provide pedestrian and bicycle transportation. Projects must be consistent with statewide and metropolitan long-range transportation plans. In metropolitan areas (urbanized areas over 50,000 population), the Metropolitan Planning Organization (MPO) selects projects for funding

through the metropolitan transportation improvement program (TIP). In nonmetropolitan areas, the state selects projects for funding through the statewide transportation improvement program (STIP). The federal share is usually 80 percent (higher in states with large amounts of federal lands).

- Safety Programs: 10 percent of STP funds are available only for safety programs.
    1. Railway-highway crossing projects are intended to eliminate hazards identified in a state survey of railway-highway crossings. Projects must take into account bicycle safety. They may be eligible for up to 100 percent federal funding.
    2. Hazard Elimination Program funds are intended to eliminate safety hazards on any public road, any public surface transportation facility or publicly owned bicycle or pedestrian pathway or trail, or any traffic-calming measure. They must be identified in a state hazard survey. They are eligible for up to 90 percent federal funding.
- Transportation Enhancements Program: 10 percent of STP funds are available only for transportation enhancement activities (see Box 4.1). Many multi-use trail projects can meet two or more of these categories. The federal share is 80 percent (higher in states with large amounts of federal lands), but

POTENTIAL FUNDING SOURCES

1. Federal government
   - Federal Surface Transportation Funds
   - Community Development Block Grants
   - Land and Water Conservation Fund
2. State government
   - Recreation, transportation, conservation, water quality programs
3. Local government
   - Taxes
   - Impact fees
   - Bond referendums
   - Capital improvements program
4. Private sector
   - Land trusts
   - Foundations
   - Local businesses
   - Individual sponsors
   - Volunteer work
   - "Buy-a-Foot" Programs

Box 4.1. Transportation Enhancement Activities

The list of qualifying transportation enhancement activities provided in 23 U.S.C. 101(a)(35) is intended to be exclusive, not illustrative. That is, only those activities listed therein are eligible to be accounted for as transportation enhancement activities.

1. Provision of facilities for pedestrians and bicycles.
2. Provision of safety and educational activities for pedestrians and bicyclists.
3. Acquisition of scenic easements and scenic or historic sites.
4. Scenic or historic highway programs (including the provision of tourist and welcome center facilities).
5. Landscaping and other scenic beautification.
6. Historic preservation.
7. Rehabilitation and operation of historic transportation buildings, structures, or facilities (including historic railroad facilities and canals).
8. Preservation of abandoned railway corridors (including the conversion and use thereof for pedestrian or bicycle trails).
9. Control and removal of outdoor advertising.
10. Archaeological planning and research.
11. Environmental mitigation to address water pollution due to highway runoff or reduce vehicle-caused wildlife mortality while maintaining habitat connectivity.
12. Establishment of transportation museums.

there are provisions for states to allow variable matching shares. Most states accept donations of funds, services, material, and land. For general information, contact the National Transportation Enhancements Clearinghouse at 800-388-6832, or www.enhancements.org. For specific state requirements, contact your state transportation enhancements program manager.

CONGESTION MITIGATION AND AIR QUALITY IMPROVEMENT PROGRAM (CMAQ). The CMAQ program funds transportation projects and programs that will contribute to attainment or maintenance of the national ambient air quality standards. Funds are apportioned to the states based on severity of air quality problems. Projects that benefit pedestrian and bicyclists, including trail projects, are eligible to the extent they can demonstrate an air quality benefit. Projects are selected by metropolitan planning organizations. For general information, see www.fhwa.dot.gov/environment/cmaq.htm.

RECREATIONAL TRAILS PROGRAM (RTP). The RTP provides funds to the states to develop and maintain recreational trails for motorized and nonmotorized trails and trail-related projects. In most states, the RTP is administered by a state resource agency. Funds may be used for maintenance and restoration of existing trails, development and rehabilitation of trailside and trailhead facilities and trail linkages, purchase and lease of trail construction and maintenance equipment, construction of new trails, acquisition of easements or property for trails, and operation of educational programs to promote safety and environmental protection related to trails. The federal share is 80 percent, but projects sponsored by a federal land management agency may allow additional federal funds from that agency. The RTP also allows federal funds from other programs to be used as the nonfederal match. The nonfederal share also may include donations of services, materials, or newly acquired rights-of-way. For general information, see www.fhwa.dot.gov/environment/rectrail.htm. For specific state requirements, contact your state trail administrator.

PUBLIC LANDS HIGHWAYS DISCRETIONARY PROGRAM (PLH). The PLH program provides financial assistance to improve access to and within the federal lands. The public lands highways projects must be under the jurisdiction of and maintained by a public authority and open to public travel. Several major trail projects on federal lands have received PLH funds since 1999. Projects are selected by the U.S. Department of Transportation, but must be submitted through the state transportation department. For more information, see www.fhwa.dot.gov/discretionary.

NATIONAL SCENIC BYWAYS PROGRAM. The National Scenic Byways Program provides financial funding for state scenic byways programs and plans; safety improvements on state or federally designated scenic byways; construction along a scenic byway of facilities for the use of pedestrians and bicyclists, rest areas, turnouts, highway shoulder improvements, passing lanes, overlooks, and interpretive facilities; protection of scenic, historical, recreational, cultural, natural, and archaeological resources in an area adjacent to a scenic byway; and developing and providing tourist information to the public, including interpretive information about the scenic byway. Projects are selected by the U.S. Department of Transportation but must be submitted through the state transportation department. For more general information, see www.byways.org. For state requirements, contact your state scenic byways program manager.

OTHER FEDERAL SURFACE TRANSPORTATION CATEGORIES. Other federal highway funding programs can benefit trails. If your trail crosses an interstate highway, it is possible to use Interstate Maintenance funds to build or reconstruct a highway crossing. If your trail is within a National Highway System corridor, NHS funds may be used for trail construction. If your trail needs to use a highway bridge, bridge program funds may be used. If your project is on federal lands, it may be eligible under the Federal Lands Highway Program.

- Community Development Block Grant Program: The U.S. Department of Housing and Urban Development (HUD) offers financial grants to communities for neighborhood revitalization, economic development, and improvements to community facilities and services, especially in low- and moderate-income areas. Several communities have used HUD funds to develop trails in these areas. Check with HUD to determine current programs, eligibility, and available funds.

- Land and Water Conservation Fund (LWCF) Grants: This federal funding source was established in 1965 to provide park and recreation opportunities to residents throughout the United States. Money for the fund comes from the sale or lease of nonrenewable resources, primarily federal offshore oil and gas leases and surplus federal land sales. LWCF funds are used by federal agencies to acquire additions to national parks, forests, and wildlife refuges. In the past, Congress has also appropriated LWCF moneys for so-called stateside projects. These stateside LWCF grants can be used by communities to acquire and build a variety of park and recreation facilities.

Stateside LWCF funds are annually distributed by the National Park Service through state natural resource departments. Communities must match LWCF grants with 50 percent of the local project costs through in-kind services or cash. All projects funded by LWCF grants must be used exclusively for recreation purposes, in perpetuity. Check with your state parks or conservation agency to determine current status.

State Sources of Funds

Since each state will have its own specific funding sources available for trail development, these are too numerous to list in this publication. Many states have statewide trails programs and associated grants. Typically, state funding sources for trails will focus on improving recreation, water resources, land conservation, and off-road transportation in the state. Your state natural resources agency or parks agency can most likely provide you with detailed information about existing trail funding sources. You should also contact your state trails coordinator or state bicycle/pedestrian coordinator (if your state has one or both of these staff positions) for more information.

Local Sources of Funds

Although local governments may have less money available for trail development than do other public sources, their funds can be used to match federal and state dollars in order to obtain a higher level of funding for the project. The following methods have been used successfully by communities to fund trail development and management.

TAXES. The development of trails can be funded through sales tax revenues. One example is Oklahoma City, where voters approved a temporary $0.01 sales tax that generated millions of dollars for acquisition and development of trails.

IMPACT FEES. Impact fees and development excise taxes are one-time charges levied by a local government on new development that can be used to finance trails and other projects located outside the boundary of development. These fees can be levied through the subdivision or building permit process and are commonly set as a charge per dwelling unit or per 1,000 square feet of nonresidential floor space. Many developing communities use impact fees to purchase trail lands. Some communities, including Colorado Springs, Colorado, require developers to provide trails. Colorado Springs also has a sales tax on bicycles that raises funds for trails.

BOND REFERENDA. Communities across the nation have successfully placed propositions on local ballots to support funding for trail development. For example, the Charlotte–Mecklenburg County, North Carolina, area passed four

Figure 4.2. One of the many trails in Mecklenburg County, North Carolina, funded by bond referenda.

consecutive referendums in recent years that generated more than $3 million for trail land acquisition and development. Since bonds rely on the support of the voting population, it is a good idea to implement an aggressive education and awareness program prior to any referendum vote (Figure 4.2).

LOCAL CAPITAL IMPROVEMENTS PROGRAM. Some local governments have initiated a yearly appropriation for trail development in their capital improvements program. In Raleigh, North Carolina, for example, trails continue to be built and maintained, year after year, thanks to a dedicated source of annual funding administered through the Parks and Recreation Department. This source could be used by local communities to acquire, develop, and manage trail corridors year after year.

RAILROAD FRANCHISE AGREEMENTS. Wherever a railroad line crosses through a street or cuts across a street, there will usually be a franchise agreement giving the railroad the right to use the property. A franchise agreement is much like a street use permit, in that it allows a private use in a publicly owned space. Most franchise agreements require railroads to remove tracks and restore the improved portions of the street when the tracks are no longer needed for rail purposes.

Since this can be relatively expensive, especially in urban areas where long sections of track may be in street right-of-way, the railroad may be willing to exchange right-of-way property for cancellation of its obligations to restore the street. The agency then takes on the responsibility for removing the track and restoring the street when it constructs the trail. While it is not free of cost, this strategy—which has been successfully implemented by the city of Seattle—allows for quick acquisition of right-of-way with no immediate outlay of cash. This can be particularly useful when land must be purchased in a short period of time.

Private Sector Funds

Although often overlooked as a source of funding for trails, the private sector can contribute significant financial support to local projects. Soliciting private sector dollars can generate communitywide support of a project while leveraging public sector funds. The following types of private sector funding opportunities have been used to develop trails.

LAND TRUSTS. A land trust is typically a private, nonprofit organization that is engaged in the protection and conservation of real estate. National, state, and local land trusts can be a great resource for protecting trail corridors. Land trusts can use a variety of tools to protect landscapes, negotiate with landowners, and raise funds from individual donors for the acquisition and conservation of land.

LOCAL AND NATIONAL FOUNDATIONS. Many communities have solicited trail funding from a variety of private foundations and other conservation-minded benefactors. As a general rule, local foundations will have a greater interest in and be more likely to fund local projects. These local sources should be approached first, before seeking funds outside the community. National foundations include the American Greenways DuPont Awards and the REI Environmental Grants. Visit your local library or the Internet to find out about national foundations that could provide grant money for your trail.

LOCAL BUSINESSES. The following methods could be used by local industries and private businesses to provide support for the acquisition, development, and management of trails:

• Donations of cash to a specific trail segment or amenity (especially if it is located near the business).

Box 4.2. Top Ten Tips for Successful Grant Writing and Fund-Raising

Every trail project needs funding and often must compete against other projects for it, so your proposal or other fund-raising strategy must stand out among the rest. These tips come from Tracy Esslinger of Denver, Colorado, president of Development Solutions, Inc. Tracy assists nonprofit organizations in raising funds for successful trails, and other types of projects.

1. **Develop a fund-raising plan for your project:** Starting with total funds needed for your project, set goals from key sources. For example, if you have a $1 million budget, break it down into realistic goals for each source—Individuals: $75,000; Corporations: $150,000; Foundations: $275,000; In-kind: $250,000; Project partners: $250,000. You will need a funding plan because foundations often require you to show percentages of funding anticipated from each source. Once you have established amounts from each source, identify potential foundations, corporations, individuals, and others, and obtain contact information for each.

2. **Identify key components of your project that can be tailored to specific funding sources:** Without compromising your project, try to develop a menu of miniprojects tailored to the interests of a number of different funding sources. Foundations can have different types of grants available, including capital improvement projects, project/program support, general operating, endowments, matching grants, and technical assistance. Identify project components that meet various types of grants. This process also helps you define (or redefine) your project. For example, identify capital improvement grants for trail construction, trailhead amenities, and other "bricks and mortar" subcomponents. Identify "program support" grants for youth/volunteer planting projects or education programs associated with your project. In addition, many corporations like to fund projects that involve employees. In order to gain corporate support, you may forgo a contractor and create a specific voluntary task such as tree planting or bench building. Foundations that fund "education" (but not trail projects) may participate if an environmental education component is added, where, for example, students are taught the history and culture of trail routes or the values and functions of wetlands along a greenway corridor.

3. **Complete all planning elements prior to submitting funding requests.** Do not seek funding prematurely. Often you get only one chance to make a positive impression on a potential funder. Make sure that planning is complete, that the right partners are in place, that you have expertise on your team to bring credibility to your project, that you have a fund-raising plan, a realistic timeline for project completion, a budget, a plan for maintenance, and a plan for

(continues)

- Donations of services by local businesses to reduce the cost of developing trails, including equipment and labor to construct and install elements of a project.
- Reductions in the cost of materials purchased from local businesses that can supply essential products for facility development.
- Contribution of employee volunteer time to work on trail projects.

This method of raising funds can require a great deal of staff coordination. Contact local businesses after completing a conceptual design for your trail, and always mention other businesses, especially competitors, that have already donated to the trail effort. This will make your effort seem more legitimate and will generate larger donations. One example of a successful endeavor of this type is the Swift Creek Recycled Greenway in Cary, North Carolina. A total of $40,000 in donated construction materials and labor made this trail an award-winning demonstration project (Figure 4.3).

Often, businesses want to see a promotional return or other direct benefit if they give money. Involving their employees in a trail volunteer workday is a great way to motivate businesses to participate. Some businesses also have employee match and "spare change" programs, in which businesses will match employee donations or ask employees to contribute a "change element" of their paycheck by rounding down to the nearest dollar.

Box 4.2. *Continued*

ongoing management. Once all of these components are in place, it will be a lot easier to prepare a grant proposal and, more important, you will position your organization as a credible applicant in the eyes of the funder. Don't forget to research potential funder profiles and interest areas. Know the areas of interest of each foundation/funding source and make sure they match your project. Don't waste time submitting proposals to sources that support causes very different from yours.

4. **Start by writing a two-page summary letter:** This helps to succinctly define your project and your request for support. Many funding sources provide guidelines for the initial "inquiry" letter. Make sure you follow their guidelines. If none are provided, a good rule of thumb is to start with the basic who, what, where, when, and why. Include a budget and any other relevant information. Many funders ask that you submit a summary letter prior to submitting a full application. This allows them to decide if they are interested in your project before you spend a lot of time writing a full proposal. This will also help you narrow your list of prospective donors. This letter can then be modified and sent to prospective individual and corporate donors.

5. **Create a credible team prior to seeking funding:** Funders are interested in not only the quality of your project, but the quality of your organization or team as well. Similar to applying for a business loan at a bank, the "owners" are evaluated on their ability to plan, implement, finance, and manage the project. Funders need to have confidence in the team behind the project. If you represent a nonprofit, you may need to bring new people onto your board or create an advisory board for your specific project. Choose credible, reputable partners or advisors. Often foundations will ask you to attach your board roster, and resumes of staff and other partners involved in your project, in order to evaluate your "team." If possible, arrange an in-person meeting or project tour with prospective donors. "People give money to people" continues to prevail. Not all donors afford this opportunity, but many do. Ask, and be sure to take along a few experts on your team to cover all aspects of the project.

6. **Establish strong partnerships and demonstrate coordination:** Funders are interested in strong partnerships and coordination among agencies. They especially like to see public and private sectors working together to leverage funds. Funders tend to favor strength in numbers so they do not feel solely responsible for the success of a project. They also want to make sure you are

not duplicating another organization's efforts. Demonstrate that you have done all the preliminary work by getting the right people and agencies together from the onset to carry out your project.

7. **Establish broad community support prior to seeking funding.** Funders like to see that your project has broad community support prior to approaching them for funding. At a minimum, all project partners should provide "lead" funding, both cash and in-kind services, where feasible. This demonstrates that the main project proponents are "putting their money where their mouth is." It is always advantageous to demonstrate that a portion of funding has been secured from "local" supporters (project partners, individuals in the community, civic groups) prior to seeking outside funding. If you do not have "lead" funding, attach support letters from individuals, local businesses, civic groups, and others to your grant requests, in order to demonstrate community support.

8. **Submit proposals:** Once you have completed your research, have partners in place, and have a solid plan, submit proposals to your target list of potential funders. Most foundations have application guidelines that are important to follow. Write clearly and concisely. Grant reviewers have to read several proposals and you want yours to be remembered.

9. **Complete all follow-up documentation; thank and recognize donors.** Have a plan in mind for how you will recognize donors (a sign at the trailhead, newsletters and publications, Web site). Check with each donor to determine preferences for recognition. Make sure that you send thank-you letters recognizing receipt of donations and complete any required follow-up documentation. Remember that you are building an ongoing relationship with each funder. You may ask for another grant in the future, so make sure you recognize that each contribution made a difference to your project.

10. **Establish long-term funding for your project by securing endowment grants:** Consider creating an endowment fund to manage and maintain your project once it is complete. Some foundations have funding available specifically for endowments. Having an endowment demonstrates an organization's foresight in long-range planning. A $50,000 endowment, for example, can generate 10 percent earnings, or $5,000 annually, which can then be earmarked for ongoing management and maintenance. Research any foundations that fund endowments and request funds for this purpose. Another approach is to request that some of your capital improvement grant is earmarked to the endowment fund. For example, for a $100,000 capital improvement grant request, you would request that 10 percent, or $10,000, be earmarked to the endowment

Figure 4.3. A ribbon-cutting to celebrate the opening of the Swift Creek Recycled Greenway in Cary, North Carolina.

SERVICE CLUBS. Service clubs have been great trail sponsors in a number of communities. Often they will hold fund-raisers and donate the proceeds to a trail or greenway project.

INDIVIDUAL SPONSORS. A trail sponsorship program allows for small and large donations to be received both from individuals and from businesses. The program must be well planned and organized, with design standards and associated costs established for the trail. Project elements that may be funded include trailheads, canoe launches, wayside exhibits, benches, trash receptacles, entry signage, and picnic areas. Usually, plaques recognizing the individual contributors are placed on the constructed amenities or at a prominent entry point to the trail (Figure 4.4). Ozark Greenways in Springfield, Missouri, pur

Figure 4.4. Along Florida's Pinellas Trail, a plaque recognizing a donation to the trail adorns a bench.

sued a $1.5 million campaign to fund its trails and greenways. Project planners employed a professional fund-raiser and appointed a steering committee consisting of local leaders. They raised over $100,000 from the steering committee alone.

VOLUNTEER WORK. Community volunteers may help with project construction, as well as fund-raising. Potential sources of volunteer labor in your community include bicycle or horse enthusiasts, historical groups, neighborhood associations, churches, conservation groups, scout troops, garden clubs, school groups, and civic clubs such as Kiwanis, Rotary, and Lions Clubs.

"BUY-A-FOOT" PROGRAMS. Buy-a-Foot programs have been successful in raising funds and awareness for trail projects across the country.

Under local initiatives, citizens are encouraged to purchase one linear foot of a trail by donating the cost of acquisition or construction. An excellent example of a successful endeavor is the High Point (North Carolina) Greenway Buy-a-Foot Campaign, in which linear greenway "feet" were sold at a cost of $25 per foot. Those who donated were given a T-shirt and a certificate. This project provided an estimated $5,000 in funds (Figure 4.5).

In addition to these sources, research the various funding opportunities that may be available within your area. Several states dedicate a por-

Figure 4.5. High Point Greenway Buy-a-Foot Campaign materials.

tion of their lottery receipts to open space acquisition and preservation. Other states may offer community development funds for trails that help spark urban renewal. Some trails, located near rivers or lakes, may qualify for fish and wildlife funds if the trail provides access to fishing areas. The possibilities are many, so do not underestimate the diverse resources available as you seek additional acquisition and development funding.

Successful Implementation: Public-Private Partnerships

Nationally, model trails and trail systems have emerged through developing partnerships between the public and private sectors. To be truly successful, implementation of a trail project should not become the sole responsibility of local government, but a collective pursuit that includes residents, businesses, and organizations. A public-private partnership can enable your trail to be developed in a cost-effective manner, maximizing all available resources in your community (see Case Study 10).

You should pursue the formation of a public-private partnership as part of your trail development efforts (Figure 4.6). Typically, these partnerships are an extension of a governmental agency or nonprofit organization and include up to fifteen representatives, or stakeholders, from the local community (see "Identifying Stakeholders" in Chapter 1). The partnership meets

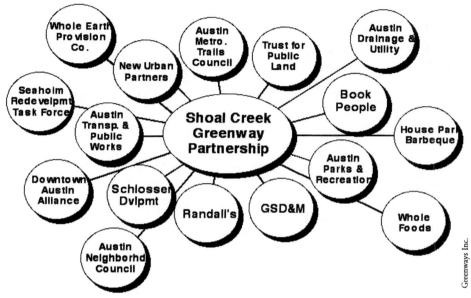

Figure 4.6. Austin's Shoal Creek Greenway partnership structure.

regularly and works to raise funds, acquire land, promote trails, and provide feedback on trail construction and management efforts. Specific roles and responsibilities of partnership members and associated agencies and organizations should be established at the onset.

Construction

After your trail design is complete, and the land has been acquired, construction documents should be developed in final preparation of groundbreaking. These documents can be com-

pleted by an engineer or registered landscape architect and contain specific guidelines for the contractor in building the trail. There are several key steps from completion of construction documents to breaking ground.

- Agency Review and Revisions: The final plans and specifications should be circulated to key interested agencies, including but not limited to drainage agencies, public works agencies, maintenance personnel, utility companies, police and fire agencies, and others who have a stake or interest in the project. Often valuable comments are received and the drawings can be revised accordingly.

TEN FUN WAYS TO FUND YOUR TRAIL

1. Rent bicycles or other equipment.
2. Sell sponsorships of feet of trail.
3. Charge concession stands a fee to operate on the trail.
4. Create a gift catalog to sell trail items.
5. Charge an entry fee for a long-distance race on the trail.
6. Ask bookstores or sporting goods stores to donate profits to the trail for one day.
7. Establish a farmer's market along the trail and charge a vendor fee.
8. Have an art show and ask artists to donate their work.
9. Hold a raffle with donated items from local businesses.
10. Charge admission to a "chowder challenge" or "blues-n-brews"(microbrewery and performers) festival

- Bidding and Bid Opening: Bidding will likely be through the responsible public agency and should be carefully monitored to assure adopted policies and procedures are followed. In general, sealed bids are submitted and are opened and read aloud. Bids are then tabulated by the administrator, and the winning contractor identified. Often your landscape architect or engineer can administer the bidding and bid-opening process.

- Contractor Approval: The bid administrator and/or your landscape architect should determine if the low bidder is in good standing, has appropriate bonding and licenses, and is capable to accept the award and build the project.

- Completion of Contract Documents: The administering agency will next assemble and execute the appropriate contract documents. They will also want to certify that the funds are available to build the project.

- Award of Contract: If all materials are in order, the agency and possibly the town council or board will approve award of contract and issue Notice to Proceed.

- Construction Observation and As-Builts: During construction, the work should be overseen by a design professional. This phase will likely include change orders and other modifications as needed. A contingency budget should be allowed for this likelihood. This may be a public agency person, your landscape architect or engineer, or a combination of both. This oversight is critical to assure a quality project and you should allow for it in your design budget. At completion of the project, the landscape architect or engineer should provide "as-built" drawings, showing the project as completed with any changes.

CASE STUDY 10
Partnering with the Private Sector

Ed McBrayer moved back to his native Atlanta in 1990 and found that, unlike the town in Colorado where he had been living, Atlanta had no trails for walking and biking. An aeronautical engineer by training, McBrayer set about to change that situation. Gathering the support of neighborhood groups and grassroots activists, the idea of building trails in Atlanta started to get some press. Up to that point, McBrayer had been putting on spaghetti dinners to raise money. Then, one day, the phone rang and McBrayer found himself talking to some of the leaders of Atlanta's business community. They liked the idea of building trails not only because they enjoyed such trails themselves but because they knew that having such a resource in Atlanta would make for a more desirable place to live and thus create a more stable workforce.

McBrayer pitched the idea to these folks, including some of Atlanta's big hitters such as Jim Kennedy of Cox Enterprises, Coca-Cola, and Turner. They offered to set up a board of directors for an organization that would spearhead trail building in Atlanta if McBrayer would quit his regular job and run the organization. He accepted the offer.

Now, ten years since the start of the PATH Foundation (www.pathfoundation.org), Ed acts as the general contractor for the trail projects. He applies to all possible public funding sources for each of these projects and then develops a capital campaign to raise money from the private sector that will be used as a match to the public funds. Jim Kennedy leads the fund-raising campaign from individuals, foundations, and corporations in the Atlanta area. Without Jim and the other eighteen board members, McBrayer says he would still be holding spaghetti dinners. To date, the board has raised over $8 million from private sources.

McBrayer finds even more support from the cities and counties in the form of in-kind contributions. These public entities turn their roadwork crews toward trail building and mainte-nance activities for the couple of months every year during the winter when roadwork ceases. The counties have also provided free fill dirt, gravel, and building permits.

While he appreciates volunteers, he finds that coordinating large volunteer activities takes more effort than the resulting work makes worthwhile, at least for major construction work. The PATH Foundation does encourage volunteer groups to adopt sections of completed trail for maintenance work.

McBrayer suggests that if a relationship with such funding partners is going to be sustained, it is critical for them to see results. Do not promise something you cannot deliver. McBrayer says his biggest problem is not in finding money for the trails he wants to build, but in waiting for the various government entities to act. Thus highlighting another virtue of having substantial private funds, it allows PATH to begin work on projects while waiting for the public funds to work through channels.

5

Managing and Maintaining Your Trail

Managing and maintaining your trail system should not be an afterthought of the planning and design process for trails. The issues of maintenance, management, and operation of the trail environment should include consideration of who should manage the trail, what type of activities are associated with successful management and maintenance, and how to design your trail so that it is easy to manage and maintain.

Who Should Manage Your Multi-Use Trail?

Determining which agency, organization, or association should manage your multi-use trail is a critical step in developing a successful project. Possibilities include local, county, state, and federal agencies, special districts, regional park authorities, nonprofit organizations, homeowners associations, joint powers authorities, and private businesses or associations. Often the choice is obvious; other times it seems as if every possible managing authority has a dozen reasons for not taking on the task. In general, determining the management for short trails is easier than doing so for long ones passing through many towns, counties, or states.

It is generally preferable to have one agency or organization, rather than a group of smaller ones, manage a multi-use trail. When managed by a single authority, the trail is more likely to have a homogeneous look, a comprehensive design, a uniform trail surface, a single set of

trail regulations, and a consistent level of maintenance along its entire length. For users, the trail experience will vary less from one community to another, and trail neighbors will be less confused about where to report problems or concerns.

On the other hand, a group of agencies or communities may be able to work together successfully when a trail runs through several jurisdictions. The key is cooperation and communication among the entities. This may be facilitated though a memorandum of understanding (MOU), a shared design and management manual, or a combination of both.

Of course, who manages the trail depends primarily on where the corridor runs and how many jurisdictions it crosses. Large agencies such as state park systems, with their advantages of size and scale, might be better suited to take on long corridors that might otherwise be fragmented or only partly developed if managed by small agencies or organizations with fewer resources and a more limited mandate. Local agencies, however, may have better rapport with local residents, landowners, and other private entities. They might also have larger amounts of available funds for management and maintenance.

Local Management

If a trail corridor is confined to one community, it may be most appropriately managed by a local agency such as a city or town department of parks, recreation, public works, or conservation,

---

TRAIL MANAGEMENT OPTIONS

- Local agency
- County agency
- State agency
- Federal agency
- Regional authority (existing or new)
- Public-public partnership
- Nonprofit organization
- Public-private partnership
- Private company or association

or even a board of supervisors or the town clerk's office. Choosing among these options is generally a matter of resources, agency commitment, orientation, and connection with other managed lands.

County and Special District Management

In general, if a corridor traverses several localities within one county, it may be best managed at the county level. A county parks department (or an equivalent agency, such as forest preserve districts in some Illinois counties and county conservation boards in Iowa) may be the most logical managing agency. If there is no county park or conservation agency in your county (as is the case in many rural areas), perhaps the county's transportation department or utility agency can manage the trail. In some cases, a county transportation or public works department develops the trail and then turns it over to a parks department for management.

Creation of a special district may be another option where the district addresses trails, open space, and other conservation benefits. In many states, a special district can be created through a vote of the residents in the district with quasi-municipal taxing and services authority that overlaps other municipal or jurisdictional lines.

State Management

Corridors that traverse more than one county are often managed best on the state level, usu-ally as state parks. Joining a state park system brings many advantages, including economy of scale, a large planning staff, diversified personnel, and often a consistent budget. The state can ensure uniformity of signs, amenities, and maintenance across county borders. Moreover, the state can plan for and develop trail extensions.

Particularly in less affluent rural areas, a state agency may more effectively preserve a unique resource of statewide interest than would local municipalities or counties trying to work together. For example, the 57-mile New River Trail State Park in the mountains of southwestern Virginia may never have been developed without the state's involvement; the small jurisdictions through which the trail passes did not have the resources to take on the project by themselves.

Of course, some people are skeptical of projects coming out of the state capital. State managing agencies may find it difficult to build a local support network. Landowners and potential users often feel more comfortable with a smaller, closer-to-home agency. For this reason, state-level trail managers should set up local advisory committees to foster community support and iron out problems at the point of conflict.

State trails don't work in every situation. Some state park systems are in such bad financial shape that they have placed a moratorium on the creation of new parks. Or your area may already have an abundance of state parks. If this is the case, a multicounty entity, special district, or regional park authority may be the answer.

Federal Management

Federal-level management is not very common for multi-use trails, although the U.S. Forest Service does manage trails within national forests that were developed from former logging railroads. Other federal multi-use trail managers include the National Park Service, the Army Corps of Engineers, and the Bureau of Land Management.

If your corridor runs across federal land, one of these agencies may well be the obvious manager, or will at least become a managing partner. If the corridor is not on public land, however, it is unlikely that a federal agency will become active as a single trail manager.

A Regional Authority

If your corridor traverses several counties but your state park agency is unable or unwilling to undertake the project, consider utilizing or forming a regional authority to manage the trail. The authority can be an existing agency, such as a council of governments, a metropolitan planning organization, a regional park authority, or a special district. Or you may want to establish a new one specifically for the trail. Two highly successful authorities that manage multi-use trails are the two-county East Bay Regional Park District, near San Francisco, and the three-county, two-city Northern Virginia Regional Park Authority, near Washington, D.C.

Regionally managed trails have all the advantages of state trails: comprehensive development, a uniform set of standards, continuity of maintenance, and greater likelihood of extension beyond the county line. In addition, the trail will be perceived as a regional rather than just a local facility, which can build public support over a broader political and geographic area. And with that support, the trail may generate higher levels of funding.

Another solution that is rapidly becoming popular is a partnership formed by different levels of government. Under one such scenario, a state transportation or natural resource agency purchases an abandoned railroad corridor with the understanding that the county or locality will develop and maintain it as a multi-use trail. Sometimes state departments of transportation purchase corridors for future road or rail use but allow them to be utilized as "interim" trails for ten, twenty, or more years. Although transportation departments typically do not want to develop and operate trails, they sometimes are willing to lease the corridors to local park agencies.

When a Single Agency Is Not Possible

If the corridor extends beyond the confines of one town, a county or state managing entity is preferable; however, if no such agency is feasible, it may be necessary to string together several local management agencies. An example of this is the Mohawk-Hudson Bikeway near Albany, New York, where three towns and two counties cooperatively—but independently—manage the 41-mile facility. Under this kind of scheme, trails usually change complexion—different signs, rules, surfaces, landscaping materials, and levels of upkeep—at each community's border.

If your trail passes through several jurisdictions but you are nevertheless unable to find or create a single managing agency, try to develop at least a cooperative management strategy for the trail. This will promote some consistency and will also establish guidelines and expectations for each agency. Some other tips to help unify the trail:

- Develop a design, management, and maintenance manual that has the support of, and will be used as a guide by, all of the entities.

- Make sure the trail has a consistent name throughout its length. (If local pride makes it necessary, individual sections can have sub-names such as "Iron Horse Trail, Montgomery County Section.")

- Make sure your trail map covers the entire length of the trail, not just the portion in your jurisdiction. (Or at least make sure all the maps of the trail are made available as a packet.)

- Support the formation of a "Friends of the Trail" organization that covers the entire facility, not just one section of it. The Friends can work to pull together bureaucracies that otherwise would not communicate (see "'Friends of the Trail' Groups," in Chapter 6).

- Periodically visit sections of the trail that are not in your jurisdiction to see and feel what average trail users experience and to get ideas of what (or what not) to do in your section. Even better, jointly sponsor a group hike, bike, or equestrian ride along the entire trail with all the other trail managers, and follow that up with a half-day discussion of all the issues affecting the trail.

Nonprofit Management

Other management possibilities include nongovernmental solutions—private foundations, land trusts, and local citizens' organizations—although this form of management is rare for a multi-use trail. While many single-use trails (e.g., hiking, equestrian, and snowmobiling trails) are run by private groups, the heavy use and complex dynamics of multi-use trails, particularly river and rail corridors, make them difficult to manage on a low budget and volunteer basis. Usually, the nongovernmental route is chosen only if no government entity can be found for the task. More often, nonprofit organizations serve a valuable role as a partner in managing and maintaining trails.

Partnering with the Private Sector

Many trails are managed through establishing partnerships between the public and private sectors in a community. Depending on the capacity of local private organizations, you might enlist local groups, homeowners associations, or local companies to perform major or minor routine maintenance tasks. Such tasks can vary from the upkeep of a wildflower plot to removing litter to regular mowing. Joint maintenance works particularly well when the corridor is shared with a utility. Often these companies are willing to do some of the maintenance.

Invite trail user organizations, community groups, civic organizations, and businesses to provide periodic maintenance work along the trail corridor as a means of improving trail safety, keeping maintenance costs down, and building goodwill with people living adjacent to the trail. An "Adopt-a-Trail" program could be established to encourage groups to improve certain areas along the trail (see Case Study 11).

Also explore the possibility of using a local conservation corps to help out with maintenance, or sponsor a summer youth program, which would provide young adults with work opportunities and expose them to the trail while providing you with a source of seasonal, temporary labor. Some communities have even used low-risk inmates from local correctional facilities to maintain trails.

Trail Management for User Safety

The most important reason to properly maintain a multi-use trail is to maximize the safety of those using the trail. A poorly maintained corridor can become a hazard to bicyclists, pedestrians, and others (and a liability problem for managers), while discouraging use and projecting a negative image of the facility and those responsible for its upkeep. Designing for maintenance up front, completing regular maintenance tasks, planning for liability protection, and undertaking measures to maximize user safety will ensure a safe, well-used multi-use trail.

Designing Trails with Maintenance in Mind

As you enter the design phase, remember that the best solution to maintenance problems is prevention. If potential problems become apparent during the planning phase, address and solve them prior to construction by preparing a comprehensive budget and management plan that includes maintenance costs. When considering maintenance costs, keep in mind this direct relationship: If you build it, you must maintain it. If you install informational and directional signs, for example, a certain percentage of them must be replaced each year. If you include an automatic sprinkler system, you will need to maintain it on a routine basis. Your trail design, therefore, must reflect the amount of money (and volunteer time) available for maintenance.

Unfortunately, maintenance dollars are difficult to secure. Foundation and government grants, while available for trail acquisition and development, are generally not available for maintenance. And it is not easy to get the public involved in raising funds for routine maintenance. The lesson is that maintenance costs are best addressed through prevention—by spending money during the design phase to avoid management problems later. For example, the single biggest cause of maintenance-related safety problems is drainage, and fixing damage caused by drainage is often the biggest line item in a maintenance budget. The solution is to solve drainage problems before a trail is built by including drainage facilities in the trail design. In the long run, it will be money well spent.

Maintenance Activities for Safety

Regular, routine maintenance on a year-to-year basis not only ensures trail safety (and reduces potential legal liability) but also prolongs the life of the trail. Maintenance activities required for safe trail operation should always receive top priority.

The following maintenance tasks are important in ensuring a safe trail facility and should be incorporated into a maintenance activity list (see "Sample Maintenance Activity List and Schedule" on page 158).

- Signs and Traffic Markings: Inspect signs for both motorists and trail users, and keep them in good condition. Make sure any pavement markings are clear and prominent.

- Sight Distance and Clearance: Do not allow sight distances, especially leading up to crossings and curves, to be impaired by vegetation. Trim trees, shrubs, and tall grass to meet sight distance requirements based on a 20-mile-per-hour trail design speed. Also, maintain adequate clearances on the sides of the trail and overhead. Trim tree branches to allow room for seasonal growth and to remove potentially dangerous overhanging dead or dying branches.

- Surface Repair: Patch or grade the trail surface on a regular basis. Ensure that finished patches are flush with the trail surface. Remove ruts and take steps to avoid their recurrence.

- Drainage: Repair any trail damage from seasonal washouts and silt or gravel washes. Identify the source of the drainage problem and take steps to remedy it. Clean all culverts, catch basins, and other drainage structures at least once a year and after major storms.

- Sweeping and Cleaning: Keep the trail free of debris, including broken glass and other sharp objects, loose gravel, leaves, and stray branches. If nearby roads are swept mechanically, make sure material is not thrown onto the trail. Frequently sweep trail edges, especially if they are made of loose material like bark or gravel.

- Ice and Snow Removal: Unless the trail is managed for skiing or snowmobiling, be sure ice and snow are properly managed. For high-use trails, this may include plowing. At a minimum, the trail should be inspected after snow or ice storms for ice buildup in potentially hazardous areas such as under bridges, in shady spots, and on slopes. Check for "black ice" (a patch of unexpected ice), which can be

extremely hazardous. Note also if there are patches of ice or snow that may force trail users off the trail and into a dangerous area, such as an adjacent street or highway.

- Structural Deterioration: Inspect structures annually to ensure they are in good condition. Pay special attention to wood foundations and posts to determine whether rot or termites are present. A thorough reporting and tracking system may reduce liability.

- Illumination: Make necessary lighting improvements, especially at busy road crossings and in tunnels. Keep lights clean and replace fixtures as required to maintain desired luminescence.

You should establish a mechanism for tracking citizen complaints and maintenance requests, or even make it easy for trail users to report problems they have found on the trail. From a liability standpoint, this is critical. Once an agency has been "put on notice" concerning a particular safety-related maintenance problem, it must correct the problem within a reasonable period of time or else it will be considered negligent.

Encourage trail users and neighbors to monitor and report maintenance problems and requests along the corridor. "Improvement Request Forms" should be available at trailheads, through user organizations, and at bicycle shops. They should also include a place for the date, the person's name and daytime telephone number, and the location and nature of the

problem. Field crews will use these forms to investigate potential maintenance problems.

Provide mile markers along the trail to use in identifying problems, and post signs with a number to call to report maintenance, safety, and security problems. Be sure there is someone to respond to maintenance concerns and follow up with both a response to the person complaining and actions taken by crews.

Risk Management Strategies

In today's society, people may be tempted to sue the managing agency for any incident that happens along the trail—regardless of fault. Although every case is different and is dependent on the specific circumstances surrounding the accident, negligence will play a key role. The law requires that the managing agency provide a reasonably safe facility. Therefore, the best solution to the liability problem is prevention: Eliminate hazardous situations before an incident occurs.

It is in your best interest to establish a risk management program that will aid you in discovering problem areas before anyone is injured and decides to sue. Risk management diminishes the potential for lawsuits, reduces insurance costs and claims, and enhances the safety of your facility.[1]

Although many risk management strategies are quite simple, they are often overlooked. First and foremost, be sure your trail conforms to state-of-the-art design standards. Examples

[1] "Risk Management: The Defensive Game Plan," *Parks and Recreation* (September 1988): 54.

include the *Guide for the Development of Bicycle Facilities,* published by the American Association of State Highway and Transportation Officials (AASHTO), as well as any applicable federal, state, and local codes, such as the Occupational Health and Safety Administration (OSHA) and Americans with Disabilities (ADA) guidelines. Be sure also to have thorough design review by key agency officials such as city engineers, public works department, maintenance crews, police and fire departments, and others who can share important expertise and experience in trail management and safety.

It is equally important to develop procedures for periodic inspection and maintenance of the trail and any support facilities. Negligence is predicated on the knowledge of a dangerous condition; governmental agencies are generally not held liable for a hazard unless they knew about it long enough before an incident occurred to have made repairs or posted warnings. For example, if a large branch has fallen across your trail and a bicyclist is injured, your agency may be less likely to be negligent if it can be proven that the branch fell a short time before the accident and that the agency routinely inspected for and removed dead or weakened overhanging branches. However, if the branch had fallen the day before and several trail users reported the hazard, then the agency would be negligent. Furthermore, if the branch had fallen several weeks earlier—even if no one reported it—the agency might be held negligent because it should have known about the hazard.

Figure 5.1. A smart risk management sign.

A second risk management principle is to provide adequate warning of risks, temporary and permanent. On multi-use trails, signs can play a key role in warning users of hazards. Place signs such as "Walk Bicycle through Underpass" or "Dismount Horse Before Crossing Bridge" in appropriate locations along your trail (Figure 5.1).

Management agencies are not the only entities that can be held liable—trail designers and developers are also at risk. If your trail was designed for a specific use, such as pedestrian-only, make sure that you provide signs to this effect in order to reduce liability. For example, if a trail is not designed to adhere to national standards for bicycle use (as described in AASHTO's *Guide for the Development of Bicycle Facilities*), but is not signed as a pedestrian-only facility,

then an agency could be held liable for improper design by a bicyclist injured on the trail.

Proper handling of a medical emergency is another important element in risk management. If someone is injured, a staff person should watch over the person while another calls for immediate help. It is wise to have staff properly trained in basic first aid and CPR, but if this is not the case, they should not attempt to treat the injured person, as they may inflict more harm. Be sure to follow up any accident with an accurate and thorough report. Failure to do so could have serious repercussions if the injured party sues. Your trail management manual should have a section on the handling of various emergencies.

A final risk management principle is documentation. Documenting regular inspections of your trail, its signs, and its support facilities can prove adherence to legal duties, which could make the difference in winning or losing a case. It is also very important to document all incidents and accidents. Try to obtain police and rescue agency reports, and keep them on file. Set up a database that contains the location, type of incident, extent of injuries or damages, treatment provided, and follow up to remedy any problems with the trail that may have been associated with the event. Use this common-sense procedure (along with the other risk management principles), and you can significantly reduce your overall chances of liability problems. That said, your ultimate protection is insurance that will pay to defend you and your agency against any lawsuit that occurs, even if it is ultimately found to be baseless.

Designing for Safety

Ideally, your trail was designed with personal safety in mind. Good design prevents many security problems. Be sure your design conforms to the standards mentioned above and that you follow a thorough and consistent design review process.

As in most parks, many security problems on trails occur in parking lots. To increase security, consider installing night security lights or gates at lot entrances. This allows for easy surveillance and patrol, and allows the lot to be closed if necessary. Fences should be installed only as a last resort, as they can discourage use by projecting a negative image. You might also think about installing night security lights at trailheads and major road crossings or activity areas if there are problems at those locations. Be sure to check with nearby residents or businesses before installing lights or making other changes. Note that many parks and trails are open only during daylight hours, and the presence of lights may encourage people to use facilities at night.

Providing security lighting along the entire length of the trail is not recommended unless the trail is anticipated to have heavy activity during evening hours (such as trails near universities). Lights are expensive to install and operate, and they often generate opposition from local homeowners adjacent to the trail. In addition, their effectiveness in reducing crime is questionable.

Consider providing emergency telephones or call box systems with direct connections to the local 911 network. The calling system may be installed at measured points along a trail and is particularly important in remote sections. This may be more effectively accomplished using a cellular phone system, especially in remote areas that do not have access to telephone lines. It will also be helpful to give the location of the call box (such as a mile marker or "street address") as well as directions to the nearest cross street or developed outpost at emergency stations.

Landscaping is also a factor in personal safety; vegetation adjacent to the trail can easily serve to hide potential offenders. Planting should be designed and maintained to minimize hiding places and allow long lines of sight. Avoid dense understory thickets near the trail. Shrubs should be appropriately groomed as required and branches should be cropped close to the trunk, at least 10 feet from the ground. Involve people of both genders and all ages in advising on vegetation management for security. (For more information, see "Landscaping" in Chapter 3).

Your trail corridor should be able to accommodate security, safety, and other emergency equipment, including fire trucks and ambulances. If you have installed motorized vehicle barriers at access points and road crossings, they should be the type that emergency vehicles can knock down, or security or safety personnel can unlock and remove, during an emergency response.

Trail Patrols

If trail security is perceived as a problem, you may want to set up a trail patrol. Although most multi-use trails do not have them, regular patrols can serve some useful functions and should be considered. A trail patrol's primary function is to provide assistance and information, not to apprehend criminals. If a serious crime does occur, members of the patrol can contact the emergency 911 network or police radios.

Trail patrols can be comprised of managing agency staff, local police, volunteers, or a combination of these (Figure 5.2). Volunteers should

Figure 5.2. A park ranger patrols Florida's Pinellas Trail on his bicycle.

Rails-to-Trails Conservancy

be properly equipped and appropriately trained to respond to medical emergencies. The use of volunteers has the added benefit of involving community members in trail operations, creating a sense of ownership. Patrol personnel should perform positive trail functions as much as possible—distributing maps and brochures, providing information, offering bicycle safety checks, and performing other service-oriented activities. Security personnel should use a bicycle or horse to patrol a trail, not a motorized vehicle. Users tend to respond favorably to someone who appears more like a trail user than a law enforcement officer.

At the beginning and end of each season, the trail patrol should conduct a field survey to measure its effectiveness and to identify potential enforcement problems. The survey, which could be done with volunteer assistance, also provides an opportunity for a count of trail users.

Trail patrols can fill another positive role: filing report forms for any incidents that occur on the trail as well as noting maintenance needs. The reports should be compiled and analyzed yearly to determine any necessary improvements in traffic control systems and patrol methods.

Where security is of particular concern, it may be advisable to form a technical security group made up of representatives from the police and fire departments, the emergency aid service, and the trail's managing agency. The security group should coordinate its trail safety roles and establish procedures for responding to emergencies. The group members should also determine how they would work together to coordinate security for special events.

Trail User Conflicts

Because they are used for a variety of purposes, multi-use trails are prone to a certain level of conflict among users, which in turn can lead to safety problems. Typically, conflicts occur on heavily used urban and suburban trails. While they may be difficult to solve, conflicts should be viewed as problems of success—an indication of the trail's popularity. It is important to document and log conflict problems in your management database. Try to identify any trends or problem spots, and remedy them if workable design or management solutions are feasible. Also try to work with user groups, such as bicycle and equestrian clubs, to identify solutions, and post "Share the Trail" and user courtesy signage along the trail and at key trailheads. Trail design can also reduce user conflicts by creating separate treads for various user types.

REGULATIONS. An important step in preventing user conflicts is the creation and adoption of trail user regulations. The regulations, developed in conjunction with trail user groups, should spell out the rules governing public conduct on the trail. They should also state the methods by which they will be enforced and the civil penalties imposed for noncompliance. Post the regulations at trailheads and include them on all trail

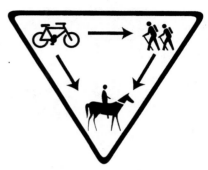

Figure 5.3. Trail etiquette sign.

brochures and maps. Unless legally required, use terms such as "trail courtesy" or "visitor responsibilities" instead of "rules and regulations."

The most common regulation for multiple-use trails is "wheels yield to heels." The self-explanatory sign shown in Figure 5.3 illustrates protocol for yielding right-of-way: bicyclists yield to all trail users, and pedestrians yield to equestrians. In addition, consider including these trail courtesy advisories:

- Be courteous to all trail users.
- Stay to the right except when passing.
- Travel at a reasonable speed in a consistent and predictable manner.
- Always look ahead and behind before passing.
- Pass slower traffic on their left; yield to oncoming traffic when passing.
- Give a clear warning signal before passing—use voice signal, not horn or bell, when passing horses.

- Keep all pets on a short leash.
- Respect the rights of adjacent property owners.
- Don't be a litterbug, and clean up after your pets.
- Move off the trail when stopped to allow others to pass.
- Yield to other users when entering and crossing the trail.
- Motorized vehicles are prohibited (except electric wheelchairs).
- Alcoholic beverages and illegal drugs are not permitted on the trail.
- Firearms, fireworks, and fires are not permitted on the trail.
- All trail users should use a light and reflectors after dusk and before dawn (if trail use is permitted at these times).
- Travel no more than two abreast.

You may also opt to establish times when the trail is closed, such as from midnight to 5:00 A.M., or from dusk to dawn.

SPEED LIMITS. A common complaint on multi-use trails is "speeding" bicyclists. But establishing a formal speed limit on trails to reduce user conflicts should be implemented only when all else fails. An effective speed limit requires consistent, ongoing enforcement, and it is unclear whether reducing the speed actually improves the real or perceived safety of the trail. Pedestrians using a trail may feel just as uncomfortable with a bicyclist passing at 12 miles per hour as at 15 miles per hour. Speed limits also may discourage those who use the trail to commute by bicycle. Finally, few bicyclists actually know the speed they are traveling. Although several multi-use trails have used speed limits effectively, consider all of these factors prior to establishing a speed limit, because it may not solve user conflicts on your trail. Speed might better be addressed through design. For example, a paved surface will encourage higher speeds than a granular stone surface. It may be worthwhile to identify alternative on-street routes for faster touring bikes and post those routes on trailhead signs.

ENFORCEMENT. Enforcement of the regulations is critical to trail safety, particularly when the trail first opens. At that time, many users of the trail are unfamiliar with the trail use etiquette. Early enforcement establishes the proper operation of the trail.

Plan to set up a system for penalizing violators of the rules. It can include fines or special duties such as trail maintenance work or other trail support activities. Reserve the stiffest penalties for safety infractions, such as speeding, failure to obey stop signs, not yielding the right-of-way, or blocking the trail. In lieu of a citation, consider offering a monthly trail safety class for violators.

However, do not assume all trail users instinctively know the rules of the trail—or the outcome if the rules are not followed. To promote goodwill on the trail, consider issuing verbal warnings to first-time offenders who may be unfamiliar with the regulations. Take time to explain why the rules were created (for example, to avoid collisions), because users will be more apt to comply with them.

Promoting Trail User Courtesy

Many managers of successful multi-use trails have promoted courtesy through encouraging compliance with regulations and cooperation among users. One of your critical roles as a trail manager will be to promote courtesy on the trail—creating a more enjoyable trail and facilitating efficient and safe circulation on the trail. One of the best ways to encourage trail user courtesy is through developing and implementing an education campaign. Several education methods are listed below.

SIGNS. Trail safety signs are one of the simplest and most effective ways to promote trail courtesy because they convey important information quickly. Develop a uniform system of trail operating and advisory signs, and post them at regular intervals along the trail. Present only one idea on each sign. Keep the message as simple as possible, and portray it so both children and adults will understand it (Figure 5.4). The signs should repeat basic trail safety and operating rules such as "Bicyclists Use Bell or Voice When Passing," "All Users Keep Right," and "Bicyclists Yield to Pedestrians." Be sure your signs con-

Figure 5.4. An innovative "Share the Trail" sign along the W&OD Railroad Regional Park.

form to the guidelines in the federal *Manual of Uniform Traffic Control Devices (MUTCD)*.

PRINTED MATERIALS. Brochures, pamphlets, and newsletters displayed along the trail route, at trailheads, and at ranger stations can help cultivate a positive user ethic. Trail regulations should be printed in all publications to reinforce trail courtesy. Be sure to post a copy of the trail user regulations at each trailhead and major rest stop to inform all users of trail rules.

Trail maps can be a tool for encouraging courtesy in a different way. Maps should include alternate routes (on parallel roads) and should suggest that fast bicyclists who may have "outgrown" the trail may find riding on the streets faster and more satisfying. Maps can be posted at trail intersections, directing fast bicyclists to alternate routes. The focus should always be on speed, not on the type of bicyclist.

SAFETY DAYS. Trail Safety Days are an enjoyable way to promote safety and courtesy. Have volunteers set up a trailside stand once a month during the trail's busiest season to provide free refreshments, safety literature, copies of the trail user regulations, brochures on helmet safety, and information concerning membership in area bicycle, equestrian, hiking, and walking organizations. During Safety Day, local law enforcement officers can perform radar-gun checks to provide riders with their actual speeds and can help them with bicycle safety checks and maintenance assistance. Generally, the program requires volunteers with safety and equipment experience, printed safety materials, and a modest service and refreshment budget.

PRESENTATIONS. Recreation clubs, schools, environmental organizations, civic groups, and religious and service organizations typically hold regular meetings and often seek interesting speakers. Consider making presentations to local clubs and schools as a way to reach out to potential trail users. The presentations allow you to introduce the trail to many people while educating them about trail use. You can foster trail courtesy even before trail users get on the trail.

Make presentations compelling by tailoring them to your audience. Particularly for children, use innovative instruction methods. For example, set up a mock trail on the school playground—complete with lines, obstructions, and signs—and then invite students to help demonstrate safe riding and walking practices. Set up a few conflicts to illustrate why the regulations were established, and then discuss how the conflicts could have been avoided.

School-age children make up a large percentage of potential trail users. If they are excited by your presentation, they will no doubt share the information with their families and friends.

PUBLIC HEARINGS. Hearings regarding trail policy changes or budget needs should be viewed as opportunities for a two-way exchange. Encourage individuals to voice concerns about user conflicts in a constructive way, and, as the manager, take the opportunity to explain conflict-prevention techniques and encourage courtesy.

MASS MEDIA. Use the media to promote courteous trail behavior. Radio, television, cable, and newspaper features can provide an effective, legitimate means of disseminating information to large numbers of people. Every publicity opportunity or media story should include proper trail use information, so show people riding and walking safely and courteously along the trail. Also, don't forget that many local recreation clubs and civic groups have newsletters and other publications that could serve as an outlet for trail information.

Maintaining Good Relations with Adjacent Landowners, Residents, and Businesses

If you followed some of the techniques to involve adjacent landowners, residents, and businesses in the trail planning process, you should not have much difficulty in maintaining good relations with them now (see "Meeting the Needs of Adjacent Landowners" in Chapter 2). If you did not use these techniques, or you still have considerable opposition, managing the trail properly and working with the landowners from now on will likely neutralize opposition and may even turn opponents into supporters.

Once a trail is open, many ardent opponents realize that their fears are unfounded and begin to recognize that the trail is a good neighbor as well as a nice amenity. In addition, some adjacent landowners may gain unanticipated social and economic benefits from the trail and suddenly become avid supporters. The owner of a bed-and-breakfast along Missouri's Katy Trail State Park, who was nervous about the trail's opening, now supports it, particularly since her business has doubled since the trail's development. Landowners and adjacent tenants can be good allies, so it is critical

to sustain and cultivate your relationships with them. They can become the "eyes and ears" of the trail and should be encouraged to play this role.

An important first step is to be sure that all adjacent owners and tenants know whom to contact about specific problems. Provide them with appropriate names and phone numbers at the trail's managing agency so they can more readily report a problem or make a suggestion. Keep a log of reports, complaints, and suggestions, and be sure to follow up with a phone call letting them know you are aware of their concern and how you intend to address it. Document the calls and follow-up actions. Remember that frequent communication is the cornerstone of successful relations with landowners. Make sure you listen to their comments, involve them in any new trail developments, respond to their needs, and maintain consistency in your discussions with them.

Always make sure the trail is maintained on a regular basis. The issues most likely to cause continuing concerns for adjacent residents are maintenance related—overgrown weeds, fallen and overhanging trees, and insufficient vegetative screening to buffer homes from the trail. Most of these problems can be solved through routine maintenance. If you do not already have a regular maintenance schedule in place, take steps to establish one (see "Maintenance Activities for Safety" earlier in this chapter). It should include a timetable for performing all aspects of trail maintenance, ranging from trash pickup to tree pruning. If possible, print the schedule and distribute it to trail neighbors.

There may be lingering problems such as unauthorized motorized vehicle use and vandalism, theft of trail-related signs, or graffiti on the trail corridor. Respond to these problems promptly. Consistent, quality upkeep of the trail corridor will build trail neighbors' confidence in your agency's ability to manage the trail. You can also build landowners' confidence by scheduling periodic meetings with them to provide an outlet for any continuing concerns.

Establish a mechanism for regular input from users and landowners, as mentioned earlier. For example, the Baltimore and Annapolis Trail in Anne Arundel County, Maryland, developed a "Good Neighbor Program" to encourage landowners to point out problems and make requests to the managing agency. The Anne Arundel County Department of Parks and Recreation staff makes periodic personal contact with each landowner. This visit is followed up with a mailing that includes general trail information (including the department's mailing address and phone number) as well as a pamphlet explaining the department's commitment to excellence and desire to be a good neighbor. The county asks the landowners to reciprocate the good-neighbor policy. The department's staff members, who are committed to listening to every comment, build landowners' confidence by responding promptly and fairly. Although the department cannot accommodate every request, it does its best to reach a mutually

acceptable solution. One of the trail's rangers has said, "Through the use of this program, landowners who were initially against the trail's construction are now our most ardent fans."

Another approach is to invite the landowners on a trail tour led by a park ranger. This gives the adjacent residents a firsthand opportunity to point out any continuing problem areas, while providing your agency a chance to showcase the wonderful facility landowners have in their own backyards. If they have not previously been on the trail, the tour may improve their view of it. They will be able to see the types of people who use the trail, and they will also view improvements that have been made along the corridor.

Still another way to win the support of landowners is to write personal letters, particularly to those residents not yet convinced of the trail's benefits. If you have received letters from local citizens supporting the trail, you might enclose a copy of one. Also, if time and money permit, send them invitations to any special events along the corridor, including trail extensions, dedications of trail support facilities, and trail festivals. These small gestures can go a long way toward maintaining good relations with adjacent landowners. The manager of the Cannon Valley Trail in southeastern Minnesota sends holiday greeting cards to residents living along his 19-mile trail.

In addition to dealing with the concerns of adjacent landowners and working to maintain good relations, you may encounter problems *caused by* adjacent residents. You will need to

handle these in a consistent and efficient manner to prevent them from getting out of control.

The main problems you will likely face are encroachment and damage—for example, landowners dumping lawn clippings on trail property, illegally using the corridor for private access, and making cuts in fences to gain trail access. The best way to overcome these problems is to set clear boundaries between the trail and private property and to make these borders known to all landowners. Take time to use some of the previously mentioned strategies (letter writing, personal visits) to encourage landowners to comply with rules and regulations of the trail. In addition, instruct patrols to watch problem areas and enforce the boundaries.

If you are unable to work out an agreement informally, you may opt to develop a lease arrangement for nontrail uses. In this arrangement the landowner is allowed continued encroachment, but he or she is charged a fee for this private use of the corridor. The lease should be a one-year, renewable agreement including a set fee. This fee would be used to cover maintenance costs or any minor damage caused by the landowner.

If this is not appropriate in your situation or if the problems persist, you may need to take a stronger stance to protect the trail. If issuing fines to violators does not alleviate the problem, you may need to consider legal action. Whatever the case, make it public knowledge—through the media, if possible—that you will not condone any inappropriate activities and that you will take serious action against illegal activities.

Developing a Fee Structure

One management issue you should consider is whether to charge fees for the use of your multi-use trail. You need to weigh the revenue possibilities with the time and effort involved in administering fees, as well as the impact a fee may have on trail use. And don't forget that fees are potentially applicable not only to trail users but also to nontrail uses within the corridor.

Trail Users: To Fee or Not to Fee?

Before deciding whether to charge a fee for use of the trail, consider the advantages and disadvantages of doing so. On the positive side, fees can generate income for trail maintenance or additional trail development. Also, by paying a fee, users may develop a stronger commitment or sense of stewardship to the trail. Depending on the structure of the fee collection system, you may collect thousands of trail users' names, which could be used in a trail activist mailing list or possibly a fund-raising list.

On the other hand, administering a fee program may cost more money than it raises, and payment may be difficult to enforce, especially if the trail has many access points. In addition, if the trail was built with taxpayers' money, local residents may protest against paying for what they perceive as a public facility, which will serve to decrease use and popularity of the facility. You may want to consider a volunteer fee system to raise funds. For example, sell a badge or bike "sticker" that says "I helped build the XYZ Trail."

If your trail is part of a large managing agency, you may have little choice about fees. The Little Miami Scenic State Park trail, for example, is part of the Ohio State Park system, and state law prohibits user fees for any Ohio state park. In contrast, several multi-use trails in Wisconsin are required by law to charge a user fee as part of that state's park system.

The following are some issues you need to address when setting up a fee structure and developing a trail use permit.

Sample Fee Structure

It is best to offer several fee options for trail users, such as $2 per day for an individual, $5 per day for a family, $8 per year for an individual, and $20 per year for a family. An annual pass option allows local trail users to enjoy the trail as often as they like for a low cost and encourages visitors to return. These prices are the average charged by several rail-trails around the nation.

Some fee structures include a higher rate for out-of-state users. The trails in Wisconsin had such an arrangement for several years, but the state decided that all users would pay the same fees to make enforcement and administration easier.

In 1991, the state of Wisconsin, which manages about ten rail-trails, raised almost $150,000 through trail pass sales. Administration costs to collect these fees are estimated at approximately $45,000, or 30 percent of the income.

If you do offer an annual trail pass, decide whether it is valid for one year from the date purchased or only for the calendar year. First-time trail users and visitors are more likely to buy an annual pass if they can use it for an entire year beginning on the purchase date.

Whom to Charge?

Different trail managers have made different decisions about who should pay a fee. On some trails, all users pay; on others, only bicyclists pay. And in some cases, all users except pedestrians (hikers, walkers, runners, and people in wheelchairs) pay to use the trail. In many cases, winter users such as snowmobilers are not charged a trail use fee because they are required to pay a registration fee that entitles them to free access to trails. Some managers base their decisions on who has the greatest impact on the trail. Managers of Iowa's Heritage Trail provided free trail passes to adjacent landowners for the first two years to build good relations with them.

Selling Trail Permits

If you do opt for a fee structure, you need to develop a system whereby trail users can prove they paid to use the trail. The best option is to develop a "permit," a pass sold at various locations that represents payment of the fee. Make the permits a size that can easily fit into a pocket or wallet. Make it as easy as possible for trail users to pay for user permits. They should be available for purchase at trailheads and at managing agency offices.

Encourage local businesses (including restaurants, bicycle stores, chambers of commerce, visitors' centers, and grocery stores) to sell trail passes. Most merchants are happy to offer this service because it brings in customers. In addition, trail rangers and people patrolling the trail should carry passes with them and offer them for sale to anyone who failed to buy one. You can make trail passes available through the mail. The state of Wisconsin set up a telephone and mail-order system so people can buy them in advance of their visit to a trail—and use a credit card to pay. You can also sell trail permits through your Web site (see "Using a Web Site to Market Your Trail" in Chapter 6).

Making Trail Users Aware of the Fee

Trail users (particularly first-time visitors) will not necessarily know that they need to obtain a trail use permit, so you need to inform them that a fee is required. You should post signs or notices at every trail access point. Post the daily fee as well as any annual fee, and include a list of locations where users can purchase permits. Also, setting up self-service registration stations at trail access points also forces people to take notice. Fees should be listed in any trail-related literature and on your Web site.

To broaden awareness, undertake additional promotion. Have local stores, restaurants, and chambers of commerce post signs such as "Get Your Trail Pass Here!" The signs will remind people that they need a permit before they get onto the trail. Consider distributing free trail passes at local festivals, presentations, or other promotional events.

Enforcement

If you really want your fee structure to succeed, you will have to enforce it, although there is no need to be heavy-handed, particularly with first-time violators. Most users who do not purchase a trail pass probably do not know one is necessary. Anyone who patrols the trail (or maintains it) can periodically ask to see trail use permits and can sell permits to those who lack one. If someone repeatedly uses the trail without a pass, you may need to issue a citation.

Joint Ventures within Your Multi-Use Trail Corridor

In the course of developing and managing your multi-use trail, you will likely encounter agencies, companies, and individuals who are interested in your trail for nontrail purposes. For example, neighboring homeowners wanting to expand their gardens onto trail property, utility companies proposing to place cables underground or overhead, or highway departments planning to construct a road across the trail would all be interested parties.

These nontrail interests may present chal-

lenges as the trail is developed and managed. Nontrail uses may threaten the linear integrity of the multi-use trail and may disturb its natural, scenic, and historic qualities. However, such uses are the result of growth in an area, so you need to develop a strategy for dealing with them and benefiting from them. Although your first priority should be to develop a high-quality trail facility, you should also consider the financial benefits of accommodating nontrail uses within the right-of-way.

Potentially Compatible Nontrail Uses

The Northern Virginia Regional Park Authority (NVRPA) owns and manages the Washington and Old Dominion (W&OD) Regional Railroad Park, a 45-mile multi-use trail developed from a former rail line. The authority has established a set of policies and procedures as well as a comprehensive licensing program to address all nontrail requests. Through coordinated planning, stringent standards, and close supervision, NVRPA has discovered not only that many uses are compatible with the trail, but that joint ventures can provide the trail with a new source of revenue.

As you plan your trail corridor, consider the following examples of potentially compatible uses that might generate income.

- Telephone cables
- Fiber-optic communication cables
- Cable television wires
- Gas pipelines

Figure 5.5. Bicyclists enjoy a utility trail developed within an electric company easement.

- Sanitary sewers
- Electric transmission and distribution lines
- Water transmission lines
- Low-volume driveways and agricultural access
- Garden plots
- Private parking lots
- Storage areas
- Road crossings, with grade-separation or with crossing signal
- Private trail connectors

A few of these uses may not be appropriate along your multi-use trail, but many others may prove compatible (Figure 5.5).

Compensation

In exchange for access to the corridor, you should seek compensation from utility companies, agencies, and adjacent landowners. The fact that your corridor has already been established makes it very valuable to utility companies. In many cases, your right-of-way may be the only continuous passage along which an agency or company can lay its cables or pipelines. Without your corridor, the utility may be forced to purchase numerous easements over private property. Clearly, your trail can benefit financially from such joint uses.

FEE STRUCTURE. Through its licensing program, the Northern Virginia Regional Park Authority has gained fair compensation for use of the W&OD trail corridor while it regulates and controls nontrail uses and protects the linear nature of the trail. The licensing program serves other uses as well: It discourages unnecessary encroachments, controls activities of licensees, minimizes inconvenience to trail users, reduces damage to the trail facility, defines standards for construction, and enables the authority to recover its administrative and overhead costs and to receive appropriate compensation.[2] The authority administers and collects fees through license agreements, which often need to be renewed annually. It also attempts to recover 100 percent of its costs. Beginning in the late 1980s, NVRPA received approximately $450,000 per year from fiber-optics license fees, onetime and recurring

rental fees (primarily for businesses using adjacent property), and administrative and review fees.

Be creative when working with companies, agencies, or individuals interested in using your trail corridor. In addition to the collection of fees, consider the following ways that your trail might benefit from nontrail uses.

LAND-USE FEES. Fees can be charged for use of trail lands for utility lines, landowner encroachments, and other purposes. This can be either a onetime payment or, ideally, a renewable rental agreement. In Montgomery County, Maryland, a local power company agreed to pay $100,000 for development of a portion of the Capital Crescent Trail in exchange for placing power lines near the corridor.

TRAIL IMPROVEMENTS. A corporation may agree to upgrade your trail in exchange for access to the property. In the East Bay region near San Francisco, a development company agreed to pave a portion of the Iron Horse Regional Trail (at an estimated cost of $350,000) in return for trail access to their office complex adjacent to the trail corridor. Other trail improvements that could serve as compensation include trailheads, parking areas, bridges, underpasses, and shelters.

OVERPASS OR UNDERPASS. If a transportation department plans to develop a road across your right-of-way, lobby for the creation of a trail bridge or tunnel traversing the road to provide a

[2] Northern Virginia Park Authority, *Manual on Policies and Procedures Governing Easements and Licenses and Non-Park Uses of Northern Virginia Park Authority Property* (Fairfax, VA: NVRPA, 1989), I:3.

safe crossing. A trail bisected by a roadway can serve as both a barrier to trail use and a safety hazard, if appropriate crossing facilities are not provided.

ADJACENT USE FEES. Local residents often like to make use of the land between the trail and their properties. Charge a small fee for them to use the land. Landowners adjacent to the W&OD Railroad Regional Park, for example, pay a $25 annual fee for garden plots within the right-of-way. A similar arrangement can be developed for private driveways, outdoor eating areas at a restaurant, or spots for a snack bar or vending kiosk.

Basically, do not underestimate the value of your trail corridor. A clear tract of linear space, particularly in a developing area, is extremely precious. Joint use of a corridor for trail and utility purposes can be mutually beneficial to all parties involved.

Protect Your Trail in the Face of Change

Changes in land-use patterns along your trail corridor are probably inevitable. Some, such as the creation of new parks or adjoining trails, may enhance the trail experience. Others, such as construction of new highway crossings or adjacent industrial sites, may significantly degrade it. Regardless of the type of change, if you are armed with a protection strategy and a base of public support for the trail, you will be better equipped to anticipate and manage change in a way that protects your trail's special qualities for present and future generations. Managers of the Wabash Cannonball Trail in Ohio have adopted a stewardship plan that outlines actions to be taken to protect the trail now and in the future, as development in the area continues.

Establishing a Trail Protection Policy

The entire right-of-way in which your trail lies may be only 100 feet wide or less, making it vulnerable to the negative impacts of surrounding development. A single highway crossing can sever a trail's continuity. Even smaller encroachments, such as adjacent buildings overlapping a corridor's boundary or private driveways bisecting the trail, can add up to an overall degradation of the trail experience. Inappropriate uses of your corridor can create safety hazards, increase maintenance needs, decrease aesthetic appeal, diminish land values, add legal liabilities, and limit future management options.

You cannot stop development, but you can prevent it from damaging your trail corridor by establishing a strong trail protection policy. The policy must set forth the "paramount," or primary, use of the corridor—recreation, transportation, or historic preservation. Any use of the trail corridor deemed incompatible with its paramount use will be denied; those compatible with the primary use will be considered and, if approved, carefully regulated.

Fiber-optic cables, sewer pipes, and water lines, for example, are well suited for placement along a recreational or commuter trail because they are underground and do not impede activities along it. But constructing a four-lane highway across a trail with no grade separation would bisect a trail, destroying its linear continuity. This is not a compatible use.

You should take steps as soon as possible to set up a truly comprehensive trail protection policy that will provide you with the authority to do the following:

- Regulate all nonparamount uses of the trail corridor in a fair and consistent manner.

- Minimize inconvenience to trail patrons, and assure protection of wildlife habitat and natural and historic resources within the trail corridor.

- Minimize damage to the trail corridor at all times.

- Establish uniform standards for construction and restoration of the trail corridor if it is damaged by a nonparamount use.

- Ensure that your agency recovers all its administrative costs and receives appropriate compensation for use of, or damage to, the trail corridor by nonparamount uses.

- Inform all public and private interests of the expectations and intentions of the trail managing agency with respect to nonparamount uses.

- Issue permits and licenses for nonparamount uses; prohibit the transfer of ownership rights through the use of easements or other mechanisms.

If you include each of the points listed above, you will have crafted a trail protection policy that is strong enough to deny harmful nonprimary uses but flexible enough to allow compatible—or even beneficial—uses. For example, you might oppose a transportation department's specific design proposal to build a road across a trail corridor, if you have determined that elements of the design would have damaging effects on trail use. However, you might approve the telephone company's proposal to pay your agency an annual fee for the right to bury and maintain a fiber-optics cable under the trail. Some trails are now allowing cell-phone towers to be built in the right-of-way as well.

If your agency does not hold full title to your trail corridor, your trail protection options may be more limited. If, for instance, your agency has a recreational easement over adjacent, privately owned land, you may not have the legal right to control other uses of that land even if it extends into the corridor.

In any event, you should communicate with all parties who have an interest in the trail corridor. You should know who holds limited title to the corridor, including individuals, local planning commission members, the department of transportation, area developers, elected officials, and recreational and environmental groups. By developing a relationship with each of these parties, you will be in a better position to discover and defuse proposed actions that may negatively impact the integrity of your trail corridor.

Regardless of the status of your agency's ownership in the corridor, a supportive citizen-based "Friends of the Trail" group may ultimately be your trail corridor's best protection. Even with a strong trail protection policy in place, your agency is probably susceptible to the political pressures that developers, commercial interests, or even adjacent landowners claiming reversionary rights can put on elected officials or pursue in the courts. Widespread, organized citizen opposition to adverse proposals, and financial support to build a legal war chest to help resist actions that would negatively impact the trail, are very effective ways to protect it (see "'Friends of the Trail' Groups" in Chapter 6).

Land Uses Adjacent to the Trail Corridor

Regulation of uses outside the corridor that adversely affect the trail's integrity is important but difficult to achieve. Problems include runoff from construction activities, deterioration of scenic vistas and viewsheds because of encroaching development, noise from development and traffic, and deterioration of wildlife habitat stemming from the loss of adjoining natural areas and open space. Some of these problems can be addressed through local planning processes and permit approval procedures for residential and commercial development. By monitoring proposals for development adjacent to the trail corridor, you may be able to work effectively with developers or with other government officials. You can also make requests for license and permit conditions that will ameliorate many of the harmful effects of a proposed development on the trail corridor.

Protection of scenic vistas and viewsheds and adjoining open space and wildlife habitat poses special and often complex problems. Two approaches are possible: Seek to protect an entire viewshed or whatever can be seen from a particular vantage point; or protect discrete ecological units, such as the area between your trail corridor and a river or a wetland adjacent to the trail corridor.

You may be able to gain some viewshed protection through federally financed or approved projects under statutes like section 102 of the National Environmental Policy Act and section 106 of the National Historic Preservation Act. However, most protection of vistas and adjoining open space, especially when related to private development, is a matter of state and local law. Thus, whatever your goal—preserving scenic vistas, maintaining a buffer zone, or safeguarding an ecological unit—you need to work within applicable laws.

Two basic legal mechanisms are available. One is zoning and land-use regulation to preserve open space. Explore such zoning categories as shoreline, floodplains, park, open space, and residential. Keep in mind, however, that "down zoning" (changing zoning from high-density to low-density use) can be a political hot potato and should not be pursued without neighborhood and property owner support. The other mechanism consists of programs to acquire or encourage the donation of development easements that restrict adjoining property to such uses as farmland, woodland, and low-density residential areas (see "Strategies to Acquire Land" in Chapter 4). Homeowners associations can also own and maintain open spaces adjacent to your trail.

Developing a Comprehensive Budget and Management Plan

Prior to construction of the trail facility, you should develop a comprehensive budget and management plan that includes all the activities and costs of maintaining the trail. This will ensure that your trail is well maintained, thereby minimizing safety risks to users, potential liability, and unexpected costs.

Key Factors

In this section, typical costs for several minor and major maintenance activities are provided. These are general estimates that can vary greatly from one trail to another. In order to estimate more accurate costs for maintaining your trail, you will need to develop a customized budget and maintenance plan. Keep in mind that developing an accurate maintenance budget is a step-by-step process, not an exact science. Differences in bookkeeping methods, wages, trail design, topography, availability of maintenance equipment, community expectations, and a host of other variables make it impossible to say categorically that a certain type of trail will have fixed maintenance costs per mile per year. Two identical trails in different communities may have radically different per-mile maintenance costs. Even so, it is feasible to develop a useful estimate of maintenance costs for a particular trail system if the following components are included.

EXISTING COSTS. An easy first step is to check the current per-mile cost for maintaining a similar existing trail in a similar community. (If your trail is the first in your area, check with a neighboring jurisdiction.) Get the maintenance costs for a trail that is nearby and analogous to your project; cost figures from distant trails may not be relevant.

When obtaining cost information, go over the budget with someone who can explain all the items included. For example, does the budget include labor and overhead costs? Does it include onetime costs on major equipment such as sweepers and trucks? Does it include charges for bringing debris to the local landfill? Do volunteers do some maintenance? Every agency budgets differently, and the answers to these questions often explain the discrepancies in per-mile maintenance for similar trails.

BOOKKEEPING. A second important step is to find out how your trail managing agency assigns charges to various maintenance activities. In particular, you will want to look at major equipment, labor, and overhead costs. If you need to purchase a sweeper for trail maintenance, for example, there may be a separate capital fund to

TYPICAL ANNUAL MAINTENANCE COSTS FOR A 1-MILE PAVED TRAIL
(based on national average; costs will vary for individual trails)

Drainage and storm channel maintenance	$ 500
Sweeping/blowing debris off trail tread	1,200
Pickup and removal of trash	1,200
Weed control and vegetation management	1,000
Mowing of 3-foot grass shoulder along trail	1,200
Minor repairs to trail furniture/safety features	500
Maintenance supplies for work crews	300
Equipment fuel and repairs	600
TOTAL	$6,500

TYPICAL COSTS OF RESURFACING TRAILS

(based on national averages; costs will vary)

Asphalt	$10 per linear foot
	($5 per linear foot to overlay
	with top coat)
Concrete	$25 per linear foot
Crushed stone	$5 per linear foot

pay for it, in which case you pay only the labor costs of the operator. Or the trail maintenance budget may be charged a per-hour fee that covers the amortized lifetime costs associated with the sweeper's purchase and maintenance. Labor and overhead costs can also vary greatly. The cost of a maintenance employee making $10 an hour may actually be charged to the budget at $20 an hour if all overhead costs are included. Some agencies maintain separate budgets for benefits, office space, and management support, while others account for these items as per-hour labor costs. The bottom line is that all agencies keep their books differently, so be sure you know how yours are set up. The bookkeeping methods used by the agency managing your trail will have a major impact on how you develop a maintenance budget.

MAINTENANCE CHECKLIST AND COST. The next step in developing a budget and plan is to create a checklist of all possible maintenance activities. Begin by listing every aspect of the trail's design. Don't forget to include costs for equipment, repair to equipment, fuel, and supplies. Also consider the long-term replacement costs of such major trail components as trail surfaces, bridges, and retaining walls. Once again, the general rule is that you will have to maintain whatever you build. Next to each maintenance activity, list its frequency, its cost per application, and the resulting annual cost. Calculating the annual cost may seem like a lot of work, but

you can do it if you understand the bookkeeping system and how charges will be assigned.

Sample Maintenance Activity List and Schedule

LIST OF MAINTENANCE ACTIVITIES. Consider this partial list of maintenance activities as you develop your maintenance budget and plan. Of course, you will need to modify it to reflect the needs and community expectations of your particular trail.

- Replace missing and damaged regulatory and directional signs.
- Repaint worn pavement markings.
- Trim trees, shrubs, and grass to maintain sight distances.
- Patch holes, fill cracks, and feather edges.
- Clean drainage systems; modify to eliminate ponding.
- Sweep to remove leaves, mud, gravel, and other debris.
- Mow trail shoulders (2 feet, 6 inches to 5 feet back from trail).
- Mow other selected areas where groomed look is desired.
- Pick up trash; empty trash cans.
- Clean out ditches, culverts, and other drainage structures.
- Maintain furniture and other support facilities.
- Clean rest rooms and drinking fountains; repair as needed.

- Remove graffiti from rest rooms, retaining walls, rocks, and other surfaces.
- Prune dense understory growth to promote user safety.
- Inspect structures for deterioration.
- Remove fallen trees.
- Clean and replace lights (in tunnels and at road crossings).
- Spray for weed control.
- Remove snow and ice.
- Maintain emergency telephones.
- Maintain irrigation lines.
- Install and remove snow fences.

ROUTINE AND REMEDIAL (MAJOR) MAINTE-NANCE. Once you have completed a draft list of maintenance activities, divide them into "routine" and "remedial" (major) maintenance categories. In general, frequent maintenance activities such as mowing are considered routine (Figure 5.6). Activities done once every several years, such as repaving a trail surface, fall under remedial maintenance. Although remedial maintenance is needed only infrequently, it should be budgeted on an annual basis to avoid the periodic need for a major infusion of cash. (See "Funding Sources for Trail Development" in Chapter 4 for maintenance funding source ideas.)

MAINTENANCE PRIORITIES. The next step is to set maintenance priorities by identifying which

Figure 5.6. Trailside maintenance along the Baltimore and Annapolis Trail in Maryland.

activities are critical to the trail's safe operation and which are key to other objectives, such as maintaining the infrastructure, protecting the environment, and protecting the overall appearance of the area.

While some priorities may vary according to local community expectations and the trail's needs, safe operation of the trail should never be compromised (see "Maintenance Activities for Safety" in this chapter). Trail maintenance should conform to the design guidelines used to build the trail. And where proper guidelines were not used, maintenance should include improvements that will enhance the trail's safety and operation.

MAINTENANCE SCHEDULE. The final task in developing a budget and management plan is to

create a schedule that ensures the timely and systematic completion of all maintenance activities. You will probably want to develop a schedule for field crews and volunteers that includes instructions on each maintenance activity and its frequency. You should also develop a system for requesting specific maintenance improvements, such as sign replacement, and a standardized work instruction form.

While there are no exact rules for calculating the frequency of maintenance activities, the guidelines in Tables 5.1 and 5.2 apply. Again,

Table 5.1. Resurfacing

Surface	Schedule
Asphalt	Every 7–15 years (resurface with top coat and replace sections)
Concrete	Every 20+ years
Boardwalk	Every 5–7 years (replace boards)
Wood chips	Every year (6 inches of wood chips)
Crushed stone	Every 7–10 years (with frequent repair)

Table 5.2. Routine Maintenance

Task	Schedule
Drainage/channel maintenance	3–5 times a year
Sweeping/blowing debris	16–24 times a year
Trash removal	16–24 times a year
Vegetation management	8–12 times a year
Mowing of shoulders	8–24 times a year

your maintenance schedule will vary based upon climate, site conditions, quality of construction, the type and amount of trail surface and amenities, level of use, and other factors.

Once the above steps have been completed, the budget and plan are ready to be put in final form. You should include a checklist of all maintenance items, the frequency of each activity as well as each activity's annual cost, and the individuals who will perform the activities. Priorities related to safe operation of the trail should be clearly identified and a tracking procedure clearly outlined.

CASE STUDY 11
Volunteer Maintenance along the Trail

Enlisting volunteer assistance to maintain trails can reduce the costs of maintenance and provide members of the community with a feeling of pride and a sense of ownership of the trail. The Lower Trail in Pennsylvania and the Musketawa Trail in Michigan provide two very different approaches for establishing volunteer maintenance help.

Rails-to-Trails of Central Pennsylvania (RTCPA), a nonprofit organization, owns the Lower Trail and is responsible for maintenance and management. From the genesis of the project, cleanup was a primary concern. Tires and other trash littered the abandoned railroad corridor, and animal carcasses left by poachers polluted waters of the canal that paralleled the trail. The trail also abuts a steep bank that had become a popular dumping ground for passing drivers. While the bank is not a part of the trail, the group organized a cleanup of the area.

RTCPA relies heavily on its membership of 602 people. Their mantra is "membership means ownership," and everyone must pitch in to help maintain the trail. The volunteer program is informal and requires no contracts, but a list of on-call volunteers is maintained. They have a diehard mowing crew of 10 people whose average age is 72. With approximately 23 acres of grass to mow, that is quite an accomplishment. On designated workdays, other members help with routine maintenance—chopping fallen trees and collecting branches—or special projects such as building rain shelters.

The Friends of the Musketawa Trail work with the Michigan Department of Natural Resources to help maintain the trail. To do this, they established a formal Adopt-a-Trail program to encourage community participation along the 26-mile trail that passes farmlands, wetlands, creeks, and villages. Any organization with six or more participants may apply to adopt a section of the trail for a two-year period. Trail crews work with the Musketawa trail manager to choose projects, such as planting trees and flowers, picking up litter, cleaning and repairing benches and picnic tables, and maintaining bird houses. Safety rules, safety vests, refuse bags, refuse pickup, a recognition sign, and an adoption certificate are provided to each group.

6

Maximizing Your Trail's Potential

Promoting and Marketing Your Trail

With so much time devoted to planning, designing, building, and managing your trail, you may not have thought about how to promote and market it. But promotion and marketing are key ingredients of a successful multi-use trail. Developing an effective promotion campaign will take time and thought, but you may be surprised to learn how much you enjoy spreading the word about your trail.

Why Publicity Is Important

Planners and Managers of multi-use trails commonly decry their lack of money. Yet often the real problem is lack of public support, which usually stems from the public's lack of knowledge about the trail or trail project. Therefore, public awareness is critical and can be increased through a variety of ways.

Your initial task is to determine how much publicity you want, because it is possible to get too much. For example, a national magazine article highlighting your trail could bring more trail users than you can handle. On the other hand, if you want to attract tourists to your area, widespread press may be a big benefit.

To determine the amount and type of exposure your trail needs, decide what audience you want to reach. People living in towns near the trail? Regional residents? Potential users throughout the state or nation? If your trail is still in its infancy, your audience will be pretty close to home. Consider the following reasons why it may be important to publicize your trail:

- *Your trail is not completed and needs increased support to get funding and visibility.* Often, when a trail project gets under way, the public assumes that it will be completed. Be sure people are aware that the trail is a "work in progress." Use the press, the Web, and other media to provide periodic updates that will keep the public excited about day-to-day or month-to-month operations of the project.

- *Your trail is complete and you want to celebrate its opening.* All the hard work finally pays off when a trail is complete, and you should call attention to this milestone. Be sure that all the communities along the trail (including any remaining opponents) are aware of any festivities, so that they assume a sense of trail "ownership" from the outset.

- *Your trail is open but not well known, and you want to increase its level of activity.* If your trail does not get much use, it may be because not enough people know about it. You have to tell the public about the opportunities your trail offers. A trail also may not be used because it is in an out-of-the-way location or because it passes through unattractive terrain. In these cases, request ideas for improvement from the public while pointing out the trail's positive aspects.

- *Your trail is open but "misused."* Misuse can range from litter to graffiti, and from speeding bicyclists to unauthorized vehicles on the trail. Publicizing "proper" trail use can go a long way toward preventing these problems. People respond better to explanations than to scolding: Litter detracts from the trail and can damage the environment; speeding cyclists can frighten senior citizens or injure an unsuspecting child; certain vehicles are prohibited because they pose a safety problem and may cause costly damage to the trail. It is important to inform the public about ways they can be better stewards of their trail. When informed, they respond.

- *You want to attract tourists to your area.* Tourists can add dollars to the local economy, particularly if your multi-use trail has features that will attract them. But tourists will not know what your trail has to offer unless you inform them. Attracting visitors typically requires a broad level of promotion.

How to Get Publicity

If you are lucky, someone in the media will hear about your trail and decide to do a story about it. More often, you will need to contact reporters and encourage them to do a story. Try to offer reporters a variety of ways in which to write about the trail.

One of the best ways to get media coverage,

while also raising trail awareness, is to hold an event. It should be all-inclusive, giving as many people as possible the opportunity to participate.

Events before Your Trail Is Complete

Here are a few ideas for events that work best prior to the trail's completion.

TRAIL CORRIDOR TOURS. Host walking, bicycling, or canoe tours of the trail corridor for donors, press, or politicians. If necessary, you may need to drive them along your trail route, though this may seem to counter the nonmotorized spirit of your trail. A firsthand view can go a long way toward turning a nonbeliever into a convert. Also, consider a tour to another established multi-use trail nearby for comparison.

"NAME THE TRAIL" CONTEST. If the trail does not have a name (or if you want to improve the current name), hold a contest with a trail-related prize for the winner and make an event out of announcing the name.

TRAIL WORKDAY. This is one of the most positive and effective ways to build community support. Encourage volunteers to spend a day helping to build a trail segment; cleaning or grooming the trail (or nearby stream); planting trees, shrubs, or wildflowers (Figure 6.1); or

Figure 6.1. Volunteer gardeners plant seasonal flowers along the Baltimore and Annapolis Trail in Maryland.

helping build trail amenities along the route. People enjoy working with others to help "get the trail on the ground" or to improve it. Arrange shifts if volunteers cannot put in a full day, and include chores for people of all ages and abilities. Workdays are also great ways to recruit corporate sponsors or teams of employees who may want to give back to the community.

Consider also an Adopt-a-Trail program, in which a business, service club, church, or family adopts a segment of the trail to maintain or improve. Credit signs similar to Adopt-a-Highway signs will go a long way to build support for this kind of long-term commitment.

PHOTO COMPETITION. To document the "before" and "after" scenarios of your trail corridor, stage a photo competition. Some older residents may even have pictures depicting former uses of the corridor. Offer prizes for various photo categories and display the winning photos in a public place.

POSTER CONTEST. Get children interested in the trail by staging a children's poster contest. Children can be awarded prizes for their trail drawings, and the best one could be developed into a poster for distribution to local businesses. If you want more sophisticated art, sponsor an adults' contest for the best logo or natural rendering of the trail.

Events on Opening Day

The following events are ideal for the day the trail opens:

"THANK YOU FOR GIVING" EVENT. As you celebrate the trail's opening, throw a party to thank the donors who made the project possible. Ask local restaurants or grocery stores to donate food for the event. Hold the party in an interesting spot along the route, perhaps at a former train station or an old canal lock.

TRAIL-ATHALON. Host a race that spans the length of the trail and involves several user groups. A horseback rider passes a baton to a runner who passes it to someone in a wheel-chair who passes it to a bicyclist. The winning team can be photographed for the local newspaper.

DECORATED BICYCLE PARADE. Have children and adults decorate their bicycles for the opening celebration, perhaps following the color scheme of the trail's logo; offer prizes. The participants should demonstrate proper bicycle safety, such as wearing helmets and following trail rules (Figure 6.2).

FLOAT COMPETITION. Encourage people to decorate floats for a trail parade. Give out prizes for the most creative floats.

Events when the Trail Is Extended

Your trail may open in phases, or it may be extended beyond its original length. Whenever you open a new section, take time to publicize it with an interesting event.

WALK-A-THON. Participants can walk the length of the existing trail and use other means where the extension is not yet passable on foot. For instance, horses can transport people through shallow water in the absence of a bridge. Thus, obstacles can be made into photo opportunities for the media.

NATURE WALK. Schedule a hike with a naturalist on the proposed extension to identify fauna

Figure 6.2. A parade of bicyclists and pedestrians at a trail opening celebration.

and flora. This could launch an interpretive sign program for the entire trail.

"BURMA SHAVE" SIGNS. You may remember the "Burma Shave" highway signs that used to be placed in series along highways. Each one contained a line from a rhyme, and the last one read "Buy Burma Shave." Develop your own set of trail rhymes and post them along the trail extension to promote it. The last sign could read "Support the Trail."

Ongoing Events

Consider the following ways to gain publicity for your trail throughout the year.

SPECIAL FEATURES TOUR. Organize a trail tour that highlights interesting sights along the route,

including historic houses, old railroad stations, gardens, and barns. This is similar to a house tour, except that the "rooms" are adjacent to the trail.

CONTESTS. You can hold a competition to find the "best" of just about anything relating to your trail. You can have writing, art, or photo contests, bicycle or foot races, and even children's tricycle contests. Anything that brings more people to the trail and draws attention to it can be effective.

NEWSPAPER COLUMN. Initiate and write a regular column in the local newspaper featuring interesting tidbits about the multi-use trail.

AWARDS. Gain national recognition by going after awards such as "Take Pride in America," "Keep America Beautiful," and "Enjoy America's Outdoors." All of these awards can generate significant trail pride and publicity (Figure 6.3).

HOLIDAYS. Use holidays as the catalyst for decorating the trail and planning events. Encourage children to place ghosts and scarecrows along the trail around Halloween, or host an "egg hunt" around Easter. Celebrate other, trail-related holidays as well, including Earth Day, National Trails Day, and Arbor Day.

FOLLOW-UP OBSERVATIONS. Scientific studies and personal observations of the completed trail

Rails-to-Trails Conservancy

Figure 6.3. Officials and volunteers of the Washington & Old Dominion Railroad Regional Park cut a ribbon after receiving an "Enjoy America's Outdoors" award.

can be interesting. This may be an opportunity for a school group to adopt the trail as an outdoor laboratory, addressing flora, fauna, or trail user issues as an ongoing school project. The "Green City" program now in Portland, Oregon, and Denver, Colorado, is an example of school kids working within a special outdoor setting.

Also, track improvements, business opportunities, and other benefits. Let the press know about any increases in property values, new businesses or improvements resulting from the trail, or individual health benefits associated with your trail. Give the press names of people they can interview to obtain a more personal view.

Working with the Media

Once you know the level and type of publicity you want for your trail and the kind of events you want to hold, the next step is to work with the media. You will need to learn the nuts and bolts of getting the newspaper, television, Internet, and radio coverage that you want.

Newspapers

One of the best (and simplest) ways to get a story into a newspaper is to issue a "press release." The form of a press release is fairly universal—one or two double-spaced, typed pages of text with a contact person and phone number listed in the upper-left corner. The release should be neat and grammatically correct and should be sent several days in advance of your event (try not to send it any earlier than this). Ideally, it should be addressed to a specific reporter with an interest in the trail.

You catch the reporter's attention by putting news in the first paragraph of the press release. Most reporters are looking for something new, current, and interesting to the public. If you do not have any specific "news," create something. Hold an event, stage a race, urge the county council to pass a bill, invite landowners to donate parcels of land, or notify the press when there will be a photo opportunity such as craning a new pedestrian bridge into place. In other words, give the reporter some news to cover

and, if possible, a photo opportunity. And be sure to phone the reporter to ensure that your release was received and to offer any additional information he or she may need. A follow-up call from you will increase the chances that a reporter will pay attention to and act on your release.

In general, it is much easier to get coverage in small local newspapers than in large metropolitan ones, but send your press releases to all press in the area. When a story appears consistently in local papers, the larger ones often realize it is newsworthy and may opt to write their own articles.

To expand your chances of coverage and readership, reach out to different sections of the newspaper. In addition to the main news section, send press releases to the editorial board, sports section, real estate, society page, and features editor. As your trail improves, seek coverage in national magazines and newspapers, particularly travel sections. This coverage can increase local use and promote tourism.

Multi-use trails lend themselves to photographs. Pictures of beautiful landscapes, smiling children, and an interesting mix of users can quickly catch a reporter's eye. You could prepare a news release based on a unique photo. This also works well if you are planning to take local dignitaries on a trail tour. And, if the media do not cover your event, send them a photograph after the fact.

Photos are not the only graphics that can

bring publicity to your trail. A cartoon could highlight some interesting or humorous aspect of the trail. Maps of the trail corridor are also helpful to the press. Make them simple and interesting.

Television and Radio

Sending news releases and photographs to television and radio stations may encourage them to cover a trail-related story. As with newspapers, you need news (and visuals like volunteers, kids, and bridge installations) to attract the cameras and tape recorders.

Television and radio also offer opportunities for public service announcements (PSAs). These usually can be made on low budgets with volunteer professionals. Most PSAs consist of thirty seconds of pre-recorded commentary. Some radio stations have their disc jockeys read short PSAs on the air.

Before you invest time and money in preparing a PSA, consider your market and what you want to say. Are you trying to raise money? Do you want to publicize an event for young people? Are you looking for volunteers? What impact do you want to make with a PSA?

Press Release (or PSA) Topics

In addition to the events previously listed, consider these creative ideas for generating media coverage for your trail:

- Trail Statistics: Offer data about your project: How many users are there? How long is the trail? What population base does it serve? How many community resources does it connect?

- Success Stories in Other Communities: Profile a trail with characteristics similar to yours. Include quotes from converted opponents to show that similar projects have had positive results in other communities.

- Questions and Answers: Prepare a fact sheet of the ten most commonly asked questions about the trail, and provide the answers.

- Trail Survey: Have volunteers conduct a survey of trail users and neighbors, and provide the results to the media.

- Interview a Favorable Politician or Landowner: Include interesting quotes and favorite trail anecdotes.

"Sound Bites"

When you work with reporters, they will take notes as you talk. Prior to talking with a reporter, know the points you want to get across. You might also think of some short, interesting quotes. The media are often searching for sound bites, catchy one-liners that convey a lot of meaning in just a few words. These are different from a motto or a mission statement that guides your agency or trail organization. An example of a sound bite is "Invest in land, they ain't making any more of it." Will Rogers said this to convey the idea that land

should be conserved because it is not in unlimited supply. Perhaps you can adapt a memorable line for your project. The line "If we build it, they will come," from the movie *Field of Dreams,* has been used by several managers in promoting their multi-use trails. If you can invent your own sound bite, you may grab the attention of a reporter and the interest of many potential trail users.

Trail Marketing Tools

Another way to spread the word about your trail is through a series of trail marketing tools that can be distributed at various locations near the trail and throughout the community, including area schools, businesses, government centers, bus stops, shopping centers, churches, and local community gatherings.

POSTERS. These should be developed and posted in the area to herald a special event, call attention to a meeting, or just to focus on the special community value of the trail. Hang posters on bulletin boards at grocery stores and restaurants; at dry cleaners' counters; in waiting rooms at gas stations; in drugstore windows, school lobbies, office lunchrooms, and town halls.

BUMPER STICKERS AND OTHER GOODIES. Bumper stickers, T-shirts, key chains, and other small items can convey key information. They are especially useful in generating support when a trail-related issue will be on the ballot. If there is an upcoming vote to fund a trail extension, your bumper sticker could say, "Vote *Yes* for the Trail." Ask local businesses to distribute the items and to post them in prominent locations.

FACT SHEET. You may want to develop a single page outlining basic facts about your trail: its length, its endpoints, interesting community resources along the route, the number of users each year, and other information. The fact sheet should be posted at trailheads and in local businesses to encourage people to experience the trail.

SCHOOL FLYERS. Ask a local school to distribute an informational flyer about the trail. Children can take flyers home to parents after school. If you have had a drawing contest for children, perhaps you can use some of their art in your flyer.

SUNDAY SUPPLEMENTS. Many local newspapers allow supplements to be inserted into their papers. You could prepare a simple, single sheet with a headline, some news about the trail, and perhaps a photo.

BROCHURES AND NEWSLETTERS. Every trail should have a general information brochure as a basic marketing tool. Many trails publish a periodic newsletter to keep trail users and neighbors up-to-date on trail news.

Publications

Printed materials are essential in promoting and marketing a multi-use trail. In addition to spreading the word about your trail, publications provide trail users with important information, direct them to sites of interest along the corridor (and in neighboring communities), highlight the area's history, and foster an appreciation of nature.

General Information Brochure

An attractive trail information brochure is a must (Figure 6.4). It should include the trail's length, permitted uses, rules and regulations, the fee schedule (if any), a trail map, a brief description and history of the trail, and the managing agency's address, telephone number, and e-mail address. Also include your Web site address, if you have a Web site for the trail. You could also include photographs or drawings showing nearby points of interest.

Make copies of the brochure available at the trail's office and post them on kiosks at all trail access points. Brochures should also be placed at local chambers of commerce and visitor centers and at nearby motels, restaurants, and other commercial establishments. They can also be distributed to local recreation clubs and civic groups and to your state or regional division of tourism. Be sure to print plenty of copies because the brochure will be a popular item.

WAYS TO GET PUBLICITY FOR YOUR TRAIL

1. Trail tours
2. "Name the Trail" contest
3. Trail workdays
4. Photo or poster competitions
5. Trail-athalons
6. Bicycle or float parades
7. Walk-a-thons
8. Guided nature walks
9. "Burma Shave" signs
10. Award ceremonies
11. Holiday celebrations
12. Success stories
13. Trail statistics

Figure 6.4. Examples of trail brochures.

Trail Map

You may decide to produce a separate, detailed map of the trail showing the facility's relation to surrounding streets and communities, especially if your trail is long, is used by bicycle commuters, or has many access points that cannot be depicted accurately in a brochure. The map should show the trail in relation to the existing road system and should highlight points of interest along the corridor. Make it a "foldable" publication that fits easily into a pocket.

Visitors Guide

Another popular piece of literature for trail users is a brochure detailing attractions, restaurants, accommodations, and trail-related facilities located near the trail. This brochure, which is particularly helpful if you are trying to promote tourism along the corridor, can provide information on everything from motels, bed-and-breakfasts, and campgrounds, to bike shops, museums, and historic sites. Several of Wisconsin's state-managed trails include a tourist guide as an insert within their general information brochures.

One effective guide is the 32-page, 5-by-9-inch color booklet describing the Northern Central Rail-Trail in Maryland. The guide combines general trail information with detailed maps that include historical information, points of interest, rest rooms, stores, and boating access. Copies of the guide are sold at the area's commercial outlets and through the managing agency, with profits going toward trail maintenance.

Newsletter

You may also want to publish a newsletter to inform trail users of any changes and improvements along the trail. Copies can be posted at kiosks at trail access points and along the corridor; additional copies may be made available at trail visitor centers. The Washington and Old Dominion Railroad Regional Park produces a simple quarterly newsletter highlighting trail etiquette, safety, and trail events. Each newsletter includes telephone numbers and an address where trail users can ask questions, make suggestions, and report any problems.

Nature Guides

A nature guide describing and illustrating plants, trees, birds, and mammals located within the corridor will interest many trail users. Minnesota's Heartland Trail publishes an excellent illustrated nature guide that includes harmful plants to avoid (poison ivy, stinging nettle), wildflowers listed by color, nonflowering plants (mosses, mushrooms), common trees, and birds and mammals. The Military Ridge State Trail in Wisconsin and the Illinois Prairie Path offer nature guides, both of which weave in the history associated with the trail route.

Local History Guide

Some multi-use trails are steeped in history because of former uses within the corridor. Boston's Minuteman Trail parallels the route of Paul Revere's famous ride during the Revolutionary Era. The North Central Railroad, now the Northern Central Rail-Trail and York County Heritage Trail, transported President Lincoln to Gettysburg, where he delivered his famous address. A local history guide is a good place to feature the interesting history and lore of your trail.

The Illinois Prairie Path's support organization developed a publication to celebrate the 150th anniversary of one of the counties through which the trail runs. Called "History Treasure Hunt," it points out historical features beginning 150 *centuries* ago, including information on 11,000-year-old elephant bones (on display at a college three blocks from the trail), Native American burial mounds dating from 300 B.C., and an eighteenth-century trading post.

Regardless of which publications you decide to develop, make sure all trail-related literature includes the name of the managing agency and its address and telephone number. Each publication should be attractive, concise, and an appropriate size for its use; dull brochures or oversized trail guides will not be effective. Be sure to consider the many types of users your trail will attract—children, senior citizens, the physically challenged, and foreign visitors.

Using a Web Site to Market Your Trail

The World Wide Web has soared in popularity in recent years. People regularly use the Web to gather information about local attractions, conduct research, plan vacations, provide input to government officials, and buy goods and services. Trail advocates, planners, and managers should take advantage of this growing phenomenon by creating Web sites in order to publicize trails of all kinds.

You can enlist the services of a professional, or work with a skilled volunteer, to create your trail's Web site. Ideally, find someone who will donate his or her time for this effort. Your site can be created as a stand-alone Web site or incorporated as pages of a larger existing site, such as that of a government agency or nonprofit organization.

Your Web site can incorporate all of the elements discussed in this chapter in order to publicize your trail. Include photographs, a trail logo, and a trail map as graphic elements. You could include contact information (including e-mail addresses) for the trail managing agency, interesting facts about the trail, visitor information (including links to the Web sites of local trail-related businesses), downloadable guides to the nature and history of the trail, the latest news about the trail, and links to the Web sites of national trail organizations. Try to keep your Web site from becoming static. Change the site regularly to include updates and newsworthy tidbits in order to encourage return visits.

Once your Web site is complete, publicize it through the other tools you are using. Include your Web site address on any flyers, press releases, and brochures that you produce. Work with your Web site developer to make your site more recognizable by various Internet search engines. Contact local organizations, the chamber of commerce, local outdoor equipment distributors, and other agencies to have them insert links to your Web site from theirs.

Think about how your Web site will be used and who will be using it. Consider integrating a form into your site for visitors to fill out, to create a database of individuals or conduct an online survey. Post a video of a recent press clip to your site. Sell trail-related T-shirts, brochures, or bumper stickers using the Web site. The possibilities are many, so try not to limit yourself when creating your Web site.

Finally, you may be able to raise money for trail development and stewardship through your Web site. Investigate opportunities for credit card contributions via your site. You may be able to arrange this through a local financial institution in return for some advertising benefits to them.

Citizen Support

Once a trail is open, the community begins to develop a tremendous sense of "ownership" toward the trail. Individuals develop strong personal attachments to a trail as it becomes part of their daily or weekly routines. Consequently, citizens frequently will be the first to recognize opportunities to expand the trail corridor and possible threats to the existing corridor.

It is critical that you work with citizens who feel some ownership of the trail if it is to be expanded. They have the interest and energy to work with elected officials and other decision makers. Help citizens focus their energy on specific tasks related to acquiring more property. And provide them with information that allows them to act in a timely way.

Citizens can be very helpful with environmental impact studies and environmental assessments, for example. By keeping a mailing list of interested and supportive citizens, you can alert them to deadlines associated with the submittal of comments and provide summaries of relevant trail issues. Another effective way to involve interested citizens is to have them help identify and prioritize property that should be acquired. With their help, you can develop a strategy to secure funding.

"Friends of the Trail" Groups

The formation of a private, nonprofit Friends of the Trail organization can be critical to the long-term success of your trail. No matter how competent and savvy the governmental agency that manages the trail, there will always be times when a group of active volunteers can provide the kind of assistance—whether through muscle power or political power—that will noticeably improve your trail. The single most important function of a Friends organization is to act as an advocate for the trail, defending it when necessary and promoting it the rest of the time.

Ideally, whenever there is a public hearing on anything remotely related to the trail facility—a nearby road project, your state's policy on parks, local open space preservation, bicycle policies, or air pollution reduction—a Friends of the Trail representative should testify and speak on behalf of the trail. If this is not possible, members of the Friends group should at least attend any meeting or hearing dealing with funding for the trail. Funding decisions often depend on public pressure, and money is generally allocated to projects with high public visibility.

Friends groups provide many other services to trails around the country. For example:

- Physical labor performed through an Adopt-a-Trail program—litter cleanup, sweeping, brush-cutting, painting, minor bridge repair, and even construction of support facilities such as benches, picnic tables, and kiosks.

- "Eyes and ears" surveillance and reporting of any problems, dangers, or inappropriate activities taking place on or near the trail.

- Fund-raising to pay for trail structures (like bridges), amenities (such as trailside rest areas), or threatened adjacent properties of environmental significance that are not included in the regular budget for the trail.

- Developing maps, newsletters, and other publications to educate users and improve the quality of their experience on the trail.

- Promoting the trail as a tourist destination throughout the state and region.

The trail managing agency should be careful to maintain legal separation from a Friends group. The trail manager, for instance, should not be an officer or a board member of the Friends. However, there is no reason that the two entities cannot communicate closely and freely. In fact, they should coordinate activities and programs to avoid making duplicate efforts or pursuing divergent goals.

Often a Friends group grows out of the original citizen organization that promoted the creation of the trail. Making this transition often requires the gradual replacement of the trail's original advocates and activists by a broad-based leadership composed of people from tourism, corporate, financial, and service agency communities. Sometimes changing the group's mission from "creating" the trail to "supporting" it can be painful for the original members, so it should be handled gradually and diplomatically.

If an effective citizen organization never formed during the trail creation period, a Friends group should be defined and set up from scratch. In this case, active members should be drawn from trail users and adjacent landowners. It is important to specify clearly the purpose and mission of the group.

Do not underestimate the ability of local citizens groups! The Friends of the M-K-T Parkway in Texas worked successfully to pass a $1.3 million local bond issue to purchase parcels of land along the parkway. No agency would have had the leverage to accomplish such a goal without citizen support.

Keeping Your Trail a Dynamic Entity

Your trail may have taken years to build and perfect, and may now be a masterpiece enjoyed by thousands. To keep your trail vital and to assure continuing public support for its use and upkeep, keep your trail dynamic. Always be thinking of ways to improve it and to involve the public in that process. Think about ways to improve the landscape, to improve the views, to promote the compatibility of surrounding land uses, to further interpret the culture, ecology, and history of the area, and to link it to other trails and trail networks. Think of your trail and the corridor it passes through as a living entity that will continue to bring joy to its users and earn the commitment and pride of generations to come.

CASE STUDY 12

Tourism Agencies Promoting Trails

The 225-miles Katy Trail, running across almost the entire state of Missouri, is the longest rail-trail in the United States. Several years ago, Renee Graham, of the Columbia Missouri Convention and Visitors Bureau, was talking with a colleague from the Sedalia, Missouri, visitors bureau about the trail and how not much, if any, marketing had been done to draw folks to it and the towns along the corridor.

At about the same time, the state department of tourism launched the cooperative marketing program, a matching funds program for local tourism agencies whereby the state would reimburse half the bill for qualified marketing efforts. Graham rallied colleagues from seven other communities along the trail to apply for funds. The group is now collectively called the Katy Central Consortium.

Over the past four years, the consortium has applied to the state program for about $30,000 a year to carry out a variety of marketing efforts centered around the Katy Trail. With the first grant, they developed a logo and a brochure. The brochure provided information not only about the trail but also about the towns along it and the various tourist services available in those towns.

They also developed a Web site, www.katy-central.com, and a toll-free telephone number that is staffed twenty-four hours a day. Inquiries are sent to a mail fulfillment house, which sends out the brochure to each caller. The mail house also provides each of the eight partners a set of mailing labels from the inquiries so that each community can follow up with its own brochures.

The consortium has also used state matching funds to place ads in various national, state, and regional publications such as *Walking* magazine, *Bicycling* magazine, *Adventure Cycling, Missouri Life,* and regional AAA publications.

The state program guidelines stipulate that the recipients must be able to track the effectiveness of their marketing efforts. Surveys have shown that the folks who use the Katy Trail are not the major demographic group that the

group originally expected. Instead of young adults and families with children, they found that the greatest economic impact comes from trail users who are age forty-five and older. The consortium has used this information to adjust its advertising to better reach both the family and adult markets.

Next up for the consortium: a renovated Web

site, an updated guide, upgraded advertising (larger, more colorful, and more frequent placements), and more research.

CASE STUDY 13

Creating and Making the Most of a Friends of the Trail Group

The Capital Crescent Trail, connecting downtown Washington, D.C., with the suburb of Bethesda, Maryland, is 11 miles long and heavily used for commuting as well as recreation. The trail, ten years in the making, still depends on the Coalition for the Capital Crescent Trail (CCCT), a Friends of the Trail group, to keep it in tip-top shape. As John Dugger of the CCCT said, "Just because the trail gets built, doesn't mean the work stops."

The story of the CCCT is instructive on what it takes to create a trail and the invaluable role such a group can play. Though the last train ran on the line until the spring of 1985, area bicycle enthusiasts had written to the Maryland–National Capital Park and Planning Commission about the possible reuse of the corridor if it were to be abandoned (Lesson 1). Once CSX

proposed abandoning the line, a key resident alerted area citizens. In November 1985, the group of activists met at a local library to discuss making the corridor into a trail. In February 1986, the group adopted the name Capital Crescent Trail for the right-of-way (Lesson 2).

The Coalition for the Capital Crescent Trail formally was formed in the spring of 1986, with founding members being area organizations including the Potomac Appalachian Trail Club, Washington Area Bicyclists Association, Virginia Volksmarchers, Capital Hiking Club, and the Audubon Naturalist Society (Lesson 3). By late spring 1986, CSX had abandoned the corridor, and the CCCT had published its first brochure about the trail (Lesson 4).

CCCT members started and maintained a campaign to highlight the trail by testifying at

local city and county council meetings, holding periodic corridor cleanup sessions, rallies, and publishing a periodic newsletter to keep people informed about the progress (Lesson 5). In early 1988, members of the CCCT met with the National Park Service to get its support (part of the Capital Crescent Trail parallels the C&O Canal, a national park, for several miles). In mid-1988, the CCCT hired a campaign coordinator to keep all the pieces of the project on track and focused. In an effort to create more visibility, CCCT staff placed CCCT decals every 20 to 50 yards along the corridor in the fall of 1988. By the end of 1988, the CCCT was comprised of thirty-five member organizations representing over 50,000 area residents.

The basic strategy of the CCCT up to this point had been to acquire the corridor. This occurred when a local developer created a foundation as a holding company for the property, and purchased and held it until such time that the National Park Service and Montgomery County can take possession of their respective pieces. With the land secure, the CCCT turned its focus on creating an image of the trail; developing a sense of reality. As part of this effort, the CCCT helped to develop a 50-page concept plan that described bridges, pathways, and other amenities.

In December 1989, students of George Washington University's Urban and Regional Planning program produced *The Crescent Connection: Reviewing Old Ties,* a development study for the trail (Lesson 6). As the project moved along, the CCCT created a trail Prep/Maintenance Committee to conduct regular trail clearing and litter pickup. In August 1991, CCCT organized a two-day trail-clearing exercise involving twenty-three students from American University. In October 1992, the first piece of rail was cut out of the corridor in a large celebration with NPS, county, and CCCT staff (Lesson 7).

Construction began in September 1993. Local businesses at one end of the trail donated $20,000 for improvements at their end, such as signs, benches, and plantings (Lesson 8). In March 1994, the CCCT signed an agreement with Montgomery County to assist with trail maintenance. As the trail was being developed, the CCCT provided the milepost markers and even donated $5,000 to Montgomery County for the development of information kiosks at the Bethesda end of the trail. CCCT volunteers planted flowers alongside trail. Throughout all of the above, the CCCT was very vocal about pushing the public agencies to continue work on the trail.

With the first phase of the trail complete, the CCCT continues to fight against various encroachments, such as a proposed gas line along the trail. With 1,300 members and an annual budget of $50,000, the CCCT is focused on extending the trail from Bethesda to Silver Spring. To accomplish this, a lot of time is spent in city and county council meetings and many letters are written. The group raises its funds by holding events on the trail, and from foundations, membership donations, and local businesses. The group continues to publish its newsletter and hold rallies on the trail (Lesson 9).

Lessons Learned

1. Always be on the lookout for a possible trail corridor even if it is not currently available.
2. Adopt a fun name for the trail early on.
3. Get established local groups to sign on early.
4. Create a concrete vision of the trail early, such as a brochure with map, photos, and descriptive text.
5. Keep a sense of momentum.
6. Get help from local experts. There's no need to reinvent the wheel. This also creates more buy-in.
7. Celebrate each achievement!
8. Local business really do like this stuff.
9. The trail is never complete.

Glossary

Compiled by Jim Schmid, State Trails Coordinator, South Carolina Department of Parks, Recreation & Tourism, 1205 Pendleton Street, Columbia, SC 29201; (803) 734-0130; (803) 734-1042 fax; www.SCTrails.net

Abney level: Handheld instrument used for measuring angles of elevation or inclination of trail.

abutment: Structure at either extreme end of a bridge that supports the superstructure (sill, stringers, trusses, or decks); composed of stone, concrete, brick, or timber.

archaeological site: Location bearing physical evidence, usually buried, of past human use or occupation.

access trail: Any trail that generally connects the main trail to a road or another trail system.

accessible: A term used to describe a site, building, facility, or trail that complies with the ADA Accessibility Guidelines and can be approached, entered, and used by people with disabilities.

acquisition: The act or process of acquiring fee title or interest of real property.

Adopt-A-Trail: A program begun by the U.S. Forest Service in which groups or businesses "adopt" trails, providing volunteer work parties at periodic intervals. Though no special trail privileges are granted, the agency generally acknowledges that a trail has been "adopted" by erecting signs saying the trail is part of the Adopt-A-Trail program and including the name of the adopter.

alignment: The layout of the trail in horizontal and vertical planes—that is, the bends, curves, and ups and downs of the trail. The more the alignment varies, the more challenging the trail.

amenities: Any element used to enhance the user's experience and comfort along a trail.

Americans with Disabilities Act of 1990 (ADA): A federal law prohibiting discrimination against people with disabilities. Requires public entities and public accommodations to provide accessible accommodations for people with disabilities.

Americans with Disabilities Act Accessibility Guidelines (ADAAG): Design guidelines for providing access to a range of indoor and outdoor settings by people with disabilities.

appraisal: An estimate and opinion of value, usually a written statement of (1) the market value of (2) an adequately described parcel of property as of (3) a specified date.

apron: One of the three main elements of a water-bar. It catches water running down the trail and directs it off the trail.

armoring: Reinforcement of a surface with rock, brick, stone, concrete, or other "paving" material.

aspect: The particular compass direction a trail or site faces. Aspect affects the amount of solar radiation and year-round moisture a site is subjected to.

asphalt (Macadam): Petroleum-based surface material that provides a smoothly paved surface that is suitable for bicycles and in-line skates. It is preferred in urban areas where trails are often used for commuting to and from work or school.

all-terrain-vehicle (ATV): A small four-wheeled vehicle equipped with low-pressure balloon tires and intended for off-highway use only.

at-grade crossing: A trail crossing a roadway on the same plane.

backfill: Mineral soil used to support a drainage structure. Backfill is used behind (downtrail) a rock or log waterbar, or to reinforce a drainage dip.

backslope: The cut bank along the uphill side of the trail extending upward from the tread. Usually sloped back by varying degrees, depending on bank composition and slope stability.

ballast: Stone, cinders, gravel, or crushed rock fill material used to elevate a railroad bed above the surrounding grade, to provide proper drainage and a level surface for the ties and rails.

barrier-free design: A trail design that promotes the elimination of physical barriers that reduce access to areas by people with disabilities.

base: The primary excavated bed of a trail upon which the tread, or finished surface, lies.

base course: The layer(s) of specified material of designed thickness placed on a trailbed to support surfacing.

batter: The angle an abutment or rock wall is inclined against the earth it retains.

bed: The excavated surface on which a trail tread lies.

bedrock: Solid rock material that is exposed when topsoil is eroded or cut away.

bench: A long seat (with or without a back) for two or more people.

bench (cut): A relatively flat, stable surface (tread) on a slope occurring naturally or by excavation. When excavated, often referred to as full or half bench.

berm: The ridge of material formed on the outer edge of the trail that projects higher than the center of the trail tread.

blaze: A trail marker. Blazes can be made on a tree by chipping away a piece of the bark and painting the chipped-out part with a 2-inch by 6-inch vertical rectangle. Plastic triangles or diamonds (known as blazers) with the name of the trail or a directional arrow imprinted can be purchased and nailed to trees to mark a trail route.

blaze, blue: On the Appalachian Trail, a blue blaze almost always means a side trail to a campsite or a town. White blazes are generally used for the main or trunk trail. Many other trails follow the Appalachian Trail example.

blaze, double: Two blazes (vertical alignment) that denote a change in direction or a junction in the trail coming up.

bleeder (kick outs, diversion dips): Graded depression angled to drain water sideways off the treadway.

boardwalk: A fixed planked structure, usually built on pilings in areas of wet soil or water to provide dry crossings.

bogs: A muddy area common where little direct sunlight reaches the trail or where there are flat areas that are difficult to drain.

bollard: A barrier post, usually 30 to 42 inches in height, used to inhibit vehicular traffic at trail access points.

borrow (pit): Soil, gravel, or rock materials used for fill taken from approved locations (pit) away from the trail to be used on the trail for tread, embankments, or backfilling.

bridge: A structure, including supports, erected over a depression (stream, river, chasm, canyon, or road) and having a deck for carrying trail traffic. If the structure is 2 feet above the surface, the bridge should have railings.

brush: Vegetation or small flora.

brushing: To clear the trail corridor of plants, trees, and branches that could impede the progress of trail users.

brushing-in: To pile logs, branches, rocks, or duff along the sides of the tread to keep users from widening the trail, or to fill in a closed trail with debris so that it will not be used.

buffer zone: Natural area or open space used between the trail and adjacent lands to minimize impacts (physical or visual).

cairn: A constructed mound of rock located adjacent to a trail used to mark the trail route. Used in open areas where the tread is indistinct.

canal: An artificial waterway for transportation or irrigation.

cap rock: Rock placed in the top or uppermost layer in a constructed rock structure, such as a rock retaining wall.

carrying capacity: The number of recreationists that can be accommodated in a specific area based on ecological, physical, facility, and/or social factors.

catch point: The outer limits of a trailway where the excavation and/or embankment intersect with the ground line.

categorical exclusion (CE): A technical exclusion for projects that do not result in significant environmental impacts. Such projects are not required to prepare environmental reviews.

causeway: Elevated section of trail contained by rock, usually through permanent or seasonally wet areas.

center line: An imaginary line marking the center of the trail. During construction, the center line is usually marked by placing a row of flags or stakes (to indicate where the center of the trail will be).

check dam: Log, rock, or wood barrier placed in deeply eroded trails or erosional channels to slow the flow of water to allow accumulation of fine fill material behind it.

chromated copper arsenate (CCA): The well-known wood preservative for boardwalks, decks, and other common trail applications where treated lumber is called for.

circle of danger: The area surrounding the trail worker that is unsafe due to tool use. The inner (or primary) circle of danger is the area the tool can reach while being used. The outer circle of danger is the area the tool could reach if the trail worker lost control or let go of the tool.

clear-cut: Area where all trees, not just mature growth, have been cut.

clearing: Removal of windfall trees, uproots, leaning trees, loose limbs, wood chunks, etc., from both the vertical and the horizontal trail corridor.

clearing height (vertical clearance): The vertical dimension that must be cleared of all tree branches and other obstructions that would otherwise obstruct movement along the trail.

clearing width (limit): The outer edges of clearing areas (cleared of trees, limbs, and other obstructions) as specified by trail use.

climbing turn: A turn that is constructed on a slope of 20 percent or less when measured between the exterior boundaries of the turn and follows the grade as it changes the direction of the trail 120 to 180 degrees.

clinometer: A handheld instrument used for measuring angles of terrain elevation or percent of trail grade or slope.

cobble: Loose rock up to 2.5 inches in diameter.

cobble drain: A cobbled improvement to the trail surface that allows drainage (usually from an intermittent wet seep) across the trail for continued passage along the trail without damage to the soil.

collector ditch: A drainage structure that intercepts water flowing toward a trail, and usually channels it underneath the trail through a culvert.

come-along: A strong cable fitted with a ratchet to gain mechanical advantage for moving heavy objects over the ground with comparative ease. It is often used in trail work to move large rocks or bridge timbers.

compacted: The degree of consolidation that is obtained by tamping with hand tools or by tamping mineral soil and small aggregate in successive layers not more than 6 inches in depth.

compaction: The compression of aggregate, soil, or fill material by tamping.

condemnation: In real property law, the process by which property of a private owner is taken for a public purpose, without property owner consent. Compensation must be paid for property taken by condemnation.

connectivity: The ability to create functionally contiguous blocks of land or water through linkage or similar ecosystems or native landscapes; the linking of trails, greenways, and communities.

contour, lines: A line on a topographic map connecting points of the land surface that have the same elevation.

contour trail: Trail constructed such that it follows a contour, with its elevation remaining constant.

control points (targets): Features that trail users will want to naturally head toward or try to avoid (views, obstacles, etc.). These features should be flagged and used to help lay out a trail.

corridor, scenic: Land set aside on either side of a trail to act as a buffer zone protecting the trail against impacts such as logging or development that would detract from the quality and experience of a trail.

corridor (trail): The full dimensions of a route, including the tread and a zone on either side (usually 3 feet) and above the tread from which brush will be removed.

course: An even layer of stones, similar to a course of bricks, that forms a foundation, intermediate layer, or capstone layer in a stone wall.

critical point: The outside edge of the trail. It's called the critical point because this is where trail maintenance problems (always related to drainage) usually begin. Rounding the outside edge helps water to leave the edge of the trail.

cross slope: The slope that is perpendicular to the direction of the trail.

crowned trail: A trail bed built up from the surrounding area (and sloped for drainage), usually by excavating trenches parallel to the trail.

crusher fines (crusher run, crushed stone): Refers to any limestone, granite, or gravel that has been run through a crusher that is used to form a hard tread surface that once wetted and compacted creates a smooth trail surface for high-use areas.

culvert: A drainage structure made of rock, metal, or wood that is placed approximately perpendicular to and under the trail tread.

cushion material: Native or imported material, generally placed over rocky sections of unsurfaced trail to provide a usable and maintained traveled way.

curvilinear: A free-flowing movement pattern characterized by the general absence of straight trail segments.

cut and fill: The process of removing soil from one area and placing it elsewhere to form a base for any given activity.

daylighting: Clearing a ditch or drain so that water can run all the way to daylight.

de-berming: Removing the ridge of material formed on the outer edge of the trail that projects higher than the center of the trail tread, allowing water to once again flow off the trail.

decking (flooring): That part of a bridge, puncheon, or boardwalk structure that provides direct support for trail traffic.

declination: The measurement describing the difference between true north and magnetic north.

designated trail: A trail that is approved and maintained by an agency.

difficulty rating: A subjective rating of trail difficulty based on an average user with average physical abilities.

- *Easy* is defined as relaxing, posing minimal difficulties, and able to be traveled with little physical effort.
- *Moderate* is defined as not requiring excessive or extreme physical effort.
- *Difficult* is defined as physically strenuous, requiring excessive or extreme physical effort.

dike (tramway, tram, levee): An embankment or dam made to prevent flooding by the sea, a stream, or a lake. The embankment is often used for a trail.

ditching, sidehill: A ditch that parallels the treadway on the uphill side to collect water seeping into the trail; usually ends in a drainage ditch that allows the water to cross the trail.

double-track trail: A trail that allows for two users to travel side by side or make passes without one user having to yield the trail. Double-track trails are often old forest roads.

downslope: The downhill side of the trail. Avoid damaging downslope vegetation that is stabilizing hillside soil.

drainage, cross: Running water in swamps, springs, creeks, drainages, or draws that the trail must cross.

drainage, sheet: Desirable condition in which water flows in smooth sheets rather than rivulets; shower flow and less concentration results in less erosion.

drainage, surface: Rain or snow runoff from the surface of the tread.

drainage dip: An erosion-control technique that reverses the grade of a trail for a distance of 15 to 20 feet before returning to the prevailing grade. The

abrupt change in grade forces water to run off the trail tread, rather than gaining additional velocity.

drainage ditch: A ditch that collects water from a wet area on the trail; used to dry and harden the treadway. A drainage ditch is also an element of a waterbar, providing an escape route for water diverted from the trail by the bar.

drop-off: Slope that falls away steeply.

duff (humus): A layer of decaying organic plant matter (leaves, needles, and humus) on the ground. It is highly absorbent and quickly erodes under traffic.

easement: Grants a nonowner the right to use a specific portion of land for a specific purpose. Easements may be limited to a specific period of time or may be granted in perpetuity; or the termination of the easement may be predicated upon the occurrence of a specific event. An easement agreement survives transfer of landownership and is generally binding upon future owners until it expires on its own terms.

ecosystem: A system formed by the interaction of living organisms, including people, with their environment.

embankment: Structure made from soil used to raise the trail, rail bed, or roadway above the existing grade.

entrenchment: Sunken tracks or grooves in the tread surface cut in the direction of travel by the passage of water or vehicles.

environmental assessment (EA): A document prepared early in a planning process (federal) that evaluates the potential environmental consequences of a project or activity. An assessment includes the same topical areas as an environmental impact statement (EIS), but assesses only the effects of a preferred action, and in less detail than an EIS. An EA results in a decision, based on a assessment of the degree of impact of an action, that an EIS is necessary, or that an action will have no significant effect and a finding of no significant impact (FONSI) can be made.

environmental impact statement (EIS): An EIS is a full disclosure, detailed report that, pursuant to Section 102(2)C of the National Environmental Policy Act (NEPA), establishes the need for the proposed action, identifies alternatives with the potential to meet the identified need, analyzes the anticipated environmental consequences of identified alternatives, and discusses how adverse effects may be mitigated. An EIS is prepared in two stages: a draft statement that is made available to the public for review and a final statement that is revised on the basis of comments made on the draft statement.

ephemeral (creek): A temporary or short-lived condition. Characteristic of some streams that change rapidly, especially after heavy rains.

erosion: Natural process by which soil particles are detached from the ground surface and moved downslope, principally by the actions of running water. The combination of water falling on the trail, running down the trail, and of freezing and thawing and the wear and tear from traffic create significant erosion problems on trails.

erosion control: Techniques intended to reduce and mitigate soil movement from water, wind, and trail user traffic.

erosion, sheet: The removal of a fairly uniform layer of soil material from the land surface by the action of rainfall and runoff water.

exposure: The relative hazard encountered when one takes into consideration obstacles, alignment, grade, clearing, tread width, tread surface, sideslope, isolation, and proximity to steep slopes or cliffs.

fall line: Direction water flows down a hill. High-use trail should never be constructed on the fall line of a hill.

fauna: The animal populations and species of a specified region.

fee simple: An interest in land in which the owner is entitled to the entire property without limitation or restriction, and with unconditional power of disposition.

fen: Low, flat, marshy land or a bog.

fill (material): Gravel or soil used to fill voids in trail tread and to pack behind retaining walls and other structures.

fill slope: Area of excavated material cast on the downslope side of trail cut (also called embankment).

fines, soil: Smallest soil particles important for binding the soil together; silt. Fines are often the first particles to move when erosion takes place.

firebreak: A strip of forest or prairie land cleared or plowed to stop or prevent the spread of fire.

fiscal year (FY): Annual schedule for keeping financial records and for budgeting funds. The federal fiscal year runs from October 1 through September 30, while most state fiscal years run from July 1 through June 30.

flagging: Thin ribbon used for marking purposes during the location, design, construction, or maintenance of a trail project.

flagline: Flagging tied to trees indicating the intended course of a trail prior to construction.

flags, wire: Wire wands with square plastic flags at one end for field layout and marking of new trail or relocations of trail sections.

floodplain: The flat, occasionally flooded area bordering streams, rivers, or other bodies of water susceptible to changes in the surface level of the water.

flora: The plant populations and species of a specified region.

flushcut: Branch or sapling cut flush with the trunk or ground.

ford: A natural water-level stream crossing improved (aggregate mix or concrete) to provide a level low-velocity surface for safe traffic (mainly saddle or pack animal) passage.

friction pile: Post hammered into muck until friction prevents further penetration; foundation for puncheon or boardwalk.

full bench: Where the total width of the trail tread is excavated out of the slope and the trail tread contains no compacted fill material.

gabion baskets: Rectangular containers made of heavy galvanized wire. Gabions can be wired together, then filled with stones to quickly make retaining walls.

gate: Structure that can be swung, drawn, or lowered to block an entrance or passageway.

Geographic Information System (GIS): A spatial database mapping system that can be used to contain location data for trails and other important features.

geotextile (geo-synthetics, geofabrics): A semi-impervious nonwoven petrochemical fabric cloth that provides a stable base for the application of soil or gravel. Most common use is in the construction of turnpikes.

Global Positioning System (GPS): A system use to map trail locations using satellites and portable receivers. Data gathered can be downloaded directly into GIS database systems.

grade: The slope the trail maintains in its direction of trail, expressed as a percentage (feet change in elevation for every 100 horizontal feet, commonly known as "rise over run"). A trail that rises 8 vertical feet in 100 horizontal feet has an 8 percent grade. Grade is different than angle; angle is measured with a straight vertical as 90 degrees and a straight horizontal as 0 degrees. A grade of 100 percent would have an angle of 45 degrees.

grade, maximum: The steepest grade permitted on any part of a trail.

grade, sustained: The steepest grade permitted over the majority of the trail length.

grade dip, rolling: A reverse in the grade of the trail accompanied by an angling outslope that will divert water off the trail.

grade-separated crossing: Trail overcrossings or undercrossings to allow trail users to cross a street at a different level than motor vehicles.

graffiti: Unauthorized scratched, painted, or sprayed inscriptions or drawings on trail structures.

grass roots (support): Efforts at the local level utilizing public interest groups and communities in support of trails or greenways.

grate: A framework of latticed or parallel bars that prevents large objects from falling through a drainage inlet but permits water and some sediment to fall through the slots.

green infrastructure: The sum of the public and private conservation lands including native landscapes and ecosystems, greenspaces, and waters.

greenbelt: Protected natural lands or working landscapes that surround cities and serve to conserve and direct urban and suburban growth.

greenspace: Natural areas, open space, trails, and greenways that function for both wildlife and people.

greenway: A linear open space established along a natural corridor, such as a river, stream, ridgeline, rail-trail, canal, or other route for conservation and recreation purposes. Greenways connect parks, nature preserves, cultural facilities, and historic sites with residential areas. May or may not be open to recreational trail use.

grubbing: To dig, or clear of roots: to uproot shallow roots near or on the ground surface; also grubbing of tree stumps.

gully: Where concentrations of runoff water cut into soil, forming large channels greater than 1 foot below postconstruction depth.

habitat: A type of place that supports an animal or a population because it supplies the animal's basic requirements: food, water, shelter, living space, and some level of security.

half bench: Where the half width of the trail tread is excavated out of the slope and the outside of the trail tread contains the excavated compacted material.

hammock: A cluster of trees, often hardwoods, on higher ground.

hard surface (paved) trail: A trail tread surfaced with asphalt or concrete.

hardening: The manual, mechanical, or chemical compaction of the trail tread, resulting in a hard and flat surface that sheets water effectively and resists the indentations that are created by use.

hardpan: A layer of rock, or a compacted clay layer of soil, that forms a durable and generally erosion-free trail surface.

hazard tree (widow maker): Tree or limb that is either dead or has some structural fault that is hanging over or leaning toward the trail or sites where people congregate.

header, stone or rock: A long, uniform stone laid with its narrow end toward the face of a retaining wall or crib, used intermittently to structurally tie in the other rocks laid in the wall.

headwall: Support structure at the entrance to a culvert or drainage structure.

height: Measure of the vertical dimension of a feature. May also be the depth of a rut or dip.

helical pier: Steel post with auger-shaped bit-end that is screwed into wet soils either by hand or with the aid of specialized hydraulic tools to establish a foundation for puncheon or boardwalk.

hiking trail: Moderate to long distance trail with the

primary function of providing long-distance walking experiences (usually 2 miles or more).

hydric soil: Soil that is saturated or flooded during a sufficient portion of the growing season to develop anaerobic conditions in the upper soil layers.

hydrology: The properties, distribution, and circulation of water on the surface of the land, in the soil and underlying rocks, and in the atmosphere.

impacts: Encompasses all physical, ecological, and aesthetic effects resulting from the construction and use of trails. Many studies have been concerned with environmental and social impacts of different users, such as tread wear, littering, conflicts between users, or vandalism.

informal trail: A trail that has developed through informal use and is not designated or maintained by an agency.

inslope (insloping): Where the trail bed is sloped downward toward the backslope of the trail; causes water to run along the inside of the trail.

intermodal: A mode is a particular form of transportation, such as automobile, transit, bicycle, and walking. Intermodal refers to connections between modes.

Intermodal Surface Transportation Efficiency Act of 1991 (ISTEA): Federal legislation authorizing highway, highway safety, transit, and other surface transportation programs from 1991 through 1997. It provided new funding opportunities for sidewalks, shared-use paths, and recreational trails. ISTEA was superseded by the Transportation Equity Act for the 21st Century (TEA-21).

interpretation: Communicating information about the natural and/or cultural resources found at a specific site or along a trail. Tours, signs, brochures, and other means can be used to interpret a particular resource.

interpretive sign or display: An educational sign or display that describes and explains a natural or cultural point of interest on or along the trail.

interpretive trail: Short to moderate-length trail ($1/2$ to 1 mile) with concentrated informational stops to explain associated views, natural flora and fauna, and other features.

intersection: Area where two or more trails or roads join together.

invasive exotic: Nonnative plant or animal species that invades an area and alters the natural mix of species.

junction: Site where one trail or road meets another.

kiosk: A structure housing informational or interpretive displays.

knob: Prominent rounded hill or mountain.

lake: Large inland body of water.

land ethic: The desire humans have to conserve, protect, and respect the native landscape and other natural resources because their own well-being is dependent upon the proper functioning of the ecosystem.

land management agency: Any agency or private organization that manages recreation and/or wilderness areas. Examples include national entities such as the USDA Forest Service, the USDI Bureau of Land Management, and the USDI National Park Service, as well as state and local park systems.

land manager: Any person who makes decisions regarding land use.

landscape: Includes a mix of both human and natural features and contains numerous interacting ecosystems such as forests, fields, waterways, and human settlements.

landslide: Dislodged rock or earth obstructing passage on a trail.

lease: The grant of an interest in land upon payment of a determined fee. The fee does not have to be monetary, but some consideration must be given for the right to use the land or the lease will not be legally binding.

license: Allows the licensed party to enter the land of the licensor without being deemed a trespasser.

limits of acceptable change (LAC): A planning framework that establishes explicit measures of the acceptable and appropriate resource and social conditions in wilderness settings as well as the appropriate management strategies for maintaining or achieving those desired conditions.

linkages: Connections that enable trails and greenway systems to function and multiply the utility of existing components by connecting them together like beads on a string.

log, trail: An inventory of physical features along or adjacent to a trail. An item-by-item, foot-by-foot record of trail features and facilities or improvement on a specific trail.

logged-out tree: Down tree across the trail with sections already removed to permit passage.

loop trails: Designing trail systems so that the routes form loops, giving users the option of not traveling the same section of trail more than once on a trip.

maintenance: Work that is carried out to keep a trail in its originally constructed serviceable standard. Usually minor repair or improvements that do not significantly change the trail width, surface, or trail structures.

maintenance (annual): Involves four tasks done annually or more as needed: cleaning drainage, clearing blowdowns, brushing, and blazing and marking.

maximum pitch: The highest percent of grade on the trail.

maximum sustained pitch: The highest percent of grade on the trail that is sustained for a significant distance.

memorandum of understanding/agreement (MOU or MOA): A signed, written agreement entered into by various governmental agencies and nonprofit groups to facilitate the planning, coordination, development, and maintenance of a trail or trail system.

mesa: Flat-topped elevation with one or more clifflike sides.

mineral soil: The layers of the subsoil relatively free of organic matter.

minor field adjustments: Deviations of the trail alignment made during the course of normal construction or maintenance, as determined by the supervisor or crew leader, and not part of an original survey.

mitigate: Actions undertaken to avoid, minimize, reduce, eliminate, or rectify the adverse impact from a management practice or impact from trail users.

mode: A particular form of travel, such as walking, bicycling, carpooling, bus, or train.

monitor: Check systematically or scrutinize for the purpose of collecting specific data in relation to a set of standards.

motorized: Off-highway recreation using motorized vehicle (motorcycle, ATV, snowmobile, four-wheel drive, or other light utility vehicle) on trails.

mulch: Organic matter spread on newly constructed trail work to help stabilize soils and protect them from erosion.

multimodal: Facilities serving more than one transportation mode or transportation network comprised of a variety of modes.

multiple-use area: A land management objective seeking to coordinate several environmental, recreational, economic, historical, cultural, and/or social values in the same geographic area in a compatible and sustainable manner.

multiple-use (multi-use) trail: A trail that permits more than one user group at a time (horse, hiker, mountain bicyclist, ATV, etc.).

National Environmental Policy Act (NEPA): Established by Congress in 1969, NEPA requires public involvement and assessment of the biological and cultural resources in the location of the proposed activity. Any ground-disturbing activity on federal land will require a NEPA analysis of some kind.

National Trails System: Federal program designed to spur the creation of a system of trails (National Scenic, Historic, or Recreation) throughout the country; authorized pursuant to the "National Trails System Act" (16 U.S.C. 1241) and administered by the U.S. Department of the Interior.

natural surface (trail): A tread made from clearing and grading the native soil, with no added surfacing materials.

nature trail: Moderate-length trail ($^3/_4$ to 2 miles) with primary function of providing an opportunity to walk and study interesting or unusual natural features at the user's pleasure.

negative grade: Trail runs downhill.

nonmotorized: Trail recreation by modes such as bicycle, pedestrian, equestrian, skate, ski, etc.

noxious plant: Plant that poses a hazard to humans or animals, such as poison oak or ivy, cacti, stinging nettles, etc.

obligate: The way project sponsors spend money, typically by putting their project under contract for construction. Grant programs often require project sponsors to obligate funds in a timely manner or lose the funds.

obstacles: Physical objects large enough to significantly impede or slow travel on a trail. Logs, large rocks, and rock ledges are common obstacles.

open space: Areas of natural quality, either publicly or privately owned, designated for protection of natural resources, nature-oriented outdoor recreation, and trail-related activities.

operating and maintenance costs (O&M): Funds for day-to-day costs of operating and maintaining costs. Costs include worker's salaries, equipment upkeep, etc.

organic soil: Soil that is made up of leaves, needles, plants, roots, bark, and other organic material in various stages of decay, and has a large water/mass absorption ratio.

outcrop: A rock formation that protrudes through the level of the surrounding soil.

outdoor recreation access route (ORAR): A continuous unobstructed path designated for pedestrian use that connects accessible elements within a picnic area, campground, or designated trailhead.

outflow (outwash): The off-treadway ditch portion of a drainage structure, intended to remove all water from the trail.

outslope (outsloping): A method of tread grading that leaves the outside edge of a hillside trail lower than the inside to shed water. The outslope should be barely noticeable—usually no more than about 1 inch of outslope for every 18 inches of tread width.

ownership-in-fee (fee purchase, fee simple): A complete transfer of land ownership from one landowner to another party, usually by purchase.

partial bench: Where part of the width of the trail tread is excavated out of the slope and the rest of the trail tread is made up of fill material.

pass: Narrow gap between mountain peaks.

path or pathway: Track or route along which people are intended to travel.

paved dip: A swale crossing paved with stones to enable water to run across a trail without erosion.

peat: Unconsolidated material, largely undecomposed organic matter, that has accumulated under excess moisture or is due to continued saturation.

pedestrian: Any person traveling by foot or who uses a manual or motorized powered wheelchair.

picnic area: Area with one or more picnic tables.

pier (bridge): Intermediate bridge supports located between two adjacent bridge spans.

pitch: An increase in the prevailing grade of a trail, used during construction to avoid an obstacle, to catch up with the intended grade, or to meet a control point.

plan and profile sheets: Drawings (usually prepared for trail construction) used to record horizontal and vertical geometry of a trail alignment as well as other required improvements to the trail corridor.

planimetric map: A map that shows features such as roads, trails, and mountains but without contour lines showing elevation changes.

portage: A situation that exists when a paddler must temporarily leave a river or stream in order to bypass hazards such as dams, downed trees, or dangerous white water.

positive grade: Trail runs uphill.

primary trails: Continuous through routes that originate at the trailhead. Primarily for directing users through an area while promoting a certain type of experience.

prism: The trail cross section as a whole.

privy: Latrine or outhouse.

puncheon (bog bridge): A log or timber structure built on the ground for the purpose of crossing a boggy area. Usually consists of sills, stringers, decking, and often a soil or loose gravel tread laid on top of decking.

put-in/take-out point: A defined area that provides public access/egress to water trails.

quit claim deed: Deed of conveyance whereby whatever interest the grantor has in the property described in the deed is conveyed to the grantee without warranty of title.

radius: An arc or curve that connects two straight trail segments in order to provide smooth horizontal and vertical alignment.

rail corridor: The path of a railroad right-of-way, including the tracks and a specified tract of land on either side of the tracks (generally 100 feet wide).

rail-trail (rail-to-trail): A multipurpose public path (paved or natural) created along an inactive rail corridor.

rail-with-trail: A trail that shares the same corridor with active rail traffic.

railbanking: Retaining a rail corridor for future railroad uses after service has been discontinued. Federal legislation regarding railbanking provides for interim public use of the corridor, allowing the establishment of recreational trails.

railing (handrail): Horizontal or diagonal structural member that is attached to vertical posts for the purpose of delineating trails, protecting vegetation, providing safety barriers for trail users at overlooks, and assisting users when crossing bridges or using steps.

ravine: Deep, narrow gouge in the earth's surface, usually eroded by the flow of water.

realignment: The process of moving a portion of an existing trail to alleviate maintenance problems or resource impact.

rebar: Steel reinforcing rod that comes in a variety of diameters, useful for manufacturing pins or other trail anchors.

reconstruction: Building a trail on a new location to replace an existing trail.

reconnaissance (recon): Scouting out alternative trail locations prior to the final trail route location being selected.

record of decision (ROD): Also called a decision memo. The portion of a Final Environmental Impact Statement that identifies the proposed action, signed by the appropriate deciding officer.

Recreation Opportunity Spectrum (ROS): A means of classifying and managing recreational opportunities based on physical, social, and managerial settings.

rehabilitation: All work to bring an existing trail up to its classification standard on the same location, including necessary relocation of minor portions of the rail.

relocation (relo): Construction of a new section of trail to replace an old stretch—to avoid problems of erosion or impact, or due to landowner or management constraints.

renovation: Activities that will significantly change the trail width, surface, or trail structures.

reroute: To alter the path of a trail to better follow land contours, avoid drainage sites, bypass environmentally sensitive areas, improve views, or for other reasons.

rest room: Public toilet facility.

retaining wall (revetments, cribbing): Structure used to provide stability and strength to the edge of a trail, usually made of log or stone.

revegetation: Process of restoring a denuded and/or eroded area close to its original condition.

reverse grade: A short rise in the trail that traverses a slope that forces any water on the trail to drain off to the side.

ridge: A long, narrow land elevation.

right-of-way: A strip of land held in fee simple title, or an easement over another's land, for use as a public utility for a public purpose. Usually includes a designated amount of land on either side of a trail that serves as a buffer for adjacent land uses.

rill: A steep-sided channel resulting from accelerated erosion.

riparian zone: The land and vegetation immediately adjacent to a body of water, such as a river, lake, or other natural perpetual watercourse.

riprap: Stones placed randomly on a bank to provide support.

rise and run: A measurement of grades and slopes, expressed as a proportion of the amount of vertical rise in a given horizontal run. For example, 1:4 means that the grade or slope rises 1 unit for each 4 units of horizontal run. Taking this one step further, 1:4 is a 25 percent grade or slope, where 25 percent is obtained by dividing 1 by 4 and expressing the result as a percentage.

root: Area where vegetation roots protrude through the tread surface.

run (running) plank: Usually wood planks laid lengthwise (along the axis) on top of bridge decking used as the tread surface.

runoff: Water not absorbed by the soil that flows over the land surface.

rut: Sunken groove in the tread, perpendicular to the direction of travel, and less than 2 feet in length.

saddle: Ridge between two peaks.

scenic viewpoints (vistas): Designated areas developed at key locations that will afford trail users an opportunity to view significant landforms, landscape features, wildlife habitat, and activities.

scoping: The procedures by which an agency determines the extent of analysis necessary for a proposed action.

scree: Gravel-sized loose rock. Scree can be used to define a trail to channel trail traffic, or along rock staircases to stabilize soils and direct trail traffic onto the staircase.

secondary trails: Short trails used to connect primary trails or branchings of primary trails. They encourage movement between two primary trails or facilitate dispersal of use through secondary branching.

segment (passage): A portion of a trail. Changes in geographic features, jurisdiction, and/or political boundaries often distinguish segments (passages).

shared use: The shared use concept contends land managers and trail user groups work together to identify common goals and share in the process to achieve them. It means sharing of knowledge, tools, trailheads, grant funds, labor, and other resources in an area. In some instances it means sharing the same trail, but doesn't always require multiple-use trails.

shared use path: Trail permitting more than one type of user, such as a trail designated for use by both pedestrians and bicyclists.

shelter: Open-front structure that includes a sleeping platform and roof.

side trails: Dead-end trails that access features near the main trail.

sidehill: Where the trail angles across the face of a slope. The tread is often cut into the slope.

sidehilling: Process of excavating or cutting a bench across the slope.

sideslope: The natural slope of the ground measured at right angles to the centerline of the trail, or the adjacent slope that is created after excavating a sloping ground surface for a trailway, often termed a cut-and-fill slope, left and right of the trail tread.

sight distance: The visible and unobstructed view seen by a trail user from a given point along the trail.

sign: A board, post, or placard that displays verbal, symbolic, tactile, or pictorial information about the trail or surrounding area.

significant: As used in NEPA, requires consideration of both context and intensity. Context means that the significance of an action must be analyzed in several contexts, such as society as a whole and the affected region, interests, and locality. Intensity refers to the severity of impacts.

sill: A crosswise member at the top of an abutment or pier that supports the stringers, beams, or trusses.

single-track trail: A trail only wide enough for one user to travel and requires one user to yield the trail to allow another user to pass.

sinkhole: A natural occurrence when the limestone crust of the earth collapses and creates a crater. Old sinkholes are often filled with water and resemble ponds.

sinks: A term given to areas where underground rivers emerge at the ground surface. Areas surrounding sinks are generally lush with vegetation.

skew angle: Less than at right angle to a trail. Usually an oblique angle of 45 degrees or less.

slackline: Rigging system with a highline that is lowered to pick up a load, then tightened to move the load.

slide: Material that has slid onto the trail tread from the backslope and possibly in quantities sufficient to block the trail.

slope: Angle of the ground from a level position measured as a ratio in percentage of rise over run, or in degrees.

slope, percent: Number of feet rise (vertical) divided by feet of run (horizontal) times 100 to get percent slope; example: 15 feet of rise over 100 feet of run is a 15 percent slope.

slough (pronounced "sloo"): Ingress, egress, or backflow from a creek or river; usually areas full of soft, deep mud.

slough (pronounced "sluff"): Material from the backslope or the area of the backslope that has been deposited on the trail bed and projects higher than the center of the trail tread.

slump: When the trail bed material has moved downward causing a dip in the trail grade.

soft-surface trail: A trail tread surfaced with soil cement, graded aggregate stone, or shredded wood fiber.

soil auger: T-shaped tool with a spiral tip for turning into soil to probe its content.

soil profile: Site-specific arrangement of soil layers from surface to bedrock.

soil stabilizer: Material, either natural or manufactured, used to hold soil in place and prevent erosion from water, gravity, or trail users. Stabilizers include soil cement, geogrid, etc.

staging area: See **trailhead**.

specifications: Standards of work and type of materials to which trails (tread, clearing, grade) and trail structures (bridge, culvert, puncheon) are built and maintained according to type of use.

spine trail: A regional trail that acts as a "backbone" to a regional trail system.

spur trail: Trail that leads from primary, secondary, or spine trails to points of user interests—overlooks, campsites, etc.

stakes, grade or slope: Temporary stakes set by the trail locator to establish the elevation and cross section of the completed tread.

stakes, line: Temporary stakes set by the trail locator to establish the centerline of the trail.

station: One hundred feet measured along the centerline of the trail.

steel rungs: Placed on rock faces or ledges to provide ladder-like access in steep terrain.

step: Structure that provides a stable vertical rise on the trail while permitting lower typical grades between steps.

step, pinned: Step held in place on ledge or a rock slab by steel pins set in holes drilled in the rock.

stepping stones: Large rocks (preferably greater than 200 pounds) set in boggy areas or shallow stream crossings to provide passage for hikers.

stile: A step or set of steps that allows hikers to pass over a fence or wall, but does not allow livestock to get out.

stob (stub): Projecting (and hazardous) piece of a branch or sapling not cut flush with the trunk or ground.

stone: A rock put to human use.

stream: Small body of running water moving in a natural channel or bed.

stream crossing: A trail crossing a body of running water at grade without the use of a developed structure or bridge.

stringer: The lengthwise member of a structure, usually resting on sills, that spans wet areas and supports the decking.

summit: The highest point of a mountain.

super-elevation: Slope or bank of a curve or trail expressed as the ratio of feet of vertical rise per foot of horizontal distance. The outside edge of a trail is raised or banked for the purpose of overcoming the force causing a vehicle (bicycle or OHV) to skid when maintaining speed.

surfacing: Material placed on top of the trailbed or base course that provides the desired tread. It lessens compaction of soil, provides a dry surface for users, and prevents potential erosion and abrasion.

survey: A physical field assessment of the trail or proposed trail, to determine maintenance tasks, hazards, impact, alignment, etc.; prior to work, or as part of ongoing trail maintenance.

sustainable development: The use of resources to meet the needs of the present without compromising the ability of future generations to meet their own needs.

swale: A low-lying natural topographic drainage feature crossing the trail alignment. A low-lying ground drainage structure (resembling a swale) can be constructed to enhance drainage across the trail.

switchback: A sharp turn in a trail to reverse the direction of travel and to gain elevation. It is constructed on a slope of more than 15 percent when measured between the exterior boundaries of the trail 120 to 180 degrees. The landing is the turning portion of the switchback. The approaches are the trail sections upgrade and downgrade from the landing.

talus: Large rock debris on a slope. The rocks are larger and have sharper edges than those found on scree slopes.

tent platform: Wooden platform used to minimize damage to fragile alpine or wetlands areas or to reduce impact on a heavily used, erosion-prone campsite.

terminus: Refers to either the beginning or the end of a trail.

topography: The slope of the land as it exists or is proposed. It is represented on drawings by lines connecting points at the same elevation; is typically illustrated by dashed lines for existing topography and solid lines for proposed.

trail: Linear route on land or water with protected status and public access for recreation or transportation purposes such as walking, jogging, hiking, bicycling, horseback riding, mountain biking, canoeing, kayaking, backpacking, and vehicular travel by motorcycle or all-terrain vehicles.

trail access information: Objective information reported to trail users through signage about the grade, cross slope, tread width, and surface of a trail.

trail bed: The finished surface on which base course or surfacing may be constructed. For trails without surfacing, the trail bed is the tread.

trailhead (staging area): The start or end of a trail, often accompanied by various public facilities such as a horse unloading dock or chute, parking areas, toilets, water, directional and informational signs, and a trail use register.

trailway: The portion of the trail within the limits of the excavation and embankment.

transportation enhancement: Projects that include providing bicycle and pedestrian facilities, converting abandoned railroad rights-of-way into trails, preserving historic transportation sites, acquiring scenic easements, mitigating the negative impacts of a project on a community by providing additional benefits, and other nonmotorized projects.

Transportation Equity Act for the 21st Century (TEA-21): Federal legislation authorizing highway, highway safety, transit, and other surface transportation programs from 1998 through 2003. It provides funding opportunities for pedestrian, bicycling, and public transit facilities, and emphasizes intermodalism, multimodalism, and community participation in transportation planning initiated by ISTEA.

travelway: The trail as a whole, including the trail tread and the cleared areas on either side of the trail.

traverse: To ascend a slope diagonally up and across in lieu of the more direct up and over approach.

tread (treadway): The actual surface portion of a trail upon which users travel, excluding backslope, ditch, and shoulder. Common tread surfaces are native material, gravel, soil cement, asphalt, concrete, or shredded recycled tires.

tread width: The width of the portion of the trail used for travel.

trestle: Midspan support for a bridge.

tree line (timberline): The farthest limit, either in altitude on a mountain, or the farthest north in the Northern Hemisphere, in which trees are able to grow. Beyond this line, the environment is too harsh for trees to survive.

turnout: A place where the trail is widened to permit trail traffic traveling in opposite directions to pass.

turnpike (turnpiking): Tread made stable by raising trail bed above wet, boggy areas by placing mineral soil over fabric between parallel side logs (3 to 5 feet apart); usually includes ditches alongside the logs. Turnpike must be "crowned" to provide drainage.

undulating trail: One that follows a wavelike course, often going in and out of gullies.

USGS topo (contour) map: Maps published by the United States Geological Survey, indicating built and natural features (buildings, roads, ravines, rivers, etc.) as well as elevation changes. Available from many government offices, outdoor shops, or map stores.

universal design: Few if any barriers exist to inhibit accessibility.

Universal Trail Assessment Process (UTAP): An inventory process that can be used by trail managers to assess a trail to determine compliance with design guidelines and to provide objective information to trail users regarding grade, cross slope, tread width, surface, and obstacles.

volunteer: Person who works on a trail or for a trail club without pay.

wall, retaining: Log or rock construction to support trail tread or retain backslope.

wash: A natural watercourse, wet or dry.

watercourses: Any natural or built channel through which water naturally flows or will collect and flow during spring runoff, rainstorms, etc.

waterbar: A drainage structure for turning water, composed of an outsloped segment of tread leading to a barrier placed at a 45 percent angle to the trail, usually made of logs, stones, or rubber belting material. Water flowing down the trail will be diverted by the outslope or, as a last resort, by the barrier.

watershed: A region or area bounded peripherally by a water-parting formation (i.e., ridge, hill, mountain range) and draining ultimately to a particular watercourse or body of water.

way (wildcat, social) trail: Unauthorized path made by trail users, often through switchbacks or between adjacent trails.

wetland: A lowland area, such as a marsh or swamp, which is saturated with water, creating a unique, naturally occurring habitat for plants and wildlife.

wheel guard: Narrow logs, poles, or lumber installed along the edges of bridge or puncheon decking designed to help keep wheeled equipment (wheelchair, bicycle, ATV) from running off the edge of the structure.

Wilderness Act of 1964 (16 U.S.C. 1131–1136): Federal law prohibiting the use of motorized vehicles and mechanized construction on certain tracts of federally managed lands.

wilderness area: An uninhabited and undeveloped area that Congress has voted to grant special status and protection under authority of the Wilderness Act of 1964.

winch: Applicable to a broad array of devices for using a drum driven by a handle and gears, around which a cable is wound, so as to provide mechanical advantage for moving heavy objects.

windfall: Anything (trees, limbs, brush, etc.) blown down on the trail by the wind.

Annotated Resource Directory

This annotated resource directory will guide you to additional information on trail planning, design, and management. Although few resources relating specifically to multi-use trail development exist, there are numerous works relating to various aspects of trail development. The following reference sources are divided into "general interest" categories, and into separate sections that correspond with the chapters of this book. Many of these resources are available from the Trails and Greenways Clearinghouse at www.trailsandgreenways.org.

General Interest: Greenways

American Trails. *Trails for All Americans: Report of the National Trails Agenda Project.* **Washington, DC: National Park Service, Summer 1990. 21 pp.**

Offers an exciting and comprehensive vision for a nationwide system of trails within fifteen minutes of every front door in the country. Discusses the wide-ranging benefits of multi-use trails, including health, economics, conservation, transportation, and recreation. Examines the role of local, state, and federal governments in providing trail infrastructure. Discussion of existing policy and programs, and recommendations for change are particularly helpful in charting the future of an American trail system.

Association of State Wetland Managers, Association of State Floodplain Managers, and National Park Service. *A Casebook in Managing Rivers for Multiple Uses.* **Philadelphia, PA: National Park Service, Mid-Atlantic Regional Office, 1991. 79 pp. Maps, photos.**

Contains eight case studies, several of which include multi-use trail development as a component of river management and preservation. Identifies the objectives, participants, innovative aspects, and accomplishments of each project and discusses their planning processes. Provides contacts within management agencies and bibliographic references.

Flink, Charles A., Robert M. Searns, and Loring Schwarz, eds. *Greenways: A Guide to Planning, Design, and Development.* **Washington, DC: Island Press and The Conservation Fund, 1993. Illustrations.**

A how-to guide for planning and designing greenway projects. The guide takes a step-by-step approach to greenway development and addresses many issues that face greenway planners and designers.

Grove, Noel. "Greenways: Paths for the Future." *National Geographic* **(June 1990): 77–98.**

Provides a well-written introduction to the greenway movement in the United States; cites examples from many greenway projects across the country.

Little, Charles E. *Greenways for America.* **Baltimore, MD: Johns Hopkins University Press, 1990. 237 pp. Color photos.**

Traces the history of the greenway movement and its efforts to preserve and restore linear open space. Describes many benefits of greenways, particularly those used as bicycle and pedestrian trails, and includes a valuable bibliography of published and unpublished sources.

Macdonald, Stuart H. "Greenways: Preserving Our Urban Environment." *Trilogy* **(November–December 1991): 95–96.**

A persuasive piece that makes a case for

urban trails and greenways and urges the urban dweller to initiate and guide trail development through citizen activism.

National Park Service and National Parks and Conservation Association. *Toward a Region-wide Network of Trails for the Mid-Atlantic States.* Washington, DC: National Park Service and National Parks and Conservation Association, 1992. 25 pp. Appendices, map.

Reports on 147 potential trail and greenway corridors and provides a 27-point action agenda identified by trail interests in the Mid-Atlantic states: Delaware, Maryland, New Jersey, Pennsylvania, Virginia, and West Virginia.

National Park Service and the National Recreation and Park Association. *Trends—Recreational Trails and Greenways.* Vol. 28. Washington, DC: National Park Service and the National Recreation and Park Association, 1991. 48 pp.

Contains eleven essays on the growth and development of multi-use trails and greenways. Topics include greenways as transportation, corporate involvement in trail development, the role of government, and prospects for a nationwide trail system.

Rodale Press, Inc. "Louis Harris Poll: Pathways for People." Emmaus, PA: Rodale

Press, 1992. Packet of three documents: Summary, Complete Survey Report, Success Stories.

Survey results show that 72 percent of Americans want safe and accessible "pathways" included in transportation planning, and that 59 percent want more government funding devoted to trail development. Packet includes a 6-page summary and 11-page detail of survey results on these and related questions. A 25-page booklet outlines sixteen success stories and includes tables and charts. Also available from Rodale Press: 1991 Harris Poll findings describing Americans' strong interest in bicycling to work when safe paths and lanes are provided.

Scenic Hudson, Inc. "Greenway Fact Sheets, 1–8." Poughkeepsie, NY: Scenic Hudson, 1991. 8 pp. each.

This series of eight pamphlets provides information to assist with the creation and maintenance of local greenways: (1) Walkway Design Guidelines; (2) Trail Construction and Maintenance; (3) Volunteers: Getting the Greenway Underway; (4) Greenway Project Fund Raising; (5) Historic Preservation in Greenways; (6) Starting Your Own Land Trust; (7) Land Preservation Techniques; (8) Liability: Protecting Yourself and Others.

General Interest: Rail-Trails

Rails-to-Trails Conservancy. *Acquiring Rail Corridors: A How To Manual.* Washington, DC: Rails-to-Trails Conservancy, 1996. 136 pp.

A step-by-step explanation of how to successfully acquire a rail corridor, including assembling a negotiating team, researching property ownership, securing funding, and negotiating with the railroad company.

Hoffman, Williams, Lafen & Fletcher. *Illinois Rail-Trails Developer's Handbook.* A component of the *Illinois Railbanking Study* produced for the Illinois Department of Conservation. Silver Spring, MD: Hoffman, Williams, Lafen & Fletcher, 1990. 56 pp. Appendix.

A guidebook to rail-trail conversion prepared for state and local park planners and managers. Outlines the conversion process from beginning to end. Includes sections on assessment, feasibility studies, gathering local support, trail design, public involvement, the railroad abandonment process; discusses issues involved in managing public review.

Mills, Judy. "Clearing the Paths for Us All Where Trains Once Ran." *Smithsonian* (April 1990): 132–41.

Provides a good overview of the rail-trail movement and discusses several rail-trails in states across the nation. Some statistics cited are now outdated.

Morris, Hugh. *Rail-Trails and Liability: A Primer on Trail-Related Liability Issues and Risk Management Techniques.* **Washington, DC: Rails-To-Trails Conservancy, 2000. 23 pp.**

This report outlines the general liability issues associated with trails, including the risks and responsibilities of various constituencies. The intent is to provide trail advocates, adjacent landowners, and trail managers with a background on liability issues to prepare them to pose appropriate questions to their legal counsel when developing a trail or when an accident occurs.

Rails-to-Trails Conservancy. *Secrets of Successful Rail Trails.* **Washington, DC: Rails-to-Trails Conservancy, 1993. 174 pp. Photos, illustrations.**

This manual outlines the many steps involved in creating a rail-trail. Topics explored include assessing the feasibility of a conversion; building a coalition; working with the STB and abandonment regulations; publicizing conversion efforts; working with government agencies; finding funds; working with corporations, elected officials, and railroads; dealing with trail opposition; and managing the trail. The guide contains appendices of relevant addresses, contacts, and resources.

Morris, Hugh, Jamie Bridges, and Richard Smithers. *Rails-with-Trails.* **Washington, DC:**

Rails-to-Trails Conservancy, 2000. Tables, appendices.

Rails-to-Trails Conservancy surveyed the managers of sixty-one trails sharing the same right-of-way with a railroad, or rails-with-trails. The report discusses safety, design, liability, and experiences along these corridors. A table lists all survey responses. Rail-with-trail managers are listed in an appendix.

Trail Studies

Federal Highway Administration, U.S. Department of Transportation. *Guidebook on Methods to Estimate Non-Motorized Travel.* **McLean, VA: Federal Highway Administration, 1999. Publication no. FHWA-RD-98-166. 170 pp. Photos, tables.**

This guidebook provides a means to better understand and estimate bicycle and pedestrian travel. It describes and compares the various methods that can be used to forecast nonmotorized travel demand or that otherwise support the prioritization and analysis of nonmotorized projects. These methods are categorized according to four major purposes: (1) demand estimation, (2) relative demand potential, (3) supply quality analysis, and (4) supporting tools and techniques. The book also provides a concise overview for each available method, including some typical

applications, pros and cons, and a quick reference guide on ease of use, data requirements, sensitivity to design factors, and whether widely used.

Gobster, Paul H. *The Illinois Statewide Trail User Study.* **Chicago: U.S. Forest Service, 1990. Available from RTC, Illinois Chapter. 61 pp. Tables, photos.**

This study's objectives were to determine trail use patterns and reasons for use, identify perceptions of trail users, and create a demographic profile of users. It focuses on recreational rather than transportation uses (all interviews were conducted on weekends). The study's major finding: That on urban and suburban trails, a significant majority of users come from nearby neighborhoods and that nearly 50 percent of local users use the trail "virtually every week."

Hoffman, Williams, Lafen & Fletcher. *Economic and Tax Implications of Rail-Trails.* **A component of the *Illinois Railbanking Study* produced for the Illinois Department of Conservation. Silver Spring, MD: Hoffman, Williams, Lafen & Fletcher, 1990. 60 pp. Tables.**

A broad examination of the social benefits and economic impacts of rail-trails: stimulation of commercial activity, recreational and other social benefits, effect on property values, environmental benefits, fiscal impacts, and potential for revenue generation through right-of-way leasing by utilities.

Hoffman, Williams, Lafen & Fletcher. *Illinois Rail-Trails: Landowner and Community Concerns.* **A component of the** *Illinois Railbanking Study* **produced for the Illinois Department of Conservation. Silver Spring, MD: Hoffman, Williams, Lafen & Fletcher, 1990. 34 pp.**

An assessment of the concerns expressed by adjacent property owners and communities about plans to retain abandoned rail lines for use as greenways and recreational trails. Includes a short section on ways for trail proponents to address concerns.

Maryland Greenways Commission. *Analysis of the Economic Impacts of the Northern Central Rail Trail,* **produced for the Commission by PKF Consulting. Annapolis, MD: PKF Consulting, 1994. 61 pp. Tables, appendices.**

This report details an assessment of the direct, indirect, and induced economic impacts resulting from the establishment of the Northern Central Rail Trail in Baltimore County, Maryland. Several types of impacts were investigated, including tourism, property values, commercial uses, local resident expenditures, public sector expenditures, qualitative factors, and overall benefits. Surveys of residents, trail users, and businesses were used to gather information. The eco-

nomic impact analysis is detailed within the report.

Moore, Roger L., et al. *The Impacts of Rail-Trails: A Study of Users and Nearby Property Owners from Three Trails.* **Washington, DC: National Park Service, 1992. 100+ pp. Charts, tables.**

This study of trail users and neighboring property owners examined two rural trails (in Iowa and Florida) and one suburban trail (in California). The study had four objectives: (1) to explore social benefits and direct economic impact of the trails; (2) to examine the trail's effects on adjacent and nearby property values; (3) to determine the types and extent of problems experienced by trail neighbors; and (4) to develop a profile of users. The findings revealed that (1) trails bring many benefits to communities, including "new money" brought in by tourists; (2) trails either enhance or do not significantly affect property values; (3) problems are minor and, by and large, benefits far outweigh negative impacts; (4) trails users are representative of local population. This is the first extensive study to examine both users and neighbors of the same trails.

Ohio-Kentucky-Indiana Regional Council of Governments. *Little Miami Scenic Trail Users Study.* **Cincinnati, OH: Ohio-Kentucky-Indiana Regional Council of Governments, 1999. 32 pp.**

This study of trail users along this trail in Ohio details the number of users, their activi-

ties, and economic impacts attributed to their visits. Benefits attributed to the trail include trip-related expenditures, durable goods expenditures, and broader public benefits.

Rails-to-Trails Conservancy. *Rail Trails and Safe Communities.* **Washington, DC: Rails-to-Trails Conservancy, 1998. 15 pp. Photos.**

The issue of crime on trails is addressed in this report, which includes the results of a study of 372 rail-trails across the country. The results indicated that trails are one of the safest places a person can be, as compared to other land uses, as evidenced by the low percentages of major and minor crimes reported. The report also includes supplementary statistical and anecdotal crime information and case studies of trail patrols.

Rails-to-Trails Conservancy. *Rail Trails and Community Sentiment.* **Washington, DC: Rails-to-Trails Conservancy, 1998. 16 pp. Photos.**

This report examines 125 trails that opened in 1994–1996 in an effort to depict the level of opposition that trail projects routinely encounter. The study finds that 85 percent of trails opened with either no opposition or with landowner and citizen concerns addressed through outreach to the community. The study also takes a closer look at rail-trail opponents, why some rail-trail projects fail, and some of the many rail-trail success stories.

Rivers, Trails & Conservation Assistance Program. *Economic Impacts of Protecting Rivers, Trails & Greenway Corridors: A Resource Book.* 2d ed. **Washington, DC: National Park Service, 1991. 80+ pp. Illustrations, tables.**

Examines the economic impacts of protecting rivers, trails, and greenway corridors in the following contexts: real property values, expenditures by residents and agencies, commercial uses, tourism, corporate relocation and retention, and public cost reduction. Includes a chapter on how to assess the benefits of projects, plus appendices that contain a sample survey. Also includes references.

Seattle Engineering Department and Office for Planning. *Evaluation of the Burke-Gilman Trail's Effect on Property Values and Crime.* **Seattle, WA: Seattle Engineering Department, May 1987. Executive summary available from Rails-to-Trails Conservancy. 42 pp. Appendices.**

Analyzing data gathered through interviews with residents near and adjacent to the trail, real estate agents, and police officers, this study concludes that property values are enhanced by the trail's proximity, and that burglaries and incidents of vandalism along the trail are below the neighborhood average.

University of Wisconsin Cooperative Extension Service. *A Look at Visitors on Wisconsin's Elroy-Sparta Bike Trail.* **Madison, WI: Recreation Resources Center, University of Wisconsin**

Extension, 1989. 45 pp. Appendices. Eleven-page summary available from Rails-to-Trails Conservancy.

Examines trip characteristics, trip-related expenditures, users' geographic origins, and other social and demographic factors. Findings reveal that (1) avoiding dangerous auto traffic was the top reason for using the trail; (2) 50,000 visitors in 1988 brought $1,257,000 to the local economy in the form of direct expenditures; and (3) over 50 percent of trail users came from out of state—20 percent from Illinois and 10 percent from Minnesota.

Utility Trails

American Trails. *Trails on Electric Utility Lands: A Model of Public-Private Partnership.* **Washington, DC: Edison Electric Institute, 1989. 50 pp.**

Contains nine case studies of trails and projects across the United States. General discussion covers maintenance, cost, liability, and the impacts of electromagnetic fields on trail users.

Trail Management

Arizona Bicycle Task Force and Arizona State Committee on Trails. "Trail Use Policy."

Phoenix: Arizona Department of State Parks, 1991. Photocopy. 5 pp.

Outlines policies for nonmotorized, recreational trail use. The discussion stresses the need for user involvement in the planning and management stages of trail development. Includes an appendix of organizations and agencies and their education programs for responsible trail use.

Bay Area Ridge Trail Council. "Landowner Options: Your Handbook on How Private Landowners Can Participate in the Bay Area Ridge Trail." **San Francisco: Bay Area Ridge Trail Council, 1992. 28 pp.**

Includes a discussion of easements, leases, and land sales or donations and their various benefits and considerations. Also contains a short list of references and resources, and includes sample easements and leases. While it was written specifically for the Bay Area Ridge Trail, much of this handbook can be applied to other projects.

Northern Virginia Regional Park Authority. *Manual on Policies and Procedures Governing Easements and Licenses and Non-Park Uses of Northern Virginia Regional Park Authority Property.* **Fairfax, VA: Northern Virginia Regional Park Authority, 1989. 75 pp.**

Outlines a set of easements, license agreements, and fees developed to protect trails and parks in the rapidly developing suburbs of Washington, D.C.

Rails-To-Trails Conservancy. "Fiber-Optics Leasing along Rail-Trails and Active Railroad Rights-of-Way." Washington, D.C.: Rails-to-Trails Conservancy, 1990. Photocopy. 6 pp.

Describes ten examples of fiber-optic lease easements and provides contacts in agencies responsible for such agreements.

Trail Design

American Association of State Highway Transportation Officials. *Guide for the Development of Bicycle Facilities.* Washington, DC: AASHTO, 1999. 78 pp. Photos, diagrams. *www.aashto.org/ bookstore/abs.html* or 800-231-3475

Many highway engineers and transportation officials consider this document the primary authority on bikeway design. It provides planning, design, and construction guidelines, and makes operation and maintenance recommendations for all types of bicycle facilities, including those independent from roadways. Note: This 1999 edition updates the earlier version.

Continental Bridge. *How to Buy a Bridge.* Alexandria, MN: Continental Bridge, 1991. 24 pp. Illustrations, photos, charts.

A helpful guide for purchasing prefabricated bridges.

Colorado State Parks Trails and Wildlife Task Force. *Planning Trails with Wildlife in Mind.* Denver: Colorado State Parks, 1998. 51 pp. Illustrations.

This handbook gives trail planners information on how to balance the benefits of creating trails with being stewards of nature, especially wildlife. An overview of important issues is provided, along with a "wildlife and trail planning checklist," and case studies of trail projects that have incorporated wildlife in the planning process. A wide variety of references are provided in the sources of information section, including Web sites, publications, and people.

Duffy, Hugh. *Surface Materials for Multiple-Use Pathways.* Lakewood, CO: National Park Service, Rocky Mountain Region, 1992. 4 pp.

Provides a framework and establishes criteria for evaluating what surface types should be considered for a multi-use path. Outlines design requirements, guidelines, and standards for surface materials. A useful introduction to an important aspect of trail design.

Federal Highway Administration, U.S. Department of Transportation. *Designing Sidewalks and Trails for Access.* Washington, DC: Federal Highway Administration, 1999. Publication no. FHWA-HEP-99-006. 169 pp. Illustrations, appendices.

There are two parts to this publication. The first part is a review of existing guidelines and practices for making sidewalks and trails accessible for people with disabilities. The second is a manual recommending accessible designs for sidewalks and trails, to be released in 2000. The second part discusses general principles of accessible design, accessibility requirements, facility design suggestions, and other considerations. A very useful document for those developing trails that will accommodate persons of all abilities.

Federal Highway Administration, U.S. Department of Transportation. *Conflicts on Multiple-Use Trails: Synthesis of the Literature and State of the Practice.* Washington, DC: Federal Highway Administration, 1994. Publication no. FHWA-PD-94-031. 70 pp. Appendices.

This report provides information on current knowledge and practice of methods to minimize trail user conflicts—either within the same user group or among different user groups. Conflict is revealed to be related to activity style, focus of trip, expectations, attitudes, level of tolerance, and different norms held by users. Each of these items is discussed, along with ways to reduce trail conflict. The report also provides twelve principles for minimizing conflict through design, information and education, user involvement, regulations, and enforcement.

Florida Department of Transportation, Safety Office. *Florida Pedestrian Safety Program.* Tallahassee: Florida Department of Transportation, 1992. 75 pp. Photos, tables, appendices.

This strong plan, formed in response to rising pedestrian injuries and deaths in Florida, outlines steps for the planning, engineering, educational efforts, enforcement, and implementation of a pedestrian safety program. Valuable reading, especially for planners of pedestrian facilities that intersect or parallel streets.

Keller, Kit, and Bicycle Federation of America. *Mountain Bikes on Public Lands: A Manager's Guide to the State of the Practice.* Washington, DC: Bicycle Federation of America, 1990. 68 pp.

Though written with backcountry trails in mind, this guide contains sections on "multiple use management," "balancing user concerns," and other topics that are valuable to planners of multi-use trails.

McCoy, Michael, and Mary Alice Stoner. *Mountain Bike Trails: Techniques for Design, Construction and Maintenance.* Missoula, MT: Bikecentennial, 1992. 18 pp. Photos, diagrams.

A well-written, concise guide intended to assist trail managers in designing and maintaining trails for mountain bike use.

Pugh, Ben. "A Bicycle Parking Cookbook." Excerpted from the 2010 Sacramento City/County Bikeway Master Plan. North

Highlands, CA: Ben Pugh, 1991. Photocopy. 32 pp. Diagrams.

Provides good information on bicycle racks (organized by security level) and includes a comprehensive set of drawings that highlight positive and negative aspects of bicycle parking facilities. Contains a partial list of equipment suppliers.

U.S. Department of Transportation. *Manual on Uniform Traffic Control Devices (MUTCD), Bicycle Facilities.* Washington, DC: U.S. Superintendent of Documents, 1988. Approx. 200 pp. Diagrams, color graphics. (Note: The *MUTCD* will undergo major revisions in 2001.)

This book is the accepted standard for all road and bikeway signs. Part IX, "Traffic Controls for Bicycle Facilities," includes 24 pages on bikeway signs. A number of sections discuss signs and signal systems for trails used by both bicyclists and pedestrians. Many color graphics show standard sign shapes, designs, and dimensions.

U.S. Equal Employment Opportunity Commission and the U.S. Department of Justice. *The Americans with Disabilities Act Questions and Answers.* Washington, DC: Government Printing Office, July 1991. 19 pp.

Provides answers to a series of questions relating to implementation of the Americans with Disabilities Act, including public spaces such as parks.

Velo Quebec. *Technical Handbook of Bikeway Design: Planning, Design, Implementation.* Montreal: Velo Quebec, 1992. 169 pp. Photos, diagrams.

A thorough handbook and reference manual for those planning bicycle facilities. Discusses many types of facilities and a detailed range of planning considerations, including grades, curves, intersections, and bicycle parking. The many photos and diagrams provide excellent visual examples of bicycle facilities. While the "Bicycle and the Law" section applies only to Canada, most information is useful to all designers and engineers.

Funding

National Park Service. *1991 Annual Report and Program Brochure—Rivers, Trails & Conservation Programs.* 16 pp. Photos.

Provides an introduction to the various technical assistance programs that the National Park Service offers to conserve rivers and establish trails on land outside the NPS system. Includes regional contacts for the Rivers, Trails and Conservation Assistance program and lists the FY91 funded projects and partners, including many rail-trails and greenways.

National Transportation Enhancements Clearinghouse. *Technical Brief: Finding*

Matching Funds for Trail Projects. **March 2000. 8 pp.**

Designed to help Transportation Enhancements (TE) trail project sponsors find their local match funds. Contains case studies of how communities around the country successfully networked for their local match funds or raised the money through creative fund-raising techniques. Also included are two lists of federal funding sources for trails: non-DOT federal funding programs, which may be used for matching a TE award, and DOT federal funds, which can be used for trail projects (but not as match for TE awards). It is available on the NTEC Web site at www.enhancements.org, or by calling NTEC toll-free at 888-388-6832.

National Transportation Enhancements Clearinghouse. *A Guide to Transportation Enhancements.* **June 1999. 32 pp.**

Designed specifically with the Transportation Enhancements (TE) project sponsor in mind.

Features information on the federal and state requirements for TE under TEA-21, the project application and development process, and available streamlining measures. Also featured are twenty-one case studies of successful TE projects, including trail and rail-trail projects. Anyone interested in TE as a source of funding would benefit from reading this publication. It is available on the NTEC Web site at www.enhancements.org, or by calling NTEC toll-free at 888-388-6832.

Trail Marketing

Carver, John. *Boards That Make a Difference.* **San Francisco: Jossey-Bass, 1990. 242 pp.**

Includes guidelines for bylaws. Chapter 10, "Focusing on Results: Clarifying and Sustaining the Organization's Mission," is especially useful.

Minnesota Department of Natural Resources. *Along the Trail: A Guide to Nature on the Heartland Trail.* **St. Paul, MN: Department of Natural Resources, 24 pp. Illustrations.**

A model trail nature guide that lists regional plants and animals, harmful plants to avoid, and wildflowers arranged by color.

Turner, Helen. *A Guide to the Illinois Prairie Path.* **Wheaton, IL: The Illinois Prairie Path, 1991. 32 pp. Illustrations.**

An innovative guide to one of the nation's oldest rail-trails. This booklet, which includes information on geology, trees, flowers, birds and animals, can serve as a model for trail managers.

About the Authors

CHARLES A. "CHUCK" FLINK is founder and president of Greenways Incorporated, an environmental planning and landscape architecture company based in Durham, North Carolina, established in 1986. He is the coauthor of *Greenways: A Guide to Planning, Design and Development* (Island Press, 1993). Flink is a graduate of North Carolina State University's School of Design and served as an Adjunct Professor of Landscape Architecture from 1994 to 1998. He served three consecutive terms as chairman of the board for American Trails, Washington, D.C. (1989–1992) and served as a member of the North Carolina Greenways Advisory Panel.

KRISTINE OLKA is a former project planner for Greenways Incorporated. Before working as a project planner, she was a special projects assistant at the Rails-to-Trails Conservancy. She is currently an editor and publications manager at IBM and continues to be active in the greenways movement through her work as a member of the Triangle Greenways Council Board of Directors.

ROBERT M. SEARNS is the founding owner of Urban Edges, Inc., a planning and development firm based in Denver, Colorado, that specializes in greenways, trails, and outdoor resource conservation. He was project director of Denver's Platte River Greenway, one of the nation's benchmark urban trail projects. He produced 10,000 Trees, an 8-mile-long river-corridor revegetation and wetland-restoration project involving 3,000 volunteers along the Mary Carter Greenway in Littleton, Colorado, and authored a greenways and trails plan for the 43-square-mile gateway into metropolitan Denver from Denver International Airport. In addition to his work in Colorado, he has helped master plan trail and greenway projects in the Chicago, Dallas, Las Vegas, Los Angeles, and Portland metro areas. He partnered with Chuck Flink in assisting Grand Canyon National Park in pursuing a precedent-setting 72-mile system of multi-use trails that provide nonmotorized access to Canyon rim. He has been an instructor and advisor for the National Park Service, the National Recreation and Park Association and the National Rails-to-Trails Conservancy. He has written articles and editorials for *Landscape Architecture Magazine* and other publications and has conducted workshops in the United States,

Canada, and Europe. He co-authored with Chuck Flink *Greenways: A Guide to Planning, Design and Development* (Island Press, 1993) and was a contributing author to *Greenways, The Beginning of an International Movement* (Elsevier Press, 1996).

Index